O Joy for me!

O Joy for me!

Samuel Taylor Coleridge
and the origins of Fell-walking in
the Lake District, 1790–1802

Keir Davidson

Wilmington Square Books
an imprint of Bitter Lemon Press

WILMINGTON SQUARE BOOKS
an imprint of Bitter Lemon Press

First published in 2018 by
Wilmington Square Books
47 Wilmington Square
London WC1X 0ET

www.bitterlemonpress.com

Text and images from the following titles are reproduced
by kind permission of the publishers:

Coleridge Collected Letters, vols 1 & 2. Oxford University Press
Coleridge Notebooks, ed. Kathleen Coburn (Routledge & Kegan Paul, 1957).
Taylor & Francis Books UK
The Pictorial Guides to the Lakeland Fells, by A. Wainwright. Frances Lincoln

A CIP record for this book is available from the British Library

ISBN 9781912242054

Printed in China
2 4 6 8 9 7 5 3 1

FRONTISPIECE: James Northcote, *Samuel Taylor Coleridge*, 1804
[courtesy of The Wordsworth Trust, Grasmere]

TITLE PAGE: The Caldew Valley from the summit of Carrock Fell [author]

Chinese Zen master Yun-men Wen-yen (864–949) was asked

'How do I find the Way?'

He replied,

'Start walking …'

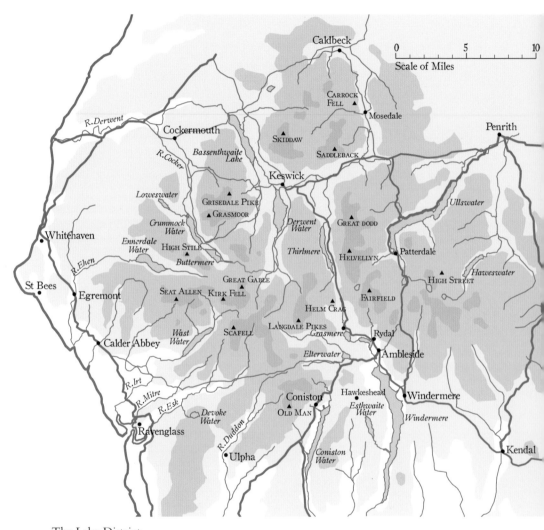

The Lake District

Contents

Foreword

Driving north from Mungrisdale to Mosedale and beyond, Carrock Fell appears as just another of the rounded, relatively low-lying fell ridges that run towards the west side of the road. It was described by Wainwright as a 'rough little height', and in spite of its apparent ordinariness, I wanted very much to visit the summit since it had been the scene of one of Coleridge's most dramatic adventures at the end of his series of walks in 1800. Illness had prevented me from visiting Carrock over the summer, but now, being here although still in recovery, I was anxious to make it to the top to find the things Coleridge had described, especially since my brother Jas had made the trip possible by volunteering to do the driving and make arrangements. As we passed below the fell, the top itself was hidden from the road beyond the shoulder of the hill, while the rising slopes on this side presented a complex wasteland of scree, gorse, crags and rock outcroppings. Clearly, I was not going to be able to negotiate that, but once we had driven further north, the broad, smooth-sided valley of the Carrock Beck offered an enticing way in, a walk of a couple of hours perhaps, up steadily rising paths to the ridge, and then along to the summit.

Although I was still struggling with a residual limp and was dependent on my walking poles to keep my balance, being here on a sunny, bright morning and seeing the fell above us, it seemed like a reasonable challenge if we took our time. We set off along the track, and it was some time later, as we were slowly making our way up the side of the beck, that we were suddenly over-taken by two collies, racing past us, purposeful and preoccupied as they quar-tered back and forth. Before long their owner had also caught us up and we fell into conversation about our reasons for making the ascent that day and about Coleridge and his eventful visit to the rocky summit in 1800. I have no recollection of how or why we started talking beyond the usual walker's greetings, or really of our companion having slowed down to join us (it may have been when we had to cross the beck), but, having fallen in with my laboured pace, she remained with us for the rest of the walk, the dogs either ranging far ahead up the track, off to the side, or checking back to see where we were. Bunty, it turned out, had worked in hill-shepherding for many years and was clearly totally at home, as were the dogs, on these windswept hillsides. Even though I was beginning to struggle somewhat as we as we made our way through the landscape of bogs and uneven clumped grass of Milton Hill and then Round Knott, the anticipation of reaching the top, taking in the views and seeing the features Coleridge had noted, grew steadily. But then, just as we passed through the tumbled stones of the ancient hill fort that surrounds the summit and reached the cairn, everything changed. All morning, low cloud had hidden the line of Cross Fell in the distance, and now it seemed to have swept across to the Lakeland fells, changing the weather completely. As the wind rose, the temperature plummeted, and instead of providing wide views, Carrock Fell became engulfed in dense mist and cloud; all of a sudden, by some strange circumstance, we began to experience something of what Coleridge had gone through in that bleak, windswept place one hundred and sixteen years earlier.

Knocked by the wind and losing feeling in ungloved hands, after a somewhat cursory look around for the sheltered place Coleridge had found, we returned to the cairn where, behind a rough wall of stones, Bunty was waiting with a most welcome cup of tea. The cold and relentless wind soon drove us off the summit, and, since there was nothing really to see, we set off to look for the most direct route down the north side to Carrock Beck somewhere below us. This, in the cold, dense, disorientating mist, proved far from easy, and in addition to searching for the track, the steepness and broken ground made it very hard for me to follow the others down. But, with my brother keeping an eye on me, and the two of us following Bunty and the dogs, we eventually made it far enough down to get below the mist and the worst of the icy wind, and locate the direct route down to the cars. Sitting in the car a little later, warming up, we reflected on what an interesting experience that had been, in spite of it having turned into such a physical challenge for me, and how different it would have been in so many ways had we not had our three companions. We felt somehow as though, quite unexpectedly, and without us really noticing, we had been joined by guides, almost as if that part of the place which had seen Coleridge safely down from his extraordinary adventure had been there too on that late October afternoon.

A couple of months later Coleridge's experiences in the Lake District came into even sharper focus at Greta Hall in Keswick, the house which has survived almost intact since Coleridge and then Southey lived there. It is run now in a magnificently informal way as a B&B, and beyond those parts lived in by our hosts, the accommodation available includes 'the Coleridge Wing' which, in turn, includes Coleridge's original 'parlour' downstairs, and three bedrooms upstairs, one of which had been Coleridge's study. Apart from the furniture, this room, with what would appear to be the original windows and fireplace, would surely still be instantly recognizable to Coleridge; as would the views from it, particularly through the window looking west/south-west, where the location of the house on its hilltop means that the views Coleridge so carefully described can still be seen over the buildings that have been built below over the years. The parlour still retains a wonderfully lived-in feeling and, sitting there, it is not hard to catch the echoes of the dramas and conversations that the room must have witnessed. Similarly, upstairs in his study, the atmosphere surrounding his life here and his long hours at his desk in this room is still palpable, strengthened by the muted sounds of bustling family life that fill the house, just as they would have done then. For anyone interested in Coleridge's life in the Lake District, a visit to Greta Hall today is a must, and we have to be thankful to Jeronime and the family for their enlightened stewardship of the house, and for sharing it and bringing it back to life in their special, unique way.

My hope is that these anecdotes will have helped to convey something of what a rewarding, and at times surprising, unexpected and challenging adventure writing this book has been, and also a sense of just how close, now and then, one can still feel to the people and events it is concerned with. None of this would be so without the help of a number of people, some of whose sudden appearances, like those mentioned above, have enriched the experience along the way, and others who have helped from the start, whether through their published scholarship, or with actively providing encouragement and ideas along the way.

I am much indebted to the work of Richard Holmes in *Coleridge: Early Visions* in which he pointed out the possible rewards of 'further exploration' of Coleridge's 'fell-walking Notebooks and letters', and provided the initial impetus for me to acquire a copy of the first volume (1794-1804) of Kathleen Coburn's edition of the notebooks. In addition to this, Holmes also credited Molly Lefebure's contribution in her book *Cumberland Heritage*, which in turn led me to reading Joseph Palmer's *Fortnight's Ramble to the Lakes by A*

Rambler in 1792, another crucial part of this story. Mention of the Coleridge notebooks requires acknowledgement of the extraordinary contribution of Kathleen Coburn, not just in transcribing and presenting the chaotic texts in some readable form, but also for the immensely detailed companion volume of Notes, valuable not just for their scholarship but also for her first-hand experience of the landscapes of the Lake District.

As mentioned above, the text of the notebooks is often very disorganized and in places very hard to interpret and make sense of, and in her Introduction to the Text, Coburn comments that 'an accurate text has been regarded as the chief editorial obligation, and the text is therefore presented as nearly as possible as Coleridge wrote it.' She goes on to point out, however, that Coleridge's 'punctuation is that of a casual or hurried memoranda, and not that of his published works; its most obvious eccentricity is his use of the oblique stroke' as a means to separate thoughts or observations that were jotted down in quick succession. In addition to this, Coleridge often misspelt or misheard a name, confused right and left or north and south, and made no attempt to link entries, making it very difficult to follow his progress or understand quite what he is looking at or which direction he is heading in. As a result, although Coburn largely left these things unaltered, commenting 'Coleridge makes better sense than we sometimes make of him', she did introduce various devices, such as to use square brackets to indicate illegible words, his inserted afterthoughts, or the 'few editorial insertions', and to 'repair an obvious omission which might otherwise mystify the reader', and add commas or full stops 'that appear to have become lost on a margin or taken for granted at the end of a line in the manuscript'. Thus, with the minimum of intrusion, Coburn sought to 'impose on the text ... that consistency and conformity to general usage that Coleridge himself practised in his published works.'

Since my intention in this book is to allow the reader to follow Coleridge's walks, and his reactions to what he is seeing along the way, both accurately and in detail, I have in turn taken the opportunity to streamline Coleridge's texts, substituting his oblique stroke with more readable punctuation, in an attempt to clarify the material, but otherwise, as Coburn writes, 'As to any other irregularities, he goes to press with all his sins upon his head.' Where the spelling of place names has altered over time, I have retained Coleridge's version in quotations from the notebooks and letters and used the modern spelling in the book text.

Conveniently the material for this book all fell within the time span of the first notebook, and it was with real pleasure that I discovered that the copy I had purchased had been previously owned by Malcolm Elwin (author of, amongst other things, *The First Romantics, Wordsworth, Coleridge, Southey*), who was given it by his wife in 1957, the year it was first published. The book came complete with Elwin's numerous marginal comments and some seven pages of his insightful typed commentary tucked in the back; it seemed like a particularly good sign.

I would also like to acknowledge the work of William Roberts for the context he has provided for the early writings about the Lake District in *A Dawn of Imaginative Feeling* (1996) and for his edition of Thomas Gray's *Journal*, and also Michael Symes for his published work on Hagley Hall and Thomas Whately, and additional comments in correspondence and conversation.

I would like to thank John Nicoll of Wilmington Square Books for his work on the manuscript and interest in the material in it, Sally Salvesen for her work on the design and Jo Christian for her help and guidance on this project. Last, but by no means least, I must acknowledge the help and support of my wife Linda Crockett, Jas Davidson for his work on the maps and drawings, as well as his company, and all those with whom I have visited the Lake District.

Finally, the maps in this book are intended only as rough guides to the routes that Palmer and then Coleridge actually took, since in many cases a lack of information means it is not possible to follow their exact paths, and, in addition to this, the route of a number of roads in the area have been altered and new ones added. It is hoped, however, that they contain enough information to give a general idea of the routes they took and the location of the sights and features they record seeing.

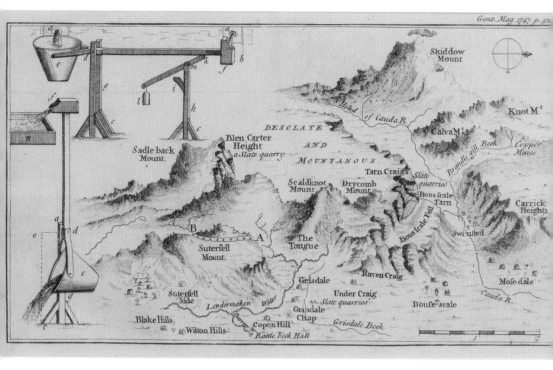

After George Smith (1700–73), *The Caudbec Fells*, 1747 [courtesy of The Wordsworth Trust, Grasmere].

    Villages, farms, mines and quarries among the 'Desolate and Mountanous' landscapes of the north-eastern fells of the Lake District.

Establishing the 'Picturesque Tour' of the Lakes: 1755–1769

It was from the 1740s onward that cartographers, poets and artists had begun to give outsiders some idea of what the Lakeland landscape of mountains and valleys, lakes, rivers, and waterfalls actually looked like, and accounts of the best, most accessible views began to be published. Following these beginnings, and as interest in the area steadily grew, by the 1760s the most convenient routes by which one could see these views had been mapped out and a 'Picturesque Tour' of the Lakes established.

Maps such as that by George Smith showing the 'Caudebec Fells' (1747) began to set the scene, giving an early and vivid impression of the terrain of, in this case, the north-eastern fells. Here, small settlements – Undercrag, Bowscale, Mosedale and Swineside – are shown, surrounded by a few protective trees, lying in the shadow of the sharply drawn perspectives of the towering cliffs, crags and precipices of 'Suterfell Mount', 'The Tongue', 'Bowscale Fell' and 'Carrock Heights'. Beyond these loom even higher peaks, Saddleback Mount, 'Blen Carter Height', Scaldknot Mount, 'Tarn Craigs' and beyond these again 'Calva Mount' and 'Knot Mt' leading up to the cloud topped summit of 'Skiddow Mount'; and much in between is simply left blank and marked with the terse, but highly expressive phrase, 'Desolate and Mountanous'.[1]

In addition, however, Smith's map also shows us something else of great interest. While to the visitor, these high fells of the Lake District may have appeared desolate and mountainous, they had, of course, teemed with life and activity for thousands of years, and looking carefully at the map, amongst what Smith describes in his accompanying article as 'insuperable precipices [and] tow'ring peaks', we find 'a slate quarry' high on 'Blen Carter Height', another tucked under the bulk of 'Tarn Craigs', and, across the 'Cauda river' valley, 'copper mines' in the wide saddle between 'Knot Mt' and 'Carrick Heights'. In addition to these we see also the isolated farms at 'Suterfell Side' and 'Swinsied', farms which, alongside the pastures close to the farm itself, also depended on access to extensive summer grazing high on the fells themselves; all of these features serve to remind us of generations of quarrymen, miners, and farmers who had long populated the landscapes of the Lakes.

From as early as the late Mesolithic period, groups of people had scrambled up the steep scree slopes below Pike o' Stickle on the Langdale ridge to quarry lumps of tuff to be fashioned into stone axes, and carried them out along well established paths which are still traceable over the otherwise apparently empty landscape. The axe quarries were in time superseded by those worked for slate and road stone, while mine levels were dug across the whole region to extract, at one time or another, wadd (graphite), lead, silver, iron ore, copper and coal. As the mining and quarrying communities grew so too did those of the sheep farmers, and with increased use, the old paths developed into networks of roads, running up and down the main valleys, and of tracks and drift roads which provided access to every corner and summit of the high fells above.

In the landscape shown by Smith, quarrymen will have routinely passed below the summits of Blencathra or Skiddaw; shepherds, often with their families, will have spent the summer months living in huts, and searched for their sheep among crags and across the ridgelines of Saddleback, Suterfell, Scaldknot Mount and Bowscale Fell, while drovers, pack teams, traders and travellers (to name but a few) will have crossed the passes offered by the 'Cauda River' flowing down from Skiddaw, 'Brandle gill Beck' and 'Lendermacken Water'; a pattern of land use repeated right across the whole region. Yet when others, both local writers and visitors from outside, began to take notice of the landscapes of the Lakes in the mid-eighteenth century, it was not these uplands and high passes, but rather the lakes themselves and their settings far below that caught their artistic eye.

One of the earliest surviving of such accounts can be found in an anonymous letter sent in to the *Gentleman's Magazine*, which describes a visit to Windermere.[2] Published in 1748, it was titled in the magazine as a *New Description of Matlock, Pool's Hole, Winander-mere &c*, and in it the author records his visit to the Lakes in 1746. After having visited the sights of the Derbyshire Peaks, including Matlock and the cavern at Poole's Hole, the author travels to the Lakes in June and goes on to give 'A Description of a Lake call'd Winander-mere'. Having arrived in Kendal:

> where we enquired after Winander-mere lake, we soon procured a guide, then quitted the high-road, and we rode 12 miles over some of the wildest hills in great-Britain. We came upon a high promontory that gave us at once a full view of the bright lake, which spreading itself under us, in the midst of the mountains, presented one of the most glorious appearances that ever struck the eye of a traveller with transport …

After reaching the lake, they immediately take a boat, leading to a long description of rowing around the islands. Eventually they stop at one of the smaller islands [possibly Thompson's Holme] 'with a small mount which rises to a considerable height'. Here they sit on benches carved from the rock and admire the view, presumably looking north, towards a sight the author describes as follows:

> [The spot] yields a prospect surpassing all that ever attracted my observation … The transparent waters of the lake extend themselves many miles before us, round which shade above shade, rock above rock, hill above hill, mountain above mountain, even up to the clouds, forming the most stupendous theatre, presenting the most sublime scenes that human sight can possibly make room for.
>
> I am yours, etc.

A brief and tantalizing glimpse of what it was that caught the eye of these early visitors, but one which, as we will see, was to become familiar to many of those who came later. After this early recognition of the beauties of Windermere, however, it was to be another lake, Derwent Water, set within the 'sweet vale of Keswick', that was soon to become the particular focus of attention.

This was a process that started when Dr John Dalton, from the village of Dean, Cumberland, and one the first local writers to be published, produced *A Descriptive Poem addressed to Two Ladies, at their return from viewing the mines near Whitehaven* in 1755.[3] After an account of their visit to explore Sir James Lowther's coal mines at Whitehaven in the first part of the poem, Dalton then takes the party on a poetic walk following the River 'Lowther' into the vale of Keswick to see the views of Derwent Water, Borrowdale and Skiddaw.

After satisfying the ladies' curiosity in the 'sulph'rous damps in caverns deep' at Whitehaven, Dalton then imagines following 'the native stream … down bending vales' to 'nature's pride / sweet Keswick vale', and once there, he sets out to describe the scene and his reaction to it:

> The muse, who trod th'inchanted ground,
> Who sail'd the wonderous lake around,
> With you will haste once more to hail
> That beauteous brook of Borrodale.
> From savage parent, gentle stream … [224–8]

And it is with this distinction between the 'savage parent', the rushing torrents in the mountains above, and the 'gentle stream' as it finally flows out of Borrowdale, that Dalton sets up the basis of his description. For him, and presumably his readers, the desolation of the mountains above and around the lake, and everything they represent, can only be appreciated if seen as an interesting contrast to the protective comfort of the placid lake and its association with the peaceful life of the village of Keswick beside it. As it flows out of the mountains, the torrent calms, and the water:

> [in] soft insinuating glide
> Silent along the meadows side,
> Smoothly o'er the sandy bottom pass … [230–2]
> To where in deep capacious bed
> The widely liquid lake is spread. [236–7]

The still, smooth and soft lake laid out amongst the meadows and woods, is seen in sharp contrast to the landscape beyond, and specifically with the waterfall of Lodore which, tumbling riotously into the lake from the heights above, forms part of the background setting with its broken rocks and savage grandeur:

> Let other streams rejoice to roar
> Down the rough rocks of dread Lodore,
> Rush raving on its boistrous sweep,
> And foaming rend the frighten'd deep … [238–41]
> The water crashes from:
> tremendous rocks amid the skies… [245]
> Till they the smoothest channel find,
> Soften the horrors of the scene,
> And thro' confusion flow serene. [247–9]

Having established the pictorial composition of the landscape, Dalton then moves on to the key theme of the poem – the possible use of sights such as these to stimulate and feed the imagination. Although this was the first known poem specifically about the Lake District, its promotion of the natural world as a place of artistic and cultural interest built on the precedent set by poems such as James Thomson's *The Seasons*, published in full in 1744. Thomson's poem reveals the poet's 'exploration of the connections between the external world of nature and the internal world of human mind and imagination … a theme of increasing importance,'[4] and this importance becomes clear in Dalton's next lines:

> Horrors like these at first alarm,
> But soon with savage grandeur charm,
> And raise to noblest thoughts your mind. [250–2]

After first recoiling in horror at the 'raving', 'boistrous', 'foaming' confusion of the rocks and water, the viewer 'soon' recovers, and the alarm is swiftly followed by a reassuringly cultivated and artistic response, the stimulation of the imagination and the raising of noble thoughts, something that lay at the heart of what the increasing numbers of picturesque tourists hoped to experience.

Now that the viewers are settled, calmed by the presence of the gentle stream and placid lake, and able to see the world beyond as contrast rather than threat, using what Thomson wrote of as 'sure Taste refin'd' they are able to take in the wider views of 'The cragged cliff, imperfect wood'[254], the 'gloomy clouds', and 'the darkened vale … '[256–8], and the 'Channels by rocky torrents torn'[265]; these wilder scenes now balanced by the central presence of the gentle lake, dotted with quiet, 'verdant' islands. And then, having established that the view down Derwent Water is 'pleasing tho' aweful', Dalton completes the scene by describing the viewing point from which it should be seen: the comfortable village of Keswick surrounded and protected by the hills around it, with the calm, 'widely liquid' lake stretching away in front, creating a sense of separation between the foreground and the distanced background of crags, the imperfect woods, the gloomy clouds, and the rocky torrents, thundering and banging their way down to the lake. The viewer is cradled within this scene, secure in the knowledge that behind them, their back is protected by 'giant Skiddow':

> Thy roofs, O Keswick, brighter rise.
> The lake and lofty hill between,

> Where giant Skiddow shuts the scene.
> Supreme of mountains, Skiddow, hail! [280–3]

In addition to this description of the place, these lines also provide one of the best descriptions of the locations chosen as the viewing points, soon to be known as 'stations', that came to form the basis of the recommended itinerary for the picturesque tour of the Lakes; a convenient spot, reassuringly close to both roads and the amenities of a town or village, which provided a view of a piece of landscape which fulfilled as many of the requirements for a good artistic composition as possible. These would include a generous foreground, and the lake (or other object of interest) stretching away within a well balanced framing of receding features on either side, and beyond these a terminating backdrop filled with interest, the grandeur of safely distanced horrors. It was compositions such as these that the painted images of Derwent Water, soon to follow, sought to reproduce.

Dalton then ends the poem by suggesting it might also be interesting for the ladies to actually climb 'Skiddow' and experience it at first hand, providing the weather was good:

> Lo, his imperious brow I see
> From foul usurping vapours free!
> 'Twere glorious now his side to climb,
> Boldly scale his top sublime … [285–8]

before concluding that, in fact, the 'softer joys' to be enjoyed safely at home are probably more preferable:

> For other scenes their minds employ,
> And move their hearts with softer joy,
> For pleasures they need never roam,
> Theirs with affection dwell at home. [293–6]

It was to be a few more years in fact before we have any recorded instance of any visitor, or 'stranger' as they were referred to locally, 'boldly scaling' the side of Skiddaw or any other Lakeland peak.

At much the same time that Dalton was escorting his 'Two Ladies' on their trip, and writing his *Descriptive Poem*, another man who had lived locally, John Brown, also wrote a description of Derwent Water, one that was to prove every bit as influential on the development and context of picturesque tours of the Lake, but, rather than being in poetic form, Brown's account of the lake was a straightforward prose description.

Although born in Northumberland, Brown grew up from a young age in Wigton, Cumberland, where his father was the Vicar, and he went on to secure a place at St John's College, Cambridge in 1732. After graduating in 1735, he returned to Wigton to serve as his father's curate, before moving to Carlisle in 1739, where he lived until 1741. From that time exact details of his life are thin, but he seems to have lived in London during the 1750s, while also holding livings at Lazonby in Cumberland and then Great Horkesley, Essex. In 1760 he moved to Newcastle where he spent the rest of his life, and although he never returned to live in Cumberland, he records that the vale of Keswick remained very important to him, and he paid 'an annual voyage to Keswick, not only as an amusement, but a religious act.'[4]

His description of Derwent Water was eventually published in the *London Chronicle* in 1766 under the title *A Description of the Lake at Keswick (And the adjacent Country) in Cumberland Communicated in a Letter to a Friend,*[5] and the text begins 'In my way to the north from *Hagley*…'. Who actually decided to call it a 'Letter' is not clear, but it has led to some confusion as to the purpose and context of what Brown wrote, other than it seems to be related to a visit to Hagley Hall. The original manuscript of this 'letter' is no longer extant, and there are 'several insoluble mysteries attached to it'; not least, was it actually a 'letter' written to George Lyttelton (1709–73) of Hagley Hall in Staffordshire?

The *Description* begins with what seems like a short explanation of its purpose:

> In my way to the north from Hagley I passed through Dovedale; and to say the truth, was disappointed in it. When I came to Buxton, I visited another or two of their romantic scenes; but these are inferior to Dovedale. They are but poor miniatures of Keswick; which exceeds them more in grandeur than I can give you to imagine; and more if possible in beauty than in grandeur.

Given the reference in the opening line to Hagley, and to his trip to Dovedale, it could be that the *Description*, if not written as a personal letter to Lyttelton, was designed to follow up on a visit Brown had paid to the Hall, and written for circulation by Lyttelton amongst the group of people who had also been present.

Some explanation of the purpose behind the style and the specific content of the *Description*, and indeed the kinds of things that may have been discussed during Brown's visit to Hagley, can be found in the fact that, building on a landscape designed with the help of Alexander Pope in the 1730s, and celebrated in part of Thomson's *The Seasons*, Lyttelton was busy working at Hagley with the landscape designer and architect Sanderson Miller from 1747, building not just a major new Neo-Palladian house between 1756–60, but also designing a number of buildings and landscape features in the park in the newly fashionable informal picturesque style.

It seems reasonable to suggest, then, that the question of what is and is not picturesque scenery was much under discussion at Hagley and amongst this circle of designers and aesthetes/connoisseurs, and that Dovedale in the Peak District had been suggested as having such qualities. Having visited it on his way north, Brown then feels obliged to argue for the vastly superior qualities of the setting of Derwent Water as both a place to stimulate the imagination and a more suitable model for landscape composition. It is also worth noting in this context that in 1750 Brown had visited Ralph Allen at Prior Park, near Bath, another place where a major programme of new landscaping was underway, and a place, as at Hagley, where the new designs modified an earlier landscape laid out with the help of Alexander Pope.

Roberts suggests that while the 1750s date is 'a plausible conjecture ... We may be on safer ground' in thinking that the letter was written nearer its publication date in 1766.[6] Either way, it is clear that the *Description* is 'the first major piece of prose writing to appreciate and analyse the beauty of wild scenery', and its brevity, lack of a wider context or discussion, the very specific subject matter and the absence of the usual niceties of letter writing, all suggest that Brown wrote it for the express purpose of conveying what he understood to be the key qualities of picturesque beauty and how these were more clearly represented by the landscape around Derwent Water than that of Dovedale. In this context, it can be seen, in fact, as part of that wider discussion about the definition of the picturesque that will have been going on at George Lyttelton's estate at Hagley, and which was to rumble on for the whole of the second half of the eighteenth century and covered, amongst other things, poetry, art, architecture and landscape design. Indeed, as the increasingly volatile situation on the Continent made travel difficult towards the end of the century, picturesque tours of the British Isles came to replace the traditional Grand Tour of classical sites in Europe as a means to further a cultural and artistic education.

Brown writes that, compared to the 'vast amphitheatre' and 'noble living lake' of Derwent Water, Dovedale can offer but a 'narrow slip of valley', a 'meagre rivulet' flowing through it, 'the little and unanimated hills', and vegetation of 'weeds, morass and brushwood.' A poor place in every respect when one has seen the vale of Keswick, with: 'the rich and beautiful landskip of cultivated fields, rising to the eye in fine inequalities, with noble groves of oak, happily dispersed, and climbing the adjacent hills, shade above shade, in the most various and picturesque forms.'

Whereas Dalton had found beauty in the poetic contrast between the 'gentle' stream that 'smoothly o'er the sandy bottom pass … ' and the waters that ' … rejoice to roar / Down the rough rocks of dread Lodore', Brown focuses on contrasts within the physical composition of the landscape itself, in the contrast between the 'cultivated fields' and 'noble groves of oaks, happily dispersed' on one shore, and the ' … rocks and cliffs of stupendous height, hanging broken over the lake in horrible grandeur, some of them a thousand feet high, the woods climbing up their steep and shaggy sides, where mortal foot never yet approached' of the opposite shore. For Brown, the landscape is then given additional picturesque atmosphere by the 'dreadful heights' of these cliffs, the places 'where eagles nest', and the 'variety of waterfalls … seen pouring from their summits, and tumbling in vast sheets from rock to rock in rude and terrible magnificence: While on all sides of this immense amphitheatre the lofty mountains rise round, piercing the clouds in shapes as spiry and fantastic', and the 'frequent and bold projection of the cliffs into the lake, forming noble bays and promontories.'

Having identified the 'immense amphitheatre' of the vale of Keswick as a superior example of a picturesque landscape compared to Dovedale, Brown then sets out to define the 'constituent principles' that make it so, identifying what he sees as 'permanent beauties' and those that are 'varying and accidental'.

Of those he considers as permanent beauties he says, 'I should tell you that the full perfection of Keswick consists of three circumstances, Beauty, Horror, and Immensity united … ', but:

> to give you a complete idea of these three perfections, as they are joined at Keswick, would require the united powers of Claude, Salvator, and Poussin. The first would throw his delicate sunshine over the cultivated vales, the scattered cots, the groves, the lake, and wooded islands. The second should dash out the horror of the rugged cliffs, the steeps, the

hanging woods, and foaming waterfalls; while the grand pencil of Poussin should crown the whole with the majesty of the impending mountains.

He then turns to the 'varying and accidental beauties' that are so important in the work of these artists. First, he 'would point out the perpetual change of prospect: The woods, rocks, cliffs, and mountains, by turns vanishing or rising into view: Now gaining on the sight, hanging over our heads in their full dimensions, beautifully dreadful; and now, by a change of situation, assuming new romantic shapes … ', before discussing the 'contrast of light and shade, produced by the morning and evening sun; the one gilding the western, and the other the eastern side of this immense amphitheatre; while vast shadow projected by the mountain buries the opposite part in a deep and purple gloom, which the eye can hardly penetrate.' Following on from this, he notes:

> The natural variety of colouring which several objects produce is no less wonderful and pleasing: the ruling tints in the valley being those of azure, green, and gold, yet ever various, arising from an intermixture of the lake, the woods, the grass, and cornfields. These are finely contrasted by the grey rocks and cliffs.'

Brown then concludes his description of the 'varying and accidental beauties' by commenting on those added to the scene by weather and moonlight. Of the former, he notes that 'the whole' scene is:

> heightened by the yellow stream of light, the purple hues, and misty azure of the mountains. Sometimes a serene air and clear sky disclose the tops of the higher hills. At others, you see clouds involving their summits, resting on their sides, or descending to their base, and rolling among the valleys, as in a vast furnace. When the winds are high, they roar among the cliffs and caverns like peals of thunder; then, too, the clouds are seen in vast bodies sweeping along the hills in gloomy greatness, while the lake joins the tumult and tosses like a sea. But in calm weather the whole scene becomes new: The lake is a perfect mirror; and the landskip in all its beauty, islands, fields, woods, rocks and mountains are seen inverted, and floating on its surface.

Of the effects of moonlight he writes:

Let me now conduct you down again to the valley, and conclude with one circumstance more; which is, that a walk by full moonlight (at which time the distant waterfalls are heard in all their variety of sound) among these enchanting dales, opens a scene of such delicate beauty, repose, and solemnity, as exceeds all description.

Thus Brown concludes his case for the superiority of the physical landscape that makes up the setting of the lake at Keswick as an expression of picturesque beauty. Although the word itself only appears once, 'in the most various and picturesque forms', the language throughout ('horrible grandeur', 'fine inequalities', 'happily dispersed', 'shade above shade', 'hanging broken', 'dreadful heights' …), builds on a growing vocabulary which came to define writing about the picturesque. But the importance of this *Description* lies not just in its identification of picturesque elements of composition, but also in its identification of that other key quality of the picturesque, noted also by Dalton: its ability to provide opportunities for the cultivated mind to transcend the immediate and mundane, to stimulate the imagination and use the artistic eye to open up new realms of consciousness.

Specifically, he describes the sheer complexity of this landscape setting:

the frequent and bold projection of the cliffs into the lake, forming noble bays and promontories: In other parts they finely retire from it, and often open in abrupt chasms of clefts, through which at hand, you see rich and cultivated vales, and beyond these at various distances, 'mountain rising over mountain', a complexity that means that 'new prospects present themselves … till the eye is lost in an agreeable perplexity…'

and it is at this moment, when the eye is lost in 'agreeable perplexity', that something magical happens, something Brown sums up as follows:

> Active Fancy travels beyond Sense
> And pictures things unseen …

This is the place to which the truly picturesque can take the viewer if they have developed their imagination enough to be capable of seeing it. In the reams and reams of writing about the picturesque that was to follow over the next fifty or so years, there were to be few better descriptions of the experience that the tourists were looking for than these two lines.[7]

Thomas Smith of Derby (c.1720/4–67), *A View of Derwentwater etc. from Crow-Park 1761*, as reissued 1767 [courtesy of The Wordsworth Trust, Grasmere].

Smith's image of the Derwent Water captures what John Brown meant when he wrote that 'the full perfection of Keswick consists of three circumstances, Beauty, Horror, and Immensity united'.

It was in response to writings such as those by Dalton and Brown that from the mid-1750s, images of the Lake District by artists such as William Bellers and then Thomas Smith of Derby began to appear and became widely available through published engravings. Largely depicting the best known and most accessible lakes, Windermere and Derwent Water, Ullswater and Haweswater, these images defined the Lakeland 'Views' which came to dominate the picturesque tour. Carefully framed, often with sets of figures in the foreground, the long view of the lake itself leading the eye deep into the dramatically emphasized forms of the mountain landscapes beyond, these images set the standard for picturesque composition; the threatening horrors and the desolation of the landscape carefully framed by the artist's skill of effect and composition, and presented as a savage grandeur that was capable of raising what Dalton had called 'the noblest thouhts of mind'.

❉ ❉ ❉

By the time Thomas Grey set out with his friend Thomas Wharton for a walking tour of the Lake District in August 1768, their aim was to experience for themselves the delights and 'horrors' of what was, by now, the increasingly popular 'Picturesque Tour'. Gray was by this time a nationally recognized poet, having published, amongst other things, 'The Elegy Written in a Country Church-yard' and the 'Pindaric Odes', and was living as a fellow-commoner at Peterhouse College, Cambridge after his return from a Grand Tour to Italy between 1739 and 1742. It was at Cambridge in 1737 that Gray had first met Thomas Wharton and the two had picked up their friendship on Gray's return. In the years that followed, Gray would visit Wharton at his home at Old Park near Durham, and it was from here that the two first set out to visit the Lake District in August 1767. Unfortunately, on that occasion, they were forced to abandon the trip when Wharton suffered a severe asthmatic attack in Keswick, and it was not until July of 1769 that they were able to set out again to finally fulfill their ambition.

Although Gray and John Brown were 'no particular acquaintances' at Cambridge, they certainly knew of each other, and after Gray's Pindaric Odes were first published in 1757, Brown remarked that 'Gray's efforts in the Pindaric mode were the best in the language.' For his part, Gray had 'read and admired both Brown and Dalton',[8] but it was Brown's pose as an informed viewer, and the content and language of his *Description*, that were to have a pervasive influence, and not only on the *Journal* that Gray wrote of his visit to the Lakes; echoes of the work, particularly the descriptive language, can also be heard in Coleridge's prose of thirty years later.

In fact on his way north in the summer of 1769 from Cambridge to Wharton's home, Gray had also taken the time to visit Dovedale, no doubt keen to see the 'narrow strip of valley' for himself in order to be able to make his own comparisons once he arrived at Keswick. The two then set off again for the Lakes, but they had barely reached the village of Brough when Wharton was again struggling for breath. Although Gray was ready once more to turn around and accompany his friend back home, this time Wharton 'managed to convince Gray otherwise', and, crucially for us, 'He may have done so ... only after extracting ... a promise – a promise that Gray keep him informed of his own progress on the journey, by writing down an extended and scrupulously precise account of his travels.'[9]

Had Wharton been well enough to continue, it is likely that the trip would, like so many others at the time and since, have gone unrecorded, and become simply a footnote in the history of Gray's life, but in the event Gray kept his promise and went on to create the first detailed account of such a visit. As his eleven days in the Lakes unfolded he used two notebooks to record where he went, what he did and saw, and his reactions to the landscapes, the people, and the experience as a whole. These accounts he then wrote up in a series of letters to Wharton between 18 October 1769 and June 1770, but it was not until 1775 that a complete '*Journal*' of the trip was published by their friend William Mason, four years after Gray's death.[10] Gray himself clearly had no intentions of this account written for his friend ever becoming public, but once it was, it became enormously influential, setting a style and standard for a new genre of travel writing, that of the picturesque tour. Most importantly perhaps, Gray had provided a context in which these 'Desolate and Mountanous' landscapes could be now be viewed by the tourist, one in which they could extract 'noble thoughts' from their experience of the otherwise 'savage grandeur'.

Gray's account of his trip actually starts with his journey across Yorkshire to Penrith, and it is not until the second day that he walks from Penrith to Ullswater. Turning off the Keswick road, he walks along beside the river Eamont before climbing a hill overlooking the lake. Once on top, he saw:

> the Lake opening directly at my feet majestic in its calmness, clear and smooth as a blew mirror with winding shores & low points of land cover'd with green inclosures, white farm-houses looking out amongst the trees, & cattle feeding. the water is almost everywhere border'd with cultivated lands gently sloping upwards till they reach the feet of the mountains, which rise very rude & aweful with their broken tops on either hand ...

He then walked on along the north shore of the lake as far as the village of Watermillock before retracing his steps. The entry ends: 'a pleasant grave day, perfectly calm & warm, but without a gleam of sunshine: then the sky seeming to thicken, the valley to grow more desolate, & evening drawing on, I return'd ... to Penrith.'

It is clear from his initial description of the lake that Gray had paid close attention to John Brown's description of Derwent Water, and carefully re-iterated Brown's focus on the contrasting elements of the landscape that composed the view. It was a focus which, with Gray's encouragement, became the filter through which visitors came to see the landscape, and knowing the rules and content of good pictorial composition became central to the picturesque experience of the Lakes.

The next day, Gray sets out for Keswick and Derwent Water, and although there are no grand compositions for him to admire, he is fully alive to the pictorial effects of the light and weather, the kind of 'varying and accidental beauties' that had been described by Brown. Along the way, for example, he passes 'at the feet of Saddleback, whose furrow'd sides were gilt by the noon-day Sun, while its brow appear'd of a sad purple from the shadows of the clouds, as they sail'd slowly by ... '

But then comes the great moment, his first view of the 'sweet vale' he had come to see, as he crests the ridge above Keswick and 'saw from an eminence at two miles distance the Vale of Elysium in all its verdure, the sun playing on the bosom of the lake, & lighting up all the mountains with its lustre'; thirty-four words which, as the *Journal* became widely read after its publication, became one of the defining descriptions of the Lakes. 'Gray's Elysium' was included in the poems and descriptions of numerous visitors who came later to find this magical spot, and this poetic re-naming of the vale of Keswick, and its setting amongst the mountains and fells, came to represent perhaps the seminal act in the transformation of the landscapes of the Lakes from the 'desolate and mountanous' realm of nature, to something that could take a legitimate and enduring place in our world of culture.

Later that day, after lunch in the Queen's Head, Keswick, and no doubt on the advice of the landlord, he heads out to admire the view from the Vicarage garden at Crosthwaite, recounting that he 'straggled out alone to the Parsonage, fell down on [his] back across a dirty lane with [his] glass open in one hand, but broke only [his] knuckles: stay'd nevertheless & saw the sun set in all its glory'.

The 'glass' Gray refers to here, known widely as a 'Claude glass', became a must-have for the tourists. It was a convex tinted mirror, sometimes rectangular, sometimes oval in shape, of a size convenient for slipping into a pocket and carrying on the tour. Its role was to help filter out the

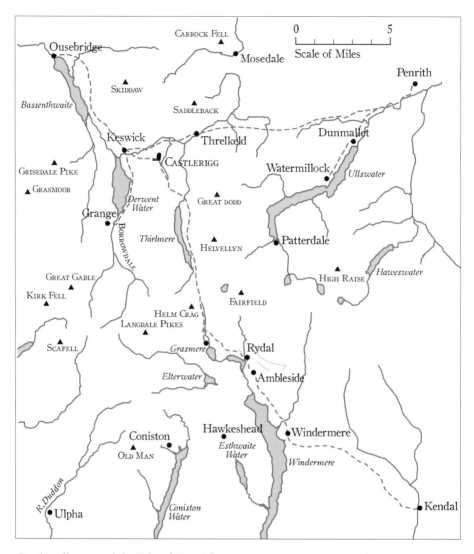

Gray's walks around the Vale of Keswick.

wider chaos of the landscape and present it as an artistic composition. Holding up the mirror, and looking at the view over their shoulders, the tourists could move the glass until its oval or rectangular shape framed the perfect composition. At the same time, the darkened glass transformed the image, smoothing out detail and providing an overall tone that was considered to replicate the kind of tonal qualities found in the paintings of Claude. In this way, the glass represents the filters of artistic conventions through which the tourists sought to transform the physical landscape into an artistic one. The fact that it is necessary to look backwards over one's shoulder to use the glass no doubt explains why Gray fell over.

The following morning, Gray set out on the first of his expeditions to experience at first hand the different elements which made up the view. 'Conducted' by his landlord, he walked round Derwent Water and into Borrowdale:

> [I] drew near the foot of *Walla-crag*, whose bare & rocky brow, cut perpendicularly down above 400 feet ... awefully overlooks the way ... [From this viewpoint beside the lake] opens both ways the most delicious views, that my eyes ever beheld. Behind you are the magnificent heights of *Walla-crag*: opposite lie the thick hanging woods ... with green & smiling fields embosom'd in the dark cliffs; to the left the jaws of *Borodale*, with that turbulent Chaos of mountain behind mountain roll'd in confusion.

Already, at the beginning of the day's walk, his frame of mind is clear. Now in amongst the landscape that Brown had described, he is determined not only to throw open his senses and soak in the atmosphere, the writing reflecting his growing anticipation of the excitements and horrors to come; but also to record moments of picturesque effect. But in spite of the lowering heights of Walla Crag behind him, whatever dangers lie within the 'jaws' of Borrowdale and amidst the turbulent chaos beyond, he is comforted by the 'smiling' fields and his ability to bring some order to this magnificent confusion through use of his glass. 'Think how the glass played its part in such a spot,' he tells Wharton.

After following the road beside the lake and 'passing a brook called *Barrow-beck*, we enter'd *Borodale*. The crags named Lodoor-banks now begin to impend terribly over your way.' At this point they briefly left the road to inspect '*Lodoor-water-fall*'. When it rains heavily 'the stream is nobly broken leaping from rock to rock, & foaming with fury. On one side a towering crag, that spired up to equal, if not overtop, the neighbouring cliffs'. Watching the water, he noted too that the cliffs 'all lay in shade and darkness', while 'on the other hand a rounder broader projecting hill shag'd with wood' was 'illuminated by the sun'; the contrasts of light and dark adding a new artistic

dimension to the scene otherwise dominated by the foaming noise and fury.

Entering Borrowdale, the walkers passed 'under *Gowder-crag*, a hill more formidable to the eye and to the apprehension than that of *Lodoor*; the rocks atop, deep-cloven perpendicularly by the rains, hanging loose & nodding forwards, seem just starting from their base in shivers … the road on both sides is strew'd with piles of fragments thrown across each other … '[11]

Suitably alarmed by the loose, nodding rocks, they passed on further into the jaws of Borrowdale, where the scene fulfilled Gray's expectations: 'The hills here are cloth'd all up their steep sides [with trees in places where] no soil appears but the staring rock, & where no man could scarce stand upright.' Yet at this point, with the whole of Borrowdale opening up before him, Gray's attention was drawn by something else, almost as though he tired of maintaining this heightened state of awareness and became interested instead in the reality of the lives of those who actually lived there. The rest of the day's entry is largely the account of meeting a 'civil young farmer' in the village of Grange, who invited him into his 'neat white house' where they were given a meal of milk, oatcakes and ale. He then spent the rest of the afternoon seeing the landscape through the farmer's eyes, watching the harvest, then in progress, and hearing of the problems and trials of the farming life. Although, looking further up the valley, he saw *Castle-crag, Eagle's-Cliff, Dove's Nest* and *Whitedale Pike*, heard tales of the wadd mines, and saw the 'summits grow loftier to the eye and of more fantastic forms … the ancient kingdom, the reign of Chaos and old Night', he was content to linger at Grange: 'For me I went no farther than the Farmer's.'

On his return to Keswick, the shadows of the afternoon sunlight had transformed the landscapes around him, 'disclosing new features', and, catching sight of a 'serene' Skiddaw, he realized that it would have been a perfect day 'for going up [it]'. Had Gray left the valley and ascended Skiddaw, the subsequent history of the picturesque tour might have been very different, but in the end he did not, being content to view such places through his glass. Gray's mission here was to understand what

Looking into Borrowdale [Derry Brabbs].

The view Thomas Gray was looking at when he wrote 'summits grow loftier to the eye, and of more fantastic forms … the ancient kingdom, the reign of Chaos and old Night'.

Brown had seen, to explore his own reactions, and the day ended not with an ascent of Skiddaw, but rather with him walking 'in the evening ... alone down to the lake' to experience what Brown had recommended, 'a walk by full moonlight.'

Following his visit to the jaws of Borrowdale, Gray spent the next day walking to two 'eminences' near Keswick, Crow-park and Cockshut Hill, from which he could catch the kind of view both Dalton and Brown had written about and Thomas Smith had painted. He then returned to the Parsonage garden 'a little before sunset, & saw in [his] glass a picture that ... would sell for a thousand pounds.' No doubt, the glass had been much in use that day.

Seeking new views the following day, Gray walked north from Keswick following the Derwent river as far as How-hill, from where he surveyed 'Bassenthwaite-water' and 'a full view of Skiddaw', formulating his plan to walk up Bassenthwaite the next day. Turning back towards Keswick he then walked round the lake, through Portinscale and on along the lake shore as far as Hawse End. That afternoon, after lunch, and perhaps another conversation with his landlord about interesting places to see, he set off to visit Castlerigg stone circle, where he admired the stones and the views of the Nadder valley, and a new range of hills, the long ridge line above 'the fells of *St. John's*, and particularly the summits of *Catchidecam* ... & *Helvellyn* said to be as high as Skiddaw.'[12]

After his long walks of the day before, the next morning Gray travelled by chaise the 8 miles up the east side of Bassenthwaite, 'directly below Skiddaw', to 'Ewes-bridge' [Ouse Bridge]. Here he took lunch at the Inn, and admired the view which 'looks directly up the whole length of the lake almost to Keswick & beyond this a ridge of cultivated hills ... ' before he returned to his hotel.

Unfortunately, he woke up next morning to a rainy 'damp' day when the 'clouds came rolling up the mountains all round' and Gray was ready to move on. He strolled to Crow Park, looking perhaps for one last effect of light or clouds to transform the scene, and, after an afternoon that was spent discussing local botany, wadd mining and local sources of food, perhaps with his obliging landlord, he took a final evening stroll along the Penrith road.

The next day brought his experience of the heart of the Lakes to an end, leaving Keswick, and walking down the length of Thirlmere, over Dunmail

The view from Castlerigg to the Helvellyn range today [stephen gillis hd9 imaging / Alamy Stock Photo].

'[T]he fells of St. John's, and particularly the summits of Catchidecam ... & Helvellyn said to be as high as Skiddaw'.

Raise into Grasmere, before carrying on past Rydal and Ambleside to arrive in Kendal.

It was a 'gloomy' morning as he set out from Keswick, but as he crossed the ridgeline at Castlerigg, he looked back one more time, down into the Vale of Elysium: 'and the sun breaking out discover'd the most beautiful (enchanting) view I have yet seen of the whole valley behind me, the two lakes, the river, & all the mountains (in all their glory). Had almost a mind to have gone back again.' But he pressed on, down into the vale of Thirlmere, along 'the foot of Helvellyn', and up over Dunmail Raise. Here, first Helm Crag to the right, 'distinguished ... by the strange broken outline of its top ... the stones flung across each

The summit of Helm Crag [Derry Brabbs].

Gray's scene of 'the strange broken outline of Helm Crag'. The road over Dunmill Raise is visible in the valley below.

other in wild confusion', caught his eye and then 'just beyond it one of the sweetest landscapes, that art ever attempted to imitate,' and, in the midst of it, 'Grasmere-water'.

For Gray, his head full of Skiddaw, Walla Crag, Gowder Crag, the jaws of Borrowdale and the 'reign of Chaos and old Night' beyond, and, indeed, the 'wild confusion' on the summit of Helm Crag, Grasmere is almost too pretty, too 'sweet', to be picturesque. The language in which he describes it is very different in tone, and here there is no 'apprehension' or sense of impending horror. Instead, 'all is peace, rusticity, & happy poverty in its neatest most becoming attire.' The lake lies, 'its margin hollow'd into small bays with bold eminences of rock'; 'a low promontory pushes itself far into the water, & on it stands a white village with the parish-church rising in the midst of it, hanging enclosures, corn-fields & meadows green as an emerald with their trees & hedges & cattle'. Beyond all this he discovers 'old woods, which climb half-way up the mountain's side, and … above them a broken line of crags, that crown the scene.' He saw nothing that 'breaks in upon the repose of this little unsuspected paradise'.

And with these observations, Gray was gone, down past the village and up over White Moss Common to Rydal; it was to be another thirty years (October 1799) before Wordsworth and Coleridge came through Grasmere vale on their own 'Pikteresk Toor', as Coleridge was to call it, and found themselves forced by bad weather to stay a few days, days in which both appear to have become, as Wordsworth put it, 'much enchanted with Grasmere and Rydal'. A few months later William and Dorothy Wordsworth moved into Dove Cottage at Town End, Grasmere, where Coleridge was to join them in the spring of 1800, and where, together, they were to find new, subtler, emotional qualities of the picturesque in the landscape around Grasmere than Gray had time to appreciate, and where they were to further develop the aesthetic consciousness of Romanticism.

For Gray though, although he was impressed by the 'huge crag call'd *Rydale-head* [probably Nab Scar]' above Rydal Water, little else caught his eye, until, walking down Windermere, he enjoyed the 'delicious views across it', probably from Low Wood, and the lake 'resembling some vast & magnificent river'. Turning from the lake he then followed the road round under Orrest Head and on into Kendal where he spent the next two nights. The *Journal* then records the final four days of his walk back to Leeds, before returning to Cambridge.

Thus, in the years c.1755–69, between them, Dalton, Brown and Gray, and artists such as Thomas Smith of Derby, had established the Lake District as one of the key locations for the picturesque tour. They had defined the purpose of the tour, the outline of an itinerary of the 'stations', and identified the frame of mind required to assume the 'role' of tourist. In the years that followed a number of others visited and toured the Lakes, some pursuing antiquarian interests, others recording agriculture and industry, a few boldly scaling Skiddaw. But it was to be another ten years before the first practical guide book, specifically defining the picturesque tour, was produced when Thomas West published *A Guide to the Lakes* in 1778.[13]

* ❋ ❋ ❋

In his *Guide*, West confirms that an interest in landscape painting in particular 'induces many to visit the lakes' and bases his descriptions of the tour largely on those in Gray's *Journal,* formalizing Gray's identification of the appropriate 'stations' from which the best views can be enjoyed. He also notes, however, that some of the earlier writers, such as Gray and Thomas Pennant, chose the wrong time of year to see the landscapes at their best. Pennant visited the Lakes on his way to make a tour of Scotland in 1772 and indeed, in his account of the trip, *A Tour in Scotland and Voyage to the Hebrides*, he thanks, amongst others, 'Mr Thomas West [who] favoured me with several things relating to the north of Lancashire'. Pennant, however, passed through in May, too early in West's view, while Gray, of course, had visited in October, too late to see things properly, rain spoiling some of his days. To avoid such problems, West advises that the tour should ideally be made between June and August.

West's *Guide* covered twelve lakes, expanding Gray's itinerary to make a more complete tour, and identifying some twenty-two 'stations' for viewing the most beautiful of the landscapes, and it is clear from this list that Derwent Water was still the pre-eminent location. Of the twenty-two, eight are on the lake or in the vicinity, and several of them are specifically located from Gray's writing, fulfilling his hope that if 'I chuse to set down these barbarous names … anybody may enquire on the place, & easily find the particular station, that I mean.' The guide itself was an immediate success and by 1784 was on its third edition, defining the tour of the Lakes for the increasing numbers of visitors who undertook it.

Yet, if West's *Guide* laid out the definitive itinerary of the tour at this time, it was to be another visitor, William Gilpin, who introduced the artistic principles that lay behind the picturesque viewpoint required to enjoy the tour, in his *Observations, relative chiefly to Picturesque Beauty* of 1786. In an earlier book (*Dialogue on Stowe*, 1748) Gilpin had 'discussed at some length the nature of views and first defined the picturesque as whatever would make a suitable picture,' before going on to elaborate his ideas in a series of books, including one on the other popular picturesque tour of the time, that down the River Wye from Ross to Chepstow.[14]

In this book, *Observations on the River Wye* (1770), Gilpin discussed in detail his analysis of those elements of the landscape through which the Wye flowed that made it picturesque – a suitable subject for the painter – and his aim on this trip down the Wye was to 'examine the face of a country *by the rules of picturesque beauty*', with an emphasis on the special combination of qualities he found as the river 'flows in a gentle, uninterrupted stream; and adorns, through its various reaches, a succession of the most picturesque scenes'. After noting the appealing 'circumstances' created by the '*lofty banks* of the river, and its *mazy course*', he writes that the resulting views should be seen to be composed of 'four grand parts: the area which is the river itself; the two *side-screens*, which are the opposite banks, and lead the perspective; and the *front-screen* which points out the winding of the river'. Having established this basic framework for the view, and the attractive 'informality' of its lines of perspective, Gilpin then discusses the 'sources of variety' which make the scene interesting to the artist, sources which include the '*contrast of the screens*: sometimes one of the side-screens is elevated, sometimes the other, and sometimes the front; or both the side-screens may be lofty, and the front either high or low.' In addition to such contrasts, variety can also be provided by 'ornaments', details in the landscape which, on the Wye, 'may be ranged under four heads: *ground, wood, rocks*, and *buildings*', features he then goes on to examine in detail. The 'rules of the picturesque' outlined in *Observations on the River Wye* were to prove particularly applicable to the Lakeland scenery, since the source of much that was beautiful in it was exactly this combination of land and water.

In his role as a picturesque tourist, Gilpin considers himself to be 'in quest of beauty', and although he finds it in certain aspects of the works of Nature, he is also often disappointed and finds himself critical of what he sees. He

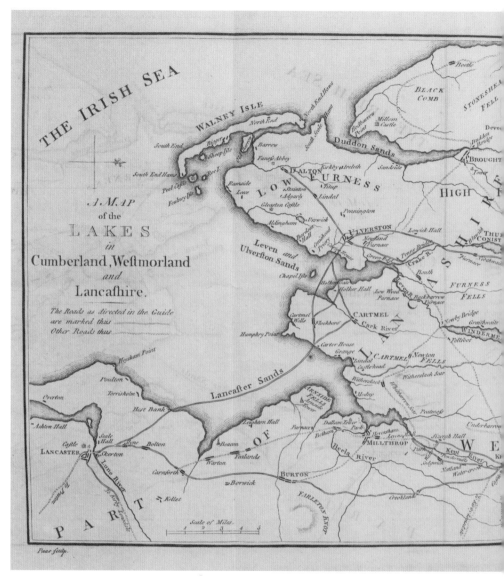

Map from Thomas West's *A Guide to the Lakes*, 3rd edition, 1784
[courtesy of The Wordsworth Trust, Grasmere].

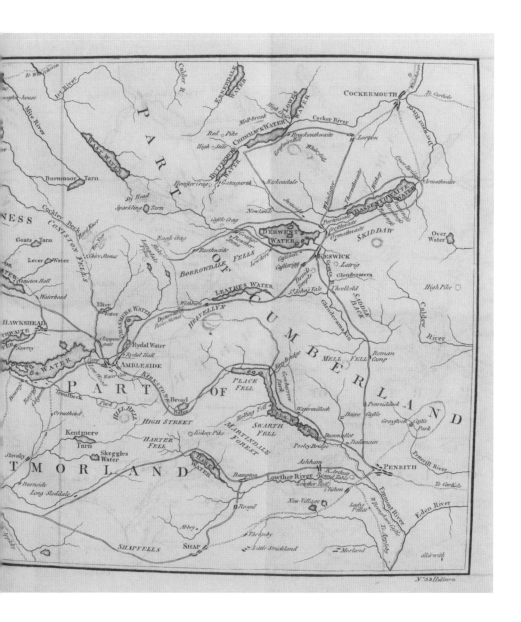

sums up the basic problem as follows: 'Nature is always great in design. She is an admirable colourist also; and harmonizes tints with infinite variety and beauty: but she is seldom so correct in composition, as to produce a harmonious whole.'

It was this same problem that had led Gray to view the landscapes of the Lakes through his 'glass' as he attempted to edit the forms provided by Nature and use the oval shape of the glass itself to frame the reflected view as a satisfactory 'artistic' composition by turning it left to right or up and down. The aim of Gilpin's books was similar: to provide a means by which the tourist could look at landscape and use their artistic eye to form an opinion about the qualities of what they see. Thus his books discussed in infinite and, at times, pedantic detail the principles which he saw as essential for transforming the natural landscape into art, from correct framing and composition, to tonal and colour qualities and suitable content, principles that he then illustrated with his own pictures.

Gilpin's *Observations, relative chiefly to Picturesque Beauty* followed a series of visits to Keswick, and his long friendship with John Brown meant that he was fully tuned in to the picturesque properties of the landscape. Over time, his books became an essential companion for the tourists, along with West's *Guide,* and his rules, particularly the division of views into sequential 'screens', or layers of recession, and the language he used to explain them, are reflected in many of the later journals, diaries and letters that recount visits to the Lakes. This can be clearly seen, for example, in the terms used by Coleridge and Wordsworth when they were to write of 'first distance', 'second distance' or 'third distance' in describing views in letters to friends and family about their walks in the Lakes in 1799.

By the end of the century then, the accepted approach to a picturesque tour of the Lakes was firmly established and very popular, as 'sensitive' visitors, tutored in the ways of the imagination, experienced the landscapes from the itinerary of carefully selected 'stations', and reacted with appropriate 'fright' and 'awe' in the face of the sublime. They were then expected to use their sense of taste and knowledge of art to form an opinion about the differing qualities discernable in each 'View', and to channel their reactions through the forms and meanings of picturesque art and romantic poetry. It was their ability to display those qualities of culture and taste, and react in this rarefied way, which, for them, set their experiences of the Lakeland landscapes apart from those of their guides and the local population in general. Aspiration to the ranks of polite society was predicated at least in part on the ability to look at a landscape, to form an educated opinion on its particular qualities, and to judge its suitability as a valid subject of art or poetry. The role of these picturesque tours was to enable the tourists to visit the choice views listed in their guidebook, and then to record a suitable reaction to what they saw, assuming, as one writer has put it, 'the role of someone who must be either pleased or displeased with the landscape they see'.[15]

Given the nature and purpose of these tours, they were usually undertaken as a group experience, travelling in carriages or on horseback, and their routes lay largely along the roads which linked the lakes and their stations. Accommodation in a series of hotels in the larger towns, particularly Ambleside and Keswick, made it possible to meet fellow tourists, with whom to exchange experiences and to take evening walks beside the lakes, to admire the effects of moonlight, and to hire guides for short excursions to particular waterfalls, or boatmen for a cruise on the lake, the latter in order to fully experience the effects of echoes created by gun or cannon shots.

Soon enough, having an opinion about these places, and having the ability to define the specific qualities of the world of natural landscape that were of value to the world of art and culture, became a mark of an individual's taste and the strength of their artistic eye. As the retired soldier and traveller Joseph Palmer was to write about the Lake District tour, by 1792 'it is now so meritoriously fashionable to make the tour, I dare say it will be thought a want of taste not to be able to speak about it; for it wants only to be made, to have preference of every summer excursion in the Kingdom.'[16]

Indeed, so popular did Gilpin's books and ideas become that by the early nineteenth century they were seen to be in danger of replacing the landscape itself as the focus of visitors' interest. Representative of this view is Coleridge's comment in his notebook in 1800: 'Ladies reading Gilpin passing by the places instead of looking at the places,'[17] Coleridge is suggesting here that, as Gilpin's definition of the picturesque as 'whatever would make a suitable picture' and his determination to codify what that meant with his lists of empirical principles, came to dominate visitor's experience of the Lakes, a crucial element of what had driven the early interest in the search for the picturesque had got lost; this was something much less tangible, much more evasive of empirical explanation – the workings of the imagination. But, in fact, by the end of the century, Coleridge himself came to play a key role in an entirely new way of experiencing the landscapes of the Lake District, the urge not to passively view the landscape as an object of artistic interest but to actively explore the natural world at first hand, and to establish some meaningful, direct connection with the life that animated it. As we will see in the next chapter, rather than simply letting 'Active Fancy' travel 'beyond Sense', and picture 'things unseen', this new interest sought to physically discover and understand, to directly experience these things.

2

Exploring the 'wild scenes of Nature', 1792–1802

One of the earliest surviving indications of this new approach to the Lakes came, in fact, some seven years before Coleridge first visited, when Joseph Palmer recorded an account of his sixteen-day 'ramble' in the Lake District in 1792. He was accompanied by a friend (never named) who knew the area, the tour very much following the traditions of the Picturesque Tour and, for guidance and further information, they took with them a copy of Thomas West's *Guide to the Lakes* of 1784. Fortunately for us, however, Palmer also took copious notes of his own, and on his return home published an account of the tour under the title *A Fortnight's Ramble to the Lakes, by a Rambler in 1792*.

Joseph Palmer (1756–1815), formerly known as Captain Joseph Budworth, became a career soldier who served with the Royal Manchester Volunteers, and was on active service during the prolonged and increasingly desperate siege of Gibraltar by the Spanish, 1779–82. During the course of this he was severely wounded, one result of which was that he either lost, or lost the use of, an arm. After the lifting of the siege, and while they were still in Gibraltar, news arrived that his regiment was to be disbanded; Palmer's comment, years later in the third edition of his *Ramble*, gives an indication of just how devastating this news was: 'so completely hath that Regiment passed away ... its officers unrewarded, unattended to, unnoticed'.

Having served with the Royal Manchester Volunteers from December 1777 to September 1783, he returned to England seriously disabled, disillusioned and on half-pay, and, failing to secure another posting on full pay, in 1784 he accepted a cadetship, a non-commissioned post, in the Bengal Artillery, in the service of the East India Company. Returning to England a few years later, he served in the North Hampshire volunteer militia before retiring, but in spite of his additional service after Gibraltar, it would seem that he had never fully recovered from his wounds. On retiring, Palmer then married Elizabeth Palmer, and in 1811, on the death of Elizabeth's brother, 'inherited the Palmer estates in Palmerston, Ireland', changing his name to Palmer. He wrote various pieces for the *Gentleman's Magazine*, and was interested in antiquities, particularly aspects of Pagan religions, both in India and, later, in England, where he pondered the 'Druidical stones' and sought to understand 'the confusion of ideas about their Cromlehs, Kistvaens, and sacred woods.' He became a Fellow of the Society of Antiquaries in 1795.

Thus it was as a retired, and to some degree disabled, soldier and freelance writer that Palmer finally found time to set out on his exploration of the Lakeland landscapes in 1792 and write up his *Ramble* for publication – an account which proved sufficiently popular for it to be reprinted in a second edition in 1795 and a third in 1810.[1] Although the tour itself may have started off in the by-then traditional manner, reading Palmer's account it soon becomes clear that, during the course it, Palmer started to become interested in aspects of the Lake District life and landscape that went beyond its purely picturesque qualities. He seems to have developed a genuine interest in the area, an interest that led him to return again in the winter of 1797–8, and his new experiences were then added to the third edition of the *Ramble*.

During his visits Palmer soon became increasingly drawn into both the landscape of the Lakes and the lives of the people he met there and came to admire, and, reading his accounts, the differences between those of 1792 and those of 1797–8 indicate that his interest in the landscape itself had developed beyond that of the initial picturesque tourist to something deeper, more engaged, and that this development had altered his sense of relationship not just to the landscape, but also to the people who inhabited it. Molly Lefebure writes of the Rambler: 'For all his ascents he employed guides and the dizzy heights and perilous paths so unnerved him that when things became too frightening he bandaged his eye … in order that he might not view the dangers that beset him.'[2] Yet against the background of his life, the fact that he had 'but one arm to trust to', and his account of his unaccompanied mid-winter walk to Scale Force in 1798, this would seem to misjudge both his experience and his achievement; here was a man for whom the Lakes, in the light of his military service, held few real surprises or dangers, and also someone who, when attempting to cross the icy planks of a rotten wooden bridge to reach the safety of the Inn in Buttermere, in waterlogged shoes and trousers and in the dark of a freezing January evening, freely admitted it when he felt 'qualms akin to fear'.

Although both shorter and less complex than Coleridge's accounts, Palmer's are particularly interesting for us because, while Coleridge, as a resident, left out much of the wider context in which his walks occurred, Palmer, with the eyes and interest of a visitor, tells us much about how the local people and the economy of the Lake District were adapting to benefit from the increasing influx of tourists. Indeed, he talks about their curiosity concerning these 'Gentlemen' and 'strangers' who came from such distant places as 'Lunnun' to pay someone to guide them up to places they themselves would never think of visiting, unless they were looking 'for runaway sheep'. Palmer's recounting of conversations, and his interest in the individuals who guided him, give us a unique insight into the world Coleridge later came to live in, and the meetings he in turn must have had, but never recorded, with the shepherds, miners, travellers, and drovers he met on the walks we will be following in this book.

Palmer's initial walk in 1792 began with a stay in Kendal to see the sights, followed by a comfortable walk down the River 'Ken' [Kent] to Levens Hall where they spent time in the park and admired the 'Dutch style' gardens round the house. He sets the tone for the *Ramble* in his Preface, where he tells us 'Whatever I have written came warm from the imagination with the views full before it', and specifies that his account 'is only offered as a Journeying Companion' rather than a guide such as Thomas West had written, adding in the third edition 'I follow[ed] no written guide, lest I should enter too fully into other people's ideas'. Although he is at pains to establish his account as something other than a guide, it is clear that he saw the whole trip very much in the spirit of a picturesque tour: 'those who make the tour of the Lakes, and will examine any of the views I attempt to describe, if they see them from the points I did … perhaps may give me the credit of delineating them faithfully.' There is a very fine line drawn here between using the word 'points' and the 'stations' of the guides, and he still emphasizes the fact that landscape had to be viewed from specific locations which gave a satisfactory artistic perspective. Note too his use of the word 'delineating', an artistic or draughting term, rather than 'describing', the term we might use today.

It is, in fact, well into the account of this first day's walk to Levens Hall before we get mention of the Lakeland hills, when Palmer notes that the view from the park of the Hall 'is now the matchless work of nature', and at the Hall itself, once they had climbed the stone winding steps of the turret,

'you have a prospect charmingly variegated and backed by high mountains.'
It is to be another two days, however, before he gets there, and when he
does it seems that there were certain views and features that he was keenly
anticipating, particularly the first glimpse of Windermere. This comes after
leaving Kendal when, from his coach, he 'caught first sight of Windermere'
where he saw 'exclusive of the islands, and mountains, and woody borders,
half a dozen boats ... sailing under a fresh westerly breeze.' As for many of the
tourists and artists at this time, for Palmer the picturesque charm of the Lakes
consisted as much of finding signs of human activity within the landscape, as
of the landscape itself. His anticipation of the view of Windermere, and his
subsequent admiration for the view to the north of the lake that he describes
as 'the long chain ... to Fairfield, which composes that grand crescent every
person upon Windermere looks up to with such respect', suggest that he may
well have read the anonymous descriptive letter published in the *Gentleman's
Magazine* in 1748 referred to earlier. Certainly the view, described in that
letter as the 'most stupendous theatre', and which he describes as 'that grand
crescent', represented for him one of the key sites in the Lakes, and a little
later, when describing Borrowdale, he comments that although it is 'a grand
assemblage of the sublime', it is 'neither so magnificent or pleasing as the
[grand crescent] around Rydal'.

By the time he reaches Ambleside, however, our Rambler is in the full
picturesque mode of Dalton, Brown and Gray when he catches sight of 'some
of the loftiest pines [he] ever saw ... though the pine is a melancholy tree, it
is here seen amongst cheerful verdures, it is worth admiring as a contrasting
shade.'

From their base at the Salutation Inn in Ambleside, where they were advised
by the Inn's resident guide Robin Partridge, Palmer and his companion start
exploring, first the falls at Rydal Hall, where 'the youngest daughter of the
head herdsman waited at the gate to attend company to the cascades', and
then the next day to Grasmere where they contacted Robert Newton at
his 'public house', recommended, no doubt by Partridge, as 'an intelligent
man' and a suitable guide. On their walk through the vale of Grasmere, they
are 'amusing [themselves] with the neat rusticity' around them, and as they
approach the village itself, he records that ' ... the steeple, and what I can see
of the church, embosomed in trees, are delightfully picturesque', while the
scene is completed by 'the Scotch cattle ... feeding amidst the woods, and
sheep ... beautifully dotted upon the hill'.

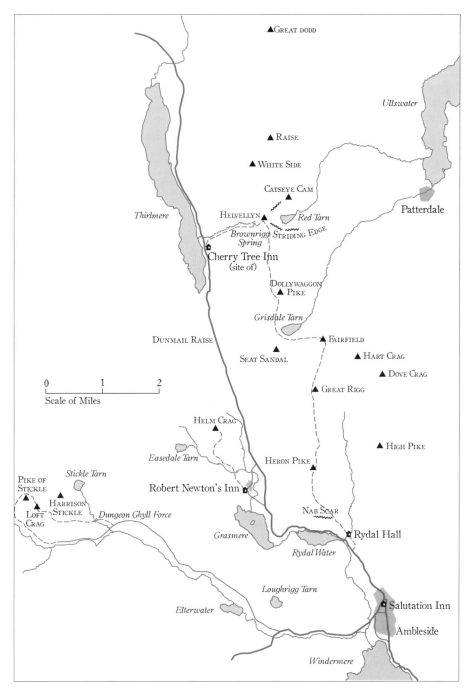

Palmer's Walks, 1. The ascents of Helm Crag and Helvellyn, 1792, and the Langdale Pikes, 1797.

Helm Crag above the roofs of Grasmere village [author].

The proximity and apparent accessibility of the rugged peak of Helm Crag to the 'delightfully picturesque' village of Grasmere seems to have caught Joseph Palmer's imagination, and persuaded him to arrange the first ascent by a 'stranger'.

But then comes something which alerts us to the fact that Palmer is not content just to look, judge and admire. After an afternoon's fishing on the lake with Newton, and tipping him 'a trifle', he arranges to return on Sunday (two days later), to 'dine at his house' and for Newton 'afterwards to go with us to the summit of Helm Crag'. While Gray had noticed the 'wild confusion' on the summit of Helm Crag only in passing, Palmer wanted to actually climb it, to experience that 'wild confusion' for himself; a significant departure from the traditional tour itinerary. After spending the next two days first taking the obligatory boat trip round Windermere and then walking over the

Kirkstone Pass to visit Patterdale and Ullswater, they duly arrive at Newton's for lunch, before setting off with their guide 'to surmount the steep ascent of Helm Crag'. The unusual nature of this expedition is underlined by the fact that neither Newton (who had himself only climbed it once) nor Partridge 'remembered that [Helm Crag] had been visited by strangers.'

Palmer's account of what followed reflects this feeling of breaking new ground. At first, the walk 'up a narrow lane' past the church was easy enough for him to look around and admire 'a new view of Grasmere valley, with a perpetual waterfall, justly from its force, called White-churn Gill [Sourmilk Gill, Easedale]; it rushes from a crescent-heathed hill'. Soon, however, things get more serious:

> The sun was hot … it was so steep we were frequently obliged to stop when we met a narrow shelf, and when we got to the first range of the hill I was glad to throw myself down panting from relief: the grass was slippery, which we guarded against by forcing our sticks as deep into the ground as we possibly could.

He continues 'When we gained the second height … the pinnacle hanging over our right [the 'Lamb' and 'the Lion'] obliged us to take a sweep, but as we had the wind and a sight of the top, we found less trouble at this stage', and they soon enough reached the summit; once there 'I allowed myself to rest a little … while I look with awful pleasure at the sight [around us].' In this line Palmer sums up the key requirement for the visitor mentioned first by Dalton – the ability to 'look with awful pleasure', conveying his sensitivity to the sublime and the knowledge of taste that enabled him to express it. After resting and getting his breath back, he 'went upon the projecting pinnacle, which just had room for two', from which he marked the views of Windermere, Esthwaite Water and Grasmere. The exhilarating experience of actually climbing the crags and being rewarded with such previously unseen views broke new ground for the Rambler and his companion, and it was something they were to immediately repeat.

The next day, intending 'an idle morning' after the exertions of the day before, they had not engaged a guide or planned a particular route but, drawn out by the beautiful weather, they set off around the top of Windermere and followed the road until they arrived at 'a purple hill, at the head of Coniston Lake, [where] you have a full view of it.' While sitting on their hill, 'making observations, a man in his harvest dress … seated himself by us, and we were soon convinced, by certain shrewd remarks, he wished to officiate as guide. On pointing to a high mountain, named the Old Man, symptoms appeared of wishing to go up it, and we did not stop to hesitate.' With the 'precaution to take some brandy … at one o'clock [we] began the arduous task', and some two hours later they gained the summit. From the top Palmer describes 'extensive views' of the sea and dozens of 'pieces of water, most of them on the summit of hills'. While they no doubt made more 'observations', it is clear that they have no curiosity, as Coleridge was to have, as to the names of the mountains, vales, passes or lakes, since most of their conversation with their guide concerns which of the visible tarns had fish in them and could provide them with sport.

After reaching the summit, they walk along the ridge 'perfectly safe', descending in time to Levers Water and its waterfall, their guide clearly knowing how to retain their interest in the walk, and after meeting one of the miners with his 'Cyclops' lamp on his head, they return to Ambleside. Following the Coniston adventure, they rest for the next couple of days, visiting Stockdale Force above Ambleside, admiring the Roman camp at Galava, and discussing their options for further adventures with Robin Partridge who, Palmer tells us, 'acts as boots, postilion, and boatman at the Salutation Inn' and is 'so bold a mountaineer, he can go anywhere a sheep can go.' Emboldened perhaps by Partridge and their success at Helm Crag and the Old Man, our Ramblers decide on their next major challenge: 'If tomorrow turns out favourable we propose mounting Helvellyn.' Interestingly enough, although they are by now regularly going beyond the normal experiences of the Tour, they are still very conscious of its conventions, and go to the trouble of 'ordering a chaise' to meet them, as they think it 'proper to enter upon a new station, with a dash that too often claims attention … ' to meet them on their planned descent to Thirlmere.

Impatient to start their new adventure, they rise the next morning between 3 and 4am: '[We] saw we had a clear sky: the full moon was just going to drop over the very point of Loughrigg Fell, and tinged all around it with solemnity.'

Starting at Rydal Hall, '[we] surmounted the first hills [taking] advantage of the morning to exert ourselves … [and] passed the long chain until we came to Fairfield, which composes that grand crescent every person upon Windermere looks up to with such respect.' Palmer's 'long chain' is, of course, the 'stupendous theatre' of our anonymous letter writer of 1748, and West went on to describe the same view, writing 'Fairfield swells in Alpine

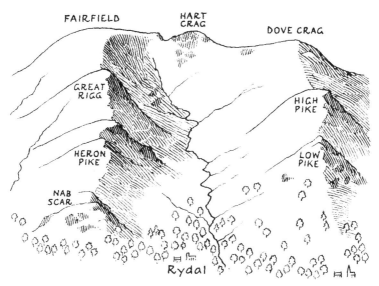

FAIRFIELD HART CRAG DOVE CRAG GREAT RIGG HIGH PIKE HERON PIKE LOW PIKE NAB SCAR Rydal

The Fairfield Horseshoe [A. Wainwright, *Eastern Fells*].

Wainwright describes this view as 'a great horseshoe of grassy slopes below a consistently high skyline, simple in design and impressive in altitude'.

pride, rivalled only by Rydal's loftier head.' It clearly became one of Palmer's favourite views, one he never forgot and which nothing he subsequently saw was to surpass. That they all noticed it suggests an early importance on the Tour which is now somewhat diminished by the subsequent growth of woodland on all sides.[3]

By 7.15am they had reached Grisdale Hause below Seat Sandal and 'descended to a tarn [Grisdale Tarn] with a bird's-eye view of Grasmere and overlooking Helm Crag' before 'clambering to a pile of stones upon … Dollywaggon Pike' and seeing 'to the west immense mountains that hide the vale of Borrowdale, showing three lakes and the sea bounding them.' Once on top of Dollywaggon Pike 'we are in the midst of sharp whirlwinds, which rustle up the dry moss, and by lifting the skirts of my coat, have given some fine coolers to my back.' Their route up from Grisdale Tarn, perhaps just off the ridgeline, seems to have meant that they did not see the sharp precipices and fissured cliffs of the line of Falcon and Tarn Crags above Cock Cove to their right.

The key to the experience of this tour for the Rambler is to see things in 'a contemplative mood', but at this point such a mood was something that eluded him, as the realities of actually climbing these mountains, rather than viewing them from stations in the valleys, become clear to him. In this instance, largely because of the 'tight tug' it had taken to get up there and his 'ungovernable thirst … [his] tongue cleaves to the roof of [his] mouth', he felt anything but contemplative even before he got to Helvellyn. He had, in fact, been tempted to drink from Grisdale Tarn and had to be dissuaded by Partridge, and it was not until they started the descent that he found a spring from which to quench his thirst.

Leaving the whirlwinds on Dollywaggon, they proceeded along to Whelp Side, from which they see Bassenthwaite, and arrive above Striding Edge, 'a hill a mile long, extend[ing] east, so narrow you might sit across any part of the ridge', before ascending to the top of Helvellyn, where they arrive at 9.30am; this was therefore a far longer ascent than Old Man had been, which he tells us had taken them two hours to ascend, or indeed Helm Crag, which had only taken an hour. On the summit they are rewarded with a wonderful view: 'Clouds fly before the wind, and reflect their shadows so fantastically that beggars what we admired at Windermere. But, as we had such a hard march, I will close this chapter.'

Much of this journal was in fact written on the spot, once he had found a comfortable place to sit out of the wind and collect his thoughts. The 1792 journal is not, therefore, as reflective as the later 1798 and 1810 editions, when he was writing after the events, at leisure, in a more contemplative mood, and which contain much more peripheral material, transcripts of conversations and poetry.

As their 'tight tug' up Helvellyn that morning had gone on, Palmer starts to notice that the 'view gets more hazy; still, the magnificence around is beyond description … mountains towering above fells … ' As Hagglund has pointed out in reference to writers on Scotland at this time, 'One of the uses of hyperbole is to emphasize the viewer as truly affected by what they have seen,'[4] and, in common with writers such as Dorothy Wordsworth later on, Palmer resorts to this kind of plea of something being 'beyond description', of its 'inexpressibility', to position himself within a certain role, within the group of the 'sensitive'. For these people, the degree of inexpressibility corresponds to, and reflects for all to see, the depth and complexity of what they are experiencing; recording a depth of feeling literally beyond words.

As Palmer grows less exhausted and his mood more contemplative, as he looks out from the summit, Helvellyn starts to come into focus as the centre of an enormous landscape: he sees Skiddaw to the north, to the west the 'immense mountains' that hide Borrowdale, south-west 'the Old Man is just in sight', and to the south, Windermere and Esthwaite Water. Turning to look east, immediately below him, 'Place Fell cuts off a branch of Ullswater', and above this, far beyond the boundaries of Lakeland, 'Cross Fell is large enough to be visible from this exalted summit, and is only exceeded by Ingleborough in Yorkshire, which holds her crowned head amidst a chain of hills'; or, as the down-to-earth Wainwright puts it, 'The Pennines in the background'. And then, beyond the actual views, Palmer suddenly seems to become aware of the moment itself, of the sensation of being amidst the life of the natural world swirling around him, breaking in on his internal dialogue: 'Ravens are croaking , and the wind which did not blow when I began to write, is coming on in flurries'; there is a spontaneity of awareness in this sudden switch of consciousness that seems to mark an unplanned sense of departure from the 'picturesque' script, and it is the first suggestion of what he is going to experience a few days later at Scale Force waterfall.

On descending from the summit towards Thirlmere, they come across Brownrigg Spring, and Palmer finally gets a chance to drink something, commenting 'None but those who know the joy of meeting a spring when it is not expected, can conceive my feelings when I found myself sitting on the wet grass' beside it. The drink and a piece of bread revive him for the descent, but it was to prove every bit as difficult as the ascent, being 'steep and unpleasant … covered in loose stones, we could not trust to', a descent which 'we were obliged to traverse with the utmost caution, the ground was so hard and step; and although I was master of my resolution, I would not whilst descending have looked at anything but my feet, for all the prospects in the universe.' Once again, as with the ravens and the wind, the true nature of the world he has entered forces itself to his attention, transcending his role as a detached viewer of the 'prospects in the universe'. He notes that 'Partridge … might have brought us down an easier descent; but as he had been out with a chaise all night, he was perhaps induced … to take us the nearest way', a note which suggests that from the spring they may have cut straight down the slope past the old lead mine to the road.[5]

Once down, 'between ten and eleven we found ourselves in the high road, and tript lightly to the Cherry Tree [the Cherry Tree Inn which stood beside Thirlmere]' where 'they gave us a breakfast fit for labouring men.' In conversation with an old lady at the Inn, they discover that she 'had been too often upon Skiddaw in her youth to be ill in her old age', having been sent up the mountain to look for lost sheep.

Palmer is also keen, and pleased, to add in the third edition of the *Ramble:* 'Some of my friends made this excursion in the summer of 1808, using my Ramble as a companion. I was gratified on being informed, that the Writer of it is spoken of with respect by many of the natives.'[6]

From the Inn they 'spanked along' the road to Keswick, and on reaching the top of the hill, turned 'to take leave of Helvellyn … in sight of Skiddaw, these mountains towering over all around them, seemed to challenge each other for pre-eminence and the decision might be on either side.' Soon the fabled Vale of Keswick came into view, but, perhaps because of magnificence of what he had already experienced that day, Palmer was decidedly underwhelmed: 'The Vale of Keswick is rich, but too broad and extensive for landscape.' Far from it being the 'Elysium' that Thomas Gray had seen in 1769, Palmer does not even consider it worth painting.

They spend that afternoon and all the next day exploring Keswick and Derwent Water, taking a boat up to the head of the lake. The village of Grange is 'unadorned and picturesque' (one of the few times he actually uses this word), and Borrowdale, although 'a grand assemblage of the sublime', is, as we have seen, dismissed as 'neither so magnificent or pleasing as the [great crescent] around Rydal'. The Rambler has become very hard to please, and it is not until a day or two later, when they walk from Keswick to Buttermere via Kescadale, that he saw the next magnificent and pleasing view: Scale Force Waterfall.

Once they arrive at Buttermere they hired a young guide and, after lunch at the Inn, set off to Scale Force 'to attend the cascade [taking] a very uneven and boggy road', the two miles being 'an uncomfortable task.' But it all proved worthwhile because, on arriving, he suddenly experienced an extraordinary shift of consciousness, which he describes as best he can as follows: 'Scale Force is 200ft perpendicular, except where it flushes over a small jut; the steep on both sides is covered with a variety of moss, fern, ash, and oak, all fed by constant spray and flourish in indescribable verdure … '. On seeing it 'I was lost in admiration in one of those vacant delights, in which the mind thinks of nothing but what is before it … and makes you feel more than a man. I required a tap on the shoulder to return to mortality.'

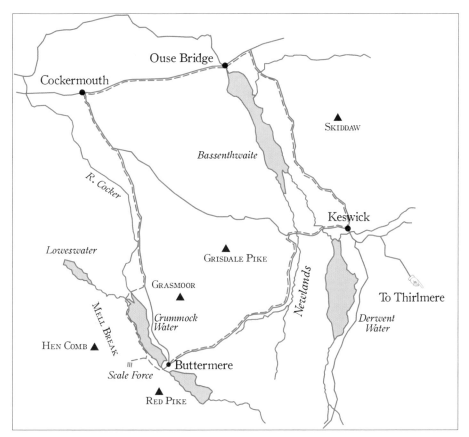

Palmer's Walks, 2. From Keswick to Buttermere, 1792, and to Scale Force via Ouse Bridge, January 1798.

And there, summed up in these words, is the reward offered by this new exploration of 'the wilds of nature' that Palmer and then Coleridge were undertaking. Once the mind and the feverish workings of the imagination are stilled by the physical exertion of these walks, once he sheds the pose of a tourist, Palmer suddenly becomes aware 'of nothing but what is before' him; he has suddenly moved beyond any distinction between self and surroundings, and he becomes 'lost' in the landscape of the natural world around him, swept away by the powerful forces swirling around him, in a state of 'vacant delight' that requires a tap on the shoulder to bring him back. He considers the waterfall 'exceeds anything of the kind I ever saw' and continues: 'every part of it was in unison with the music it created; the

The setting of Scale Force, seen across Crummock Water [author].

The waterfall tumbles down through the sunlit trees visible between the Gale Fell in the centre and the slopes of Blea Crag to the left.

mind comprehended it and carried away one of the inimitable scenes that ever enriched the fancy of man.' He had suddenly found a unity of self and setting that surpassed anything that his fancy could have conceived. In fact, he was so taken with the fall and what he experienced there that he made a special trip in January 1798 specifically to see it again, this time covered, he hoped, in spectacular icicles.

The Ramble actually lasted another four days, but by comparison with Helm Crag, 'as it had never been visited by strangers and the ascent is so very difficult', the sensation of being on top of Helvellyn alone with the ravens, and also the extraordinary 'vacant delights' of Scale Force, in the end things turned out to be something of an anticlimax. They duly climbed Skiddaw, on the top of which he describes the views, wrote his notes, and threw stones at a group of dotterels, but is otherwise unmoved. They took a boat and a gun onto Derwent Water, where 'we tried 3 discharges' to which 'the echoes answered by rushing from several hills', but neither the experience of Skiddaw nor the echoes on the lake seem to have caught his imagination as the earlier experience had done. A late exception was a boat trip they took down Ullswater during which, in addition to the 'superb view of Helvellyn', he found 'every arm presents new beauties – the interior mountains – the village and plain of Patterdale – Place Fell – the islands – the tower – Gowbarrow Park – the view of Martindale – the rough mountains, the fertile ones – Dunmallet Head … there is a chasteness about the whole which makes it the choicest gift of Nature I ever saw'; it is nominated as his favourite lake. The wider impact of the trip is summed up, I think, by his account of a walk he took in Penrith after leaving Ullswater: He says they took an '

> evening walk into the Shrubbery – I forget the name of the place' but after a while '[I] was glad to get out of the shrubbery, for shrubberies are plentiful in the south, and my head was too full of mountains, lakes, and valleys, to wish to be interrupted by the most perfect pleasure ground in the world: I am not yet far enough from the wild scenes of Nature to be pleased with anything that is studied.

How different is this reaction to admiration for the formal 'Dutch-style' gardens of Levens Hall just two weeks before, and how different to the kind of writing that had gone before.

If in Palmer's account of his first trip to the Lakes we see some hints of the kind of writing about the natural world that broke the mould of the Picturesque Tour, and suggested what was to come, this was to be reinforced by the experiences he added to the third edition of the book from his subsequent visits in 1797 and 1798, when we see his curiosity about the 'wild scenes of Nature' leading him off the well trodden route of the tourists again and into the type of direct experience of the landscape that would be undertaken by Coleridge, and which walkers would recognize today. These come in the short accounts he gives of a guided climb up the Langdale Pikes in November 1797, and his solo walk in January of 1798 to see Scale Force again; both experiences, for different reasons, took him far out of his comfort zone and exposed him to physical dangers again that few 'strangers' would ever have known. Little needs adding to his own words, in which he includes conversations written to catch the local dialect.[7]

On 7 November 1797, he engaged the services of a farmer's son by the name of Paul Postlethwaite 'residing in the extremity of Langdale Valley, and who promised …to attend me the next day to the summit of Langdale Pike … They first offered me refreshment, as I was given to understand it was a stout undertaking; and that I should be 'heaf famish't, if yoa ar naw quoite knockt-up' – as they never remembered 'foine folk aiming at it afore.'

After refreshment, they started the climb. Postlethwaite

> then got a long pole with a pike to it, similar to the one I had, and we started like hardy mountaineers, and indeed Paul would have made half a run if I had not soon checked him. He said he'd 'a moind to try me'; but when I gave him to understand that he was above a match for me, he felt the victory, and was as obedient as possible. We had many rough rocks to scramble up, and in a deep recess, impenetrable to the sun, I observed a large quantity of snow that I would suppose never completely dissolves. We had again to haul ourselves by rocks to bring us to the crown of the Langdale Pike [probably Loft Crag], which is about twenty yards in circumference; in the centre is a natural stone seat, with moss and small rock around it.

Once on top, and after catching his breath, Palmer gives a brief description of the views in various directions, which are 'terrifically grand', but:

> Nothing can exceed the delight with which I look upon Windermere. Not a breath of air … Harrison's Pike and Pica Stickle, that I had wound partially about in my advance, are below me.[8] … Skiddaw is covered with snow. The Hills I passed over, abound in foxes, sweet martens and fulimarts (noted for their offensive smell), and which give name to Mart-Crag. There are likewise plenty of Grouse and Partridges. In a recess below me the last Eagle in England was destroyed.

But he really seems more interested in Paul Postlethwaite than in recording his reactions to the landscape, and recounts that his guide 'sat down by me, and, after answering my questions, thought he had a natural right to make his own:

> PP: ' … wot a broughtin yoa here?'
>
> Rambler: 'Curiosity, Paul.'

PP: 'I think yoa mun be kurious enuff; I never cum here but after runaway sheep, and I'm then so vext at um, I cud throa um deawn th' Poike. An ye evour bin te Lunnun Sur? an wot mack on a please is'n it?'

R: 'Why, Paul, were I to begin to tell thee what I know of it, we might stay here all night.'

P: 'An t[h]en, eh fackins, youdn be as coud as death; but tell me ten, what mack on a bildin is my neame seake San Paul's? is it as big as th' little Poike?'

After answering some of his original remarks, I took my turn,

R: 'And now, Paul, how far hast thou ever been from home?'

PP: 'Why … I bin at Hawkshead, at a feor, an I bin at Ambleside, an a bin at Grasmere, an I bin heor oth' Poike oftnor an he loiked'

After a while on the top, sitting and talking, it is time to go, and a tense passage in the writing describes what happened next:

On our preparing to descend, he said 'Would you like a nearer way hoam agen, tan th' road we cum up?' On my approving his proposal, we began our decent opposite from our ascent. We were obliged to be very cautious, and to cling close to the rocks; and when we got a good way down, we came to a part where we had to pass over a large bulging part of the mountain, across a sward nearly perpendicular, and of an immoderate height: he was going unconcernedly to cross by a sheep-track; I checked him, and asked him what he meant by bringing me into such a situation? I looked up to return to the summit again, but it had too laborious an appearance, and the distance was great; and knowing that taking time to resolve when danger is near ever increases it, I tied up my right eye, which could not have borne the vast precipice almost perpendicular under me. I laid hold of one end of his pole, cautioned him as to his pace, and with my left-eye on the sheep-walk, not more than three inches broad, my head almost close to the mountain, and thus piloted, we were in about eight minutes safe moored; and when I looked back I had reason to be thankful.

Paul said, he had crossed it hundreds of times, or he must have gone a great round; and he literally said what I had remarked to Bob Partridge, to the effect that 'a man might surely go where a sheep could'.

Few tourists would ever have experienced such exposure, and, although it was something that Coleridge would come to know well some four years later, it remains a seminal moment in the early history of recorded fell-walking; it is also likely that, as at Helm Crag, Palmer's was the first 'visit by a stranger', or 'fine folk', to the top of the Langdale Pikes. It could be, from this description, that the route Paul chose was straight down off Loft Crag, past the cliffs of Gimmer Crag, and then across the open slopes diagonally down to Dungeon Ghyll, a route which takes the narrow path out and around a number of rock outcrops on the way. Whether they passed this way or took another route, Palmer had been severely tested and, as Coleridge was to write, may well have 'laughed at [himself] as a Madman.' Having survived the test, Palmer goes on to concede that:

> it did save me several miles, and, after a considerable descent we came to a chasm, where a tremendous stream roared into it, and was instantly lost … I rested myself here for some time, and the mind was actively employed. We had some roughness still to pass before we got into Langdale Valley, about three miles from the farm-house we started at, and which was so much again towards my return. Paul and I took leave here, and, after shaking hands, and giving him five shillings, he looked at me with pleasure, and at the money as if a larger sum than he had ever been before in possession of …

As intrepid as this adventure had been, however, it was followed a couple of months later by another, equally committed and unusual, this time when Palmer set out to re-visit Scale Force waterfall in the depths of winter. In the third edition of the *Ramble*, when discussing his original visit to Scale Force Waterfall in 1792, Palmer adds: 'I attempted to reach this waterfall in January 1798, to see it adorned with icicles, but, from slipperiness and rotten grass, could not surmount it.'[9]

In these words we get a hint of what happened. The full story had originally been published in the *Gentleman's Magazine* in 1800, before being included as an Appendix in the third edition in 1810, and it makes for very interesting reading. It begins with his reasons for going: 'Being amongst the English Lakes part of the winter of 1797–98 I felt an irresistible urge to re-visit Buttermere; that I might see, what I formerly called 'the incomparable Scale Force waterfall', bound up in icicles.' Later on he adds, 'Not that I supposed the effect would be so enchanting as the state I had described it; for motion is the very life of cascades: but I conceived its then Gothic style would be a *new* kind of beauty to me.'

This was in fact a highly unusual undertaking. It was an entirely solo, self-guided walk by a visitor in the middle of winter, leaving from the Salutation Inn, Ambleside – his 'home' in the Lakes – walking round the top of Bassenthwaite, and then on by way of Cockermouth and Lorton Vale, through the winter landscape to Buttermere. He actually admits to having two aims in mind: first to see Scale Force in winter, but second to see Mary at the Inn, whom he had immortalized as 'Sally of Buttermere' in his original journal. Much of this account is taken up by his story of the great dance that was held at the Inn the night he stayed, and his conversations with both Mary and many of the locals at the dance, who thought him 'the cheeriest stranger they had ever seen in Buttermere'.

Unfortunately, even though he had clearly come somewhat prepared, with cleated boots and a stick with a pike on it, he was defeated in the end by the winter conditions; nevertheless, he certainly did not give up without a struggle and, given his physical limitations, he showed the kind of courage and commitment that we will see again in Coleridge's exploits.

After stopping for breakfast at Robert Newton's, he set off over Dunmail Raise, and after skirting Keswick, which he sought to avoid, he walked up past Little Crossthwaite 'beneath the giant Skiddaw', before spending the night at the Inn at 'Ewes-Bridge' [Ouse Bridge]. The next day he walked on to Cockermouth, visited the castle, and set off to walk up Lorton Vale to Loweswater at the foot of Crummock Water. So far, the walk had been relatively easy, if chilly, but from here things get a little more difficult. From the village, instead of following the road beside Crummock Water to Buttermere, he appears to have followed the path running along the south-western shore of Crummock Water under Mellbreak to approach the waterfall, a route which certainly shortened the walk, but which was something of a challenge. Leaving Lowes Chapel, he says: 'I had many formidable strides to take, over rugged and unbeaten ground, before I could be within a certain compass of my first object Scale Force Waterfall.'

On finally arriving on the slopes below the fall, Palmer rested awhile; 'I sat for some time upon a stone, very much pleased with my solitary situation, and the manly thoughts which crowded upon me … [but] the time of day would not allow me to rest long.' So, while appreciating the sensation of being in the midst of this cold, white, silent landscape, with no one else around, he nevertheless soon found the conditions too difficult:

I made very many efforts to overcome the glassy hill; and although I had sharp nails in the balls of my shoes, and large stubs to the heels, with a pike to my hazel stick, my efforts were useless; I tumbled twice, and slid bodily down the hill again ... I changed my mode of attack, and took a sweep to the left; the rise through which we had in the summer 1792 been wet by splashes from loose stones.

And to make things worse, he was soon soaking wet,

Although the surface was ice, the rough grass and water oozing through had made it both hollow and rotten. I soon got over my shoe-tops, and up to one knee, and then I felt myself conquered, and gave up.

Defeated by the conditions, he turned back down, heading up the valley to the Inn at Buttermere, noting 'I had a bad mile and a half of this uneven and slippery road, and the night was closing fast.' There are all the elements of exposure and danger here that we will see later in some of the situations that Coleridge was to find himself in, and this underlines, I think, the ground-breaking nature of what Palmer undertook here; other 'strangers' may well have visited these places at this time yet left no records, but few, one has to believe, undertook to do so in such circumstances, since, even when Palmer reached the valley floor, things got no easier. Not only was the light of a short winter's day failing rapidly, but, as it did so, the temperature dropped rapidly, turning the puddles and wet surfaces into sheets of ice. His most difficult moment came when attempting to cross the river which flows from Buttermere into Crummock Water. While the lights of the village must have seemed tantalizingly near, he still had to negotiate the splintered and broken planks of the rotten, ice-covered bridge in the dark, tentatively sliding his feet forward, testing the next plank with his weight, and doing his best to avoid the gaping holes through which he could sense rather than see the freezing water rushing on its way below. Chilled to the bone, and expecting at any moment to be pitched into the dark water when the next plank gave way, he tells us that 'there were certain qualms about me ... which were somewhat akin to fear.'

Finally, shivering and exhausted, he reached the Buttermere Inn where he was delighted to be greeted by Mary herself. She found him a bed, but warned him that he may be 'much disturbed, as they were going to have an annual dance, for the benefit of one Askew, a blind fiddler from Whitehaven.'

Palmer's route alongside Crummock Water, from Loweswater to Scale Force [author].

'I had many formidable strides to take, over rugged and unbeaten ground, before I could be within a certain compass of my first object Scale Force Waterfall.' The 'formidable' nature of Joseph Palmer's route, from Loweswater village (off to the right), to Scale Force along the shore of Crummock Water is clear from this view of it from across the lake.

His cheerful response is: 'Nothing would delight me more', and, after a change of clothes is found for him, he thoroughly enjoys himself, sitting in the corner by the fire, smoking his pipe and watching all the goings on, commenting that the locals he met agreed that he 'was yan of the cheeriest strangers they had e'er seen in Buttermere … '

In addition to these lively accounts of his walks, Palmer also published *Windermere, A Poem* in 1798, in which he sets out to describe and then assess the qualities of the landscapes of the lake and its wider setting; to share the experience and his thoughts with all those for whom 'Nature in thy nature bears a part.'

What makes the poem particularly interesting, however, is not so much the picturesque descriptive passages, but rather that he writes the poem from the viewpoint, rarely expressed before, if at all, that in its way the landscape of the Lake District is equal to any one might see in the Alps or similar place abroad. In the third verse, Palmer writes:

> Let other climes their southern wonders boast,
> Their wide-extended lakes, midst varied coast …
> Be 't yours, advent'rous Britons, to admire,
> With that enthusiasm the scenes require;
> Yet, ere we wish, in search of such to roam,
> View them in perfect miniature – AT HOME.

Interestingly enough, it is this verse that Coleridge quotes in full in a notebook entry for November 1799 during his tour of the Lakes with Wordsworth, indicating that they too saw the Lakes in this way, as unique and interesting in their own right. It is also possible that in addition to reading Palmer's poem, he had also read Palmer's account of the winter walk to Scale Force, since it was initially published in the *Gentleman's Magazine* in January 1800.[10] This means that Coleridge may well have read both before he started his series of walks.

Although there is no evidence that either Coleridge or Wordsworth ever met Palmer, they certainly knew of him and his exploits. Not only had they read his poem and possibly the account of the walk to Scale Force, but they also stayed for several days at Robert Newton's Inn at Grasmere during their walk in 1799, and it is hard to imagine that Newton did not recount the ascent of Helm Crag, at the very least, not to mention Palmer's passing through for breakfast on his way to Scale Force in January of 1798. Given this, and the number of other people they must have met who also knew Palmer, it seems highly likely that they had also read *A Fortnight's Ramble*; and, if Coleridge had read it, it not only helps to place his subsequent walks into some sort of context, but it might also explain some of the routes he took and the places he was looking for.

❀ ❀ ❀

On arriving to live in the Lake District in June 1800, Samuel Taylor Coleridge had been initially, like Palmer before him, very much of the 'picturesque' frame of mind; visiting all the proper 'stations', using the sights and situations he experienced as material for poems, and sharing his reactions with his closest friends. After staying initially with Dorothy and William Wordsworth, who had settled at Dove Cottage in the winter of 1799, Coleridge, his wife Sara and their surviving son, the four year old Hartley, then moved to Greta Hall in Keswick in July.[11] Coleridge had married Sara Fricker in October 1798 and the two of them moved to their 'pretty cot!', as he described it, in Clevedon, near Bristol. Although Coleridge had doubts about how much he loved Sara, their early life together seems to have been happy, the period at Clevedon culminating in the birth of Hartley, their first child. By the time they reached Greta Hall two years later, however, there were severe strains on their marriage. Part of the problem lay in the closeness of the relationship Coleridge had established with William and Dorothy Wordsworth over the intervening years, a relationship that largely excluded Sara; and part was due to the long periods of time that he had spent away from his little family, studying in Germany for over a year. Although now re-united, the tensions in the Coleridge marriage continued until the couple finally separated in 1808, and things were clearly not helped at this time by the proximity of their new home to the Wordsworths and the amount of time Coleridge was to spend with them, as he and William worked towards the second edition of the *Lyrical Ballads*.

Wordsworth went on to lasting fame by creating poetry steeped in both his childhood memories of growing up in the Lakes and the experience of living there as an adult, while his sister Dorothy, to considerably less acclaim until our modern times, went on to create an extraordinary record of these years in her *Journals*, an achievement largely overlooked by contemporaries because they were in prose rather than poetry. Prose at this time, and indeed for some time to come, was a medium which lacked the elevated status of the poem as a means of conveying our interaction with the natural world.

Furthermore, while poetry had long been considered a suitable medium for exploring the role of the world of nature as a commentary on the world of art and culture, this use of prose was, like Coleridge's walks, something new; a new way of writing about the natural world for what it *actually was*, writing free from the requirement to comment, free from the reduction of the natural world to a role as symbol; it was a form of writing we now take for granted as the discrete genre of 'nature writing'. In the 1790s, however, writing to discover and record a deeper understanding of the forms and processes of the world of nature rather than our own, was new, and only just evolving from the prose forms of letter-writing, journals and notebooks.

In fact, in addition to the poetry on which his modern reputation largely rests, Coleridge also wrote a great deal of prose as a journalist/commentator, essayist and letter-writer, and, although he never kept systematic diaries or journals as Dorothy Wordsworth did, throughout most of his adult life Coleridge also kept a series of private notebooks. Everything and anything would get written down, or sometimes drawn, but for Coleridge himself, the contents of these notebooks had no significance beyond accumulating source material for other things and recording thoughts and ideas of interest. This has meant that unless the material in them was later written up as a letter, essay or lecture, or until an initial line or phrase had become a poem, the contents of the notebooks have remained largely unread.

While Coleridge's poetry had been published from as early as 1796 (*Poems on Various Subjects*), the first biography appeared in 1838, an edition of his *Essays* in 1850, and the first collection of his *Letters* only in 1895; it was not until 1957 that the *Notebooks* began to be published in a readable form. Although others may have existed, a series of sixty-seven notebooks, dating from 1794 until his death in 1834, have survived, and the texts of these, accompanied by full notes, were edited and published through the extraordinary work of Kathleen Coburn. Of all this enormous undertaking, this book draws only on Volume I,[12] which runs from June 1794 to January 1804, and contains, along with a wealth of other material, accounts of some twenty walks that he undertook, largely on his own, between 1794 and 1802.

Richard Holmes, in his biography of Coleridge, suggests the importance of these notebook accounts:

He recorded [these] in a brilliant series of running *plein-air* sketches [some later developed into letter-journals] which catch not only the physical sensation of the climber … but also the spiritual effect of moving alone through such high, wild, naked landscapes. These prose-notations were a new form of Romantic nature-writing, as powerful in their way as his poetry; rapid, spontaneous, miraculously responsive to the changing panorama of hills he moves through, and containing a sort of telegraphic score of his emotional reactions.

Holmes goes on to note:

The originality and power of Coleridge's fell-walking Notebooks and letters has only recently received some attention. His use of emotional notations comparable to a musical score; his breaking of the conventional eighteenth-century picturesque window or frame of description – using panoramic sweeps rather than fixed perspectives; and his subversion of the old guide-book formulas; all deserve further exploration … Gittings and Manton sensitively contrast his descriptive style with that of Dorothy's *Journals* (but in the latter's favour).

and he adds:

Among many other aspects, Coleridge is the first to introduce the impression of physical effort, traveling bodily through a landscape, and perilous immediacy (with the implied doubt that he will ever return). His greatest inheritor is, perhaps, Alfred Wainwright. [13]

This impression of 'physical effort' and sense of 'perilous immediacy' is caught perfectly in this passage from one of those letters:

The next three drops were not … a foot more than my height – But every drop increased the palsy of my Limbs – I shook all over … and now I had only two more to drop down – to return was impossible – but of these the first was tremendous, it was twice my own height, & the Ledge at the bottom was [so] exceedingly narrow, that if I dropt down upon it I must of necessity have fallen backwards & of course killed myself. My limbs were all in a tremble – I lay upon my back to rest myself, & was beginning according to my Custom to laugh at myself for a Madman. [14]

This is part of Coleridge's dramatic account of his descent from the top of

Scafell on 5 August 1802. He had chosen what he thought would be the easiest route down towards Eskdale, but found himself instead stranded halfway down Broad Stand, a notoriously dangerous rock outcropping, and one which Wainwright describes as 'the greatest single obstacle confronting ridge-walkers on the hills of Lakeland'. Dramatic as it is, his account only tells half the story, since, by the time he arrived there, he had been walking for five days, he lacked sleep, it was late in the afternoon, he was 'hunger'd & provisionless', and 'the wind is strong, & the Clouds hast'ning hither from the Sea – the whole air sea-ward has a lurid Look – we shall certainly have Thunder'; a storm was racing in to engulf the mountain, he was miles from the nearest house and, in preparation for all this, his knapsack contained 'a shirt, cravat, 2 pair of Stockings, a little paper & half a dozen Pens, A German Book (Voss' poems), & a little Tea & Sugar, with my Night Cap'.

Yet, as we will see, Coleridge made it down, and, as though nothing out of the ordinary had happened, he continued his walk, taking another three days to walk home to Keswick via Ambleside and Grasmere, breezily summing up the whole experience as 'a very delightful & feeding Excursion'. Still laughing at himself perhaps, he may have seen this as simply a delightful excursion, but in fact this nine-day tour, which had taken him all the way from Keswick to the coast at St Bees and back via the summit of Scafell, came as the culmination of an unprecedented series of walks he had made through the landscapes of the Lake District starting in August and October of 1800. The importance of these walks is summed up by Holmes, who wrote that Coleridge 'was in effect inventing a new kind of Romantic tourism, abandoning the coach and the high-road for the hill, flask and the knapsack' and creating 'the first literary description of the peculiarly English sport of fell-walking'.[15]

Piecing together his accounts from the Notebook and from the letters he subsequently wrote to friends and family recounting his adventures, we will now follow Coleridge's discovery of the sheer joy of walking the fells, the revelations he experiences in situations where he finds himself far from his comfort zones and face to face with the raw elements of the natural world, and his growing sense of great and unimaginable energies pulsing through that world as he experienced it; his instinctive recognition that in his tiny insignificant way he too is a part of this, of what he describes as 'a *one*ness, not an intense Union, but an Absolute Unity.'

Broad Stand [A. Wainwright, *The Southern Fells*].
Broad Stand on Scafell, described by Wainwright as 'The greatest single obstacle confronting ridge-walkers on the hills of Lakeland'.

Coleridge wrote on one walk 'Here it was 'every man his own path-maker', & I went directly across it – upon soft mossy Ground, with many a hop, skip, & jump … observing the old Saying: where Rushes grow, a Man may go.'[16] and these words sum up Coleridge's attitude, an entirely new perception of what walking on the Lakeland fells could mean. At one point on his ascent of the Helvellyn ridge he records his ecstatic reaction to seeing new views open up before him – 'O Joy for me' – a cry which we can almost hear, and which seems to capture perfectly his excited mood of discovery of the landscape. One which will be recognisable to so many today, not necessarily looking for inspiration for art or poetry, but reflecting the sheer pleasure of walking and immersing oneself in the boundless and constantly changing world of nature; not necessarily following a set route, but finding one's own way, discovering what lay beyond the accepted picturesque compositions. This was something still very new to him, something which transcended his everyday life and induced an overwhelming sense of the sheer joy of being alive. These were journeys into Palmer's 'wild scenes of Nature', journeys into George Smith's 'desolate and mountainous' places, areas that had been of no interest, and that had remained out of sight and mind.

'Pedestrian Tours' and 'Peregrinations':
Coleridge's Early Walks, 1794–1799

The anonymous introduction to the Frederick Warne collection of Coleridge's poetry of c.1890, includes an interesting anecdote.[1] Touching on the likely reason that Coleridge's career as a Light Dragoon had lasted less than six months, the writer states that 'it was thought that his then democratical feelings made his officers willing to get rid of him; it is a fact, he could not be taught to ride.' Coleridge went on to describe himself as 'a very indocile Equestrian', and this aversion to horses would seem to go some way to explain the fact that from his very first foray into the countryside he chose always to walk. Discharged from the army in April 1794, he returned to Cambridge to continue his studies, and it was from there in August 1794 that he set off in the company of a fellow Cambridge under-graduate, Joseph Huck, on a tour of North Wales. On 14 June he wrote to Samuel Butler to say 'Tomorrow morning early I set out on a pedestrian tour scheme for Oxford – from whence … I proceed to Wales, make a tour of the northern part, and return to Cambridge. My whole peregrination will take about six weeks.'[2] On their arrival in Oxford, however, one of the first people Coleridge met was Robert Southey, a student at Balliol, with the result that the peregrination was then delayed for three weeks. Southey, who already had a reputation both as a poet and as a committed republican, and Coleridge seem immediately to have recognized fellow spirits in each other and, after spending the next weeks 'disputing on metaphysical subjects', as Southey put it, they agreed to meet up again in Southey's home town of Bristol after the Welsh tour ended.

Over the next month Coleridge and Huck's walk covered some 500 miles, running 'from Gloucester to Anglesey through the Welsh hills' and back by the coast and the Wye Valley to Bristol. Although the trip started off very much in the style of the increasingly popular picturesque tour, and indeed Coleridge and Huck met up with fellow Cambridge undergraduates following the same route during their summer break, it is clear from the start that Coleridge undertook this trip very much in his own unique style.

To start with, as Holmes points out, 'Coleridge insisted on wearing rough workmen's jackets, loose trousers (rather than gentlemen's breeches and stockings) and carrying canvas knapsacks ',[3] and carried with him 'a strange Walking Stick, 5 feet in length ...' covered in carvings. In addition to this, he had also insisted on walking the route rather than taking horses, or a carriage such as the post-chaise in which the fellow 'Cantabs of [his] college' were 'vigorously pursuing their tour', but at times, he clearly found the tour at odds with the experience he was looking for. In one instance, for example, when he 'wandered for an hour and a half last evening' in the ruins of Denbigh Castle which 'surpasses everything [he] could have conceived', he was initially delighted when another visitor proposed to play his flute. Primed by the atmosphere of the ruins in the twilight, and ready to be transported by the romance of the occasion, he is appalled when, instead of the romance of a suitable air, the young man struck up 'Mrs Casey', a popular vulgar song.

Apart from such disappointments, his accounts of the countryside on this tour, one of his first exercises in describing the landscape, are much as we would expect:

> From Oxford to Gloucester, to Ross, to Hereford, to Leominster, to Bishop's Castle, to Welsh Pool, to Llanvillin [Llangollen] nothing occurred worthy of notice ... from Llanvillin we penetrated into the interior of the country to Llanvunnog [Llangynog], a Village most romantically situated [and] from Llanvunnog we walked over the mountains to Bala – most sublimely terrible! ... The rugged and stony Clefts are stupendous – and in winter must form Cataracts most astonishing – At this time of year there is just water enough dashed down over them to 'soothe not disturb the pensive Traveller's Ear'. I slept by the side of one an hour or more. As we descended the Mountain the Sun was reflected in the River that winded thro' the valley with insufferable brightness – it rivalled the Sky. At Bala is nothing remarkable except a Lake of 11 miles in circumference.[4]

The increasing brevity of his descriptions of this tour suggest, however, that it was not altogether enjoyable, and we are told very little of what happened when they reached Snowdonia, other than the fact that when 'at imminent hazard to our Lives' he and his fellow Cantabs 'scaled the very Summit of Penmaenmawr – it was a most dreadful expedition.'[5] Nor do we learn anything of his walk home down the Wye after Huck had left him. By the time he reflects on this tour in a letter of September 1800, his outlook and what interests him have changed radically following his initial walks in the Lake District:

> Of North Wales my recollections are faint … As far as my memory will permit me to decide on the grander parts of Caernarvenshire, I might say, that the single objects are superior to any, which I have seen elsewhere – but there is a deficiency in combination. I know of no mountain in the *north* altogether equal to Snowdon, but then we have an encampment of huge Mountains, in no harmony perhaps to the eye of a mere painter, but always interesting, various, and, as it were, nutritive. Height is assuredly an advantage, as it connects the Earth with the Sky, by the clouds that are ever skimming the summits, or climbing up, or creeping down the sides, or rising from the chasms like smokes from a Cauldron, or veiling or bridging the higher parts or the lower parts of the water-falls…Besides … Mountains & mountainous Scenery, taken *collectively* & *cursorily*, must depend for their charms on their novelty – they put on their immortal interest … when we have resided among them, & learnt to understand their language, their written characters, & intelligible sounds, and all their eloquence so various, so unwearied.[6]

On his return from Wales, Coleridge immediately picked up his new friendship with Southey in Bristol, where together they continued their debates on metaphysical subjects, and where, with their shared republican sympathies, they began to plan an ideal community together, the '*Pantisocracy*'. Christened such by Coleridge, this was to be 'an experimental society, living in pastoral seclusion, sharing property, labour, and self-government equally among it adult members, both men and women.'[7] Plans for this community got as far as selecting an ideal location, somewhere along the banks of the Susquehanna river in Pennsylvania, but were soon to founder on serious differences of opinion on the structural details, and subsequently on mutual recrimination about just who reneged on the idea and backed out. For Coleridge, however, this intense period of friendship and planning had lasting significance, since it was during this time that Southey was courting Edith Fricker, and Coleridge formed an attachment to her sister, Sara. The Frickers were central to the group of friends in Bristol, spending a great deal of time in each other's company and planning their communal future. A rupture between Coleridge and Southey was then initiated when Southey announced he would not join the Pantisocracy at that time, leaving Coleridge greatly upset by Southey's rejection of the Pantisocratic ideal. Eager, perhaps, not to lose everything, Coleridge went on to marry Sara Fricker in October 1795. The rupture between Coleridge and Southey was then deepened when the latter married Edith towards the end of the year, and left with her for a trip to the Continent. Coleridge was devastated, feeling, as Holmes puts it, that 'Southey ... had abandoned every duty – political, Pantisocratic, fraternal – and left him to fight alone.'[8]

With the breakup of their group in Bristol, Coleridge and Sara took a small 'cot' in Cleveden, and it was just before they moved there following their marriage that Coleridge met in person a poet whose work he had been aware of since he was a student, William Wordsworth, who had been living in Dorset with his sister Dorothy but visited Bristol to attend literary events. Following their meeting, the two began a correspondence, discussing their poetic interests and ideals and exchanging poems, an excited swopping of ideas which steadily developed into a deep and significant friendship for both of them.

Throughout this busy period, partly in response to the initial cooling of his friendship with Southey and the collapse of the Pantisocracy, but also from his eager search for a new dream, together with Wordsworth's interest and encouragement of his poetry, Coleridge had been nursing a new vision of a rural life, one secluded amidst 'a beautiful country' where he would live in peace with his wife, drawing inspiration for new poetic works and deeper reflections on such things as 'the foundations of religion and morals'. This new vision came into focus in early 1797, when he was offered a small cottage in Nether Stowey, Somerset, by his friend and fellow democrat, Thomas Poole, a local business man whom he had met with Southey after his first arrival in Bristol.

Something of Coleridge's new optimistic mood following this move is caught in a letter he wrote at the time: 'I never go to Bristol – from seven to half past eight I work in my garden; from breakfast till 12 I read and compose; then work again – feed the pigs, poultry, etc, till two o'clock – after dinner work again till Tea ... So jogs the day ... We are *very* happy.'[9]

This happiness, in turn, enabled him to begin a new kind of exploration, that of the landscape of the Quantock hills above his new home.

WALKS AROUND NETHER STOWEY, SOMERSET, JUNE 1797–JULY 1798

While Coleridge had been dissatisfied with the reactions of his fellow students to the experience of landscape in north Wales, everything changed for him in July 1797, when he was able to convince his new friends William and Dorothy Wordsworth to leave their house in Dorset, and join him in Nether Stowey where the Wordsworths settled at Alfoxden House, just outside the village. Now he could explore the landscape with like-minded people, sensitive individuals who could understand what he was looking for, and, because they were capable of experiencing the natural world with a consciousness that went beyond the 'eye of mere painters', they could enhance his experience with their thoughts and ideas, making it truly 'nutritive'. That they shared an intense meeting of minds in the months that followed is clear from the fact that walks, once or sometimes twice daily and often at night, on the hills around their respective homes at Nether Stowey and Alfoxden, became a central part of a shared and intimate existence between July 1797 and September 1798.

In *Biographia Literaria*, the 'Biographical Sketches of my Literary Life and Opinions' that Coleridge published in 1817, he remembered this time: 'My walks therefore were almost daily on the top of Quantock, and among its sloping coombs, with my pencil and memorandum book in hand, I was *making studies*, as artists call them.' But he goes on to qualify this: 'and often moulding my thoughts into verse, with the objects and imagery immediately before my senses'.[10] What he was looking for in the landscapes he walked amongst was inspiration for poetry, typified by his projected poem 'The Brook', which was inspired by discovering the Holford stream, a small brook flowing off the hills to the coast. He writes in the *Biographia*:

> I sought for a subject, that should give equal room and freedom for description, incident, and impassioned reflections on men, nature, and society, yet supply in itself a natural connection to the parts and unity to the whole. Such a subject I conceived myself to have found in a stream, traced from its source [to the sea].

The words 'a natural connection to the parts and unity to the whole' can be seen as an early reference to his idea of 'oneness' that was to emerge later. He then went on to record the stream, from:

> its source in the hills among the yellow-red moss and conical glass-shaped tufts of bent, to the first break or fall, where its drops become audible, and it begins to form a channel; thence to the peat and turf barn, itself built of the same dark squares as it sheltered; to the sheepfold; to the first cultivated plot of ground; to the lonely cottage and its bleak garden won from the heath; to the hamlet, the villages, the market-town, the manufactories, and the sea-port.

The poem was eventually abandoned unfinished, the humble Holford stream unable perhaps to carry such a weight of cultural matter as far as the sea, but, however careful his initial observation of the stream was, there is no more mention of it, or its development, once it has formed a channel and flowed past 'the peat & turf barn'. At this time, except for it providing a 'natural connection', he had no further interest in the stream itself; that interest was to come later. These walks were all about inspiration for the new poetic forms that Coleridge and Wordsworth were shaping into the *Lyrical Ballads*.

The close relationship of the three persisted after they left Somerset in late 1798 for a trip to Germany, but within a couple of months there they had split up, Coleridge remaining in the north to study, the Wordsworths travelling south to spend the winter in Goslar. In the end, they briefly met up again in Göttingen in April 1799, before the Wordsworths returned to England leaving Coleridge to his own devices. This pattern was repeated again when they all met up again in the Lake District in the spring of 1800, and an intense period of interaction was followed by a period of estrangement. It became apparent that, for all their shared interests and lasting mutual admiration, Coleridge was simply too disruptive a presence for the Wordsworths, and ultimately, for any number of reasons, there was no room for him in the closed world of Dove Cottage.

Tour of the Harz Mountains, Germany, May 1799

In the spring of 1799, Coleridge travelled south from Hamburg, where he had been studying, to visit Göttingen University with a group of friends. While there he was visited by the Wordsworths, who were leaving for England and who tried to convince Coleridge that he too should return and rejoin his

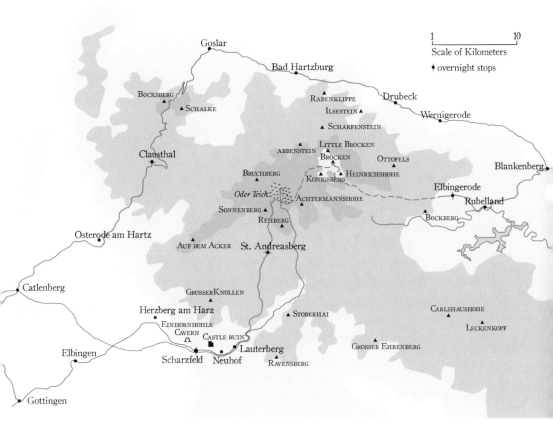

The Harz Mountains walk, May 1799.

wife and children in Somerset. Coleridge, however, was not ready to leave, his immediate reason being that he had decided on a tour of the Harz Mountains, and, after assuring the Wordsworths that he would soon follow them, he set off on 11 May. Making the trip into the mountains on this new venture with Coleridge were John Chester (a Nether Stowey neighbour who had accompanied him to Germany), and some English students he had met at Göttingen who were attracted to this charismatic new arrival: Charles and Frederick Parry, Charles Bellas Greenough, Clement Carlyon, and 'one German'. They appear to have had local guides with them each day during the walk through the mountains.

Once again with his 'pencil and memorandum book in hand' he was '*making studies*', but we see immediately that he is in a different frame of mind from hitherto. Perhaps because he was not with the Wordsworths, he is no longer strictly focused on finding images for his poetry, but rather his 'studies' emerge as an attempt to simply record the detail of the landscape he was seeing. The circular route was designed to take the group up to the summits of the Blocksberg and on to the Great Brocken where Coleridge was hoping to experience the renowned apparition know as the *Brokengespenstes* [Brocken spectre].¹¹

From the first day of the walk, as Coleridge sets out to describe the landscape as they pass through it, the texts of his notebook and letters are accompanied by little diagrams showing the location of streams, hills, houses and other features. He is clearly concentrating on the contrasting shapes and forms of the landscape and the spacing of these, and their changing relationships as he moves along and records these elements as both a visual experience in themselves and in terms of picturesque conventions.

In Hessen Driesch, for example, they 'passed immediately from the Inn, in a narrow path thro' a very lofty fir-wood – the bright green Moss on the Ground speckled with sun …'. At Poele, he describes:

> Mountains in the distance, but ever by our road the Skirts of the Green-wood. A very rapid River [the Oder] ran by our side. And now the Nightingales were all singing [and the] tender verdure grew paler in the moonlight – only the smooth parts of the river were still deeply purpled with the reflections from the fiery red Lights in the West. So surrounded & so impressed,

and when they arrive at Poele he saw 'a dear little Cluster of Houses in the middle of a semi-circle of woody hills the area of the semi-circle scarcely larger than the breadth of the village.'

The next day they reach Neuhof, where they:

> descended the Hill, at the foot of which lies the village of Neuhof – went up the hill … thro' a valley, the Hills of which on both sides were prettily wooded, & a lively rapid river ran to it – the valley is about 2 miles & half in length, almost at the end of it lies the village of Lauter-Berg – the houses neat – Here the country very much resembles Dulverton – just at the entrance two streams come from two deep & wooded coombs … at the end an high woody Hill faces you – and from the great barrier of the valley, you leave the valley thro' a narrow pass at the left hand.

After the 'narrow pass', they left the last of the plains to their right and entered the steep valleys as they headed north into the heart of the mountains, walking past the swamps of the Oder Teich and up to the peaks of the Brocken. The landscape now '... extremely resembles some parts of the River Wye & still more the Coombes about Porlock, except that here the valley is somewhat broader ...' and as 'we had been ascending [and] we left the third apartment of the valley, & entered the fourth, we found all the verdure gone, the Trees leafless, & low down & close along the banks of the River the Conical Fir Trees, in great multitudes – a melancholy & romantic Scene that was quite new to me...'

On the way to Andreasberg, Coleridge describes a particular scene that caught his attention:

> Low down in the valley ... herds of Cattle [were] wandering about, almost everyone with a cylindrical Bell around its neck ... As they moved scattered over the narrow vale & and [up] among the Trees on the Hill, the noise was like that of a large city ... when all the Steeples all at once are ringing.

Then, as they approached the wilderness around the Oder Teich, a large lake 'made they say by man', the trees closed in on the path:

> Now on all sides Firs, nothing but Firs, (violet tone) below, above and around us – Saw the little dancing Cataracts thro' the Firs in various Parts of the vale or deep Bason below – & now from the very high Hill above us, from the very Top, came down a very considerable Stream, dancing over the Rocks, & seen ever & anon thro' the Breaks of the Fir boughs ...

Annotating this entry, Coburn adds this interesting extract from the 'MS Journal':'How awful is that deep unison of their undividable Murmur – what a *one* thing it is, that witnesses the dim notion of the omnipresent.'[12]

This growing awareness of a sense of a 'unison', a one thing permeating the natural world around him, is our first indication of how the mountains were starting to influence Coleridge's consciousness and open up his imagination beyond the conventions of the picturesque tourist. It was later to emerge as his recognition of himself as part of a 'oneness'. At the same time, however, as the walk unfolds and the entries accumulate, he becomes aware of a problem – how best to describe what he is seeing. In this same way, as the tour enters the mountains, he starts to despair of conveying any real sense of what is in front of him: 'on the left a most majestic Hill indeed! the effect of whose simple outline *Painting* could not give & how poor a Thing are *Words*?' Then in a letter to Sara, he attempts to define the problem:

These Letters, & the Descriptions in them, may possibly recall to *me* real forms…but I fear that to you they must be insupportably unmeaning – accumulated repetitions of the same words in almost the same Combinations – but how can it be otherwise? In Nature all things are individual; but a Word is but an arbitrary Character for a whole Class of Things; so that the same description may in almost all cases be applied to twenty different appearances – & in addition to the difficulty of the Thing itself I neither am or ever was a good hand at description – I see what I write but alas I cannot write what I see.[13]

It is also at this point, as they approach and pass the Oder Teich, that Coleridge starts to focus on detailed descriptions of waterfalls. In his notebook he writes of 'little dancing Cataracts thro' the Firs' and a 'considerable Stream, dancing over the rocks,' and then 'In a quarter of a mile when our road was crossed by the Rehbach, or the Brook of Roes, a picturesque Waterfall or rather aggregation of little dancing Kittenracts over mossy stones with young little Firs growing in the midst crossed the road, & falls down as before down the Hill beneath us.' Not satisfied to simply use the generic word 'picturesque', he starts to playfully invent words, the 'kittenracts', to better describe what he is seeing. Then, as they pass the Oder Teich, 'we descended into the Ravin [sic] & stood at the foot of a noble cascade which rushed out of the Fir Wood, the rocky caves which formed it were particularly wild in shape.' Writing to Sara, he added to this description, 'The rocks over which it plunged were unusually wild in their shape, giving fantastic resemblances of men and animals – & the fir-boughs by the side were kept almost in a *swing*, which unruly motion contrasted well with the stern Quietness of the huge Forest.'[14] It is interesting to contrast this description with those he was to write later in the Lakes when, as we will see, rather than noticing the rocks that formed the cascade, his attention has been drawn to the impact on him of the forms and energy of the falling water itself.

Leaving the Oder Teich, they climb steadily up towards the high peaks, and, writing to Sara, Coleridge describes the scenes as they reach the summit of the Great Brocken:

The Great Brocken without a rival the highest Mountain in all the north of Germany, & the seat of innumerable Superstitions. On the first day of May all the Witches dance here at Midnight … We visited the Blocksberg, a sort of Bowling Green inclosed by huge Stones, something like those at Stonehenge; & this is the Witches Ball-room. Thence proceeded to the house on the hill [an Inn] where we dined and now we descended …

By the end of the day, however, Coleridge was feeling the strain, and on arriving that evening in Elbinrode, writes: 'My Toe was shockingly swollen, my feet bladdered, and my whole frame seemed going to pieces with fatigue', and yet even this does nothing to subdue his enthusiasm, as one of the group, Clement Carlyon, reports. In his wonderful description of Coleridge 'who drove them on relentlessly and never stopped talking' in full flow, Carlyon says:

When we were ascending the Brocken, and ever and anon stopping to take breath, as well as survey the magnificent scene, a long discussion took place on the sublime and beautiful. We had much of Burke, but more of Coleridge … Many were the fruitless attempts to define sublimity satisfactorily, when Coleridge, at length, pronounced it to consist in the suspension of the powers of comparison.[15]

This account not only points up the fundamental flaw in picturesque vocabulary – what do these words (sublime, beautiful, frightful, aweful, horror and so on), perceived to express essential elements of the picturesque, really mean? – but also gives us a glimpse of the 'more of Coleridge' which may have caused Joseph Huck to abandon the Welsh tour five years earlier.

After spending the night at Elbinrode, they:

came to Rubelland, enchanting scene – a few sweet cottages in a vale that formed a very small amphitheatre, a stream flowing thro' it c. the stream; B.b.b an half moon Hill with first one over the over like Spectators in Theatre with masses of rock-like Obelisks & Walls; a. a low green Hill with Cottages at its foot; D. Bare high Crags with some 20 scattered Firs …

What is so interesting about this drawing and description is that, like those of Poele and Neuhof, Coleridge seems drawn to identify the places where people choose to live, the relationship of house and hamlets to the landscape around them, and this is something which becomes a central theme of his early descriptions of the Lake District when he first settles at Greta Hall.

By the fourth day, having got lost leaving Blankenburg, they find their way from Werninger [Wernigerode] to Drubeck, and Hartsburg to Goslar, but by this time exhaustion is setting in and as Coburn points out, 'The entries are sparse and the writing tired here … [it] was their longest day's march.'[16] They had covered some 40 miles and Coleridge describes the ordeal: 'We travelled on and on, O what a weary way! now up, now down, now with path, now without it, having no other guides than a map, [and] a compass'. Yet in spite of his growing weariness, it is this new brevity and a growing precision of word use which leads to the first emergence of the kind of descriptive language that he was to use when he started his walks in the Lake District, language which moves beyond that of the picturesque vocabulary, to describe what he is seeing:

> Hills ever by our sides, in all conceivable variety of forms & garniture – It were idle in me to attempt by words to give their projections & their retirings & how they were now in Cones, now in roundnesses, now in tonguelike Lengths, now pyramidal, now a huge Bow, and all at every step varying their outlines; or how they now stood abreast, now ran aslant, now rose up behind each other, or now, as at Hartsburg presented almost like a Sea of huge motionless waves, too multiform for Painting, too multiform even for the Imagination to remember them – yea, my very sight seemed *incapacitated* by the novelty & Complexity of the Scene.[17]

It is as though he has realized, through his attempts to describe this walk to others, that he needs to find enduring and unchanging themes below the surface of what he is seeing to carry a description through the bewildering 'multiform' detail of such complex sights; by the end of 1802, and his walks in the Lakes, not only was he on his way to identifying the central theme of 'oneness', but he was recording his experiences in a simplified straightforward prose, avoiding the thick descriptive layers and ambiguities of picturesque language, and allowing these deeper themes to emerge.

Towards the end of the walk, tired and talked out, Coleridge seems ready, finally, to follow the Wordsworths home, and his mood becomes increasingly tinged with a nostalgia for England. Now they had left the mountains, things were altogether more familiar, the landscape increasingly reminding him what it was he liked about that of England:

A hilly, pleasant country, the Fields heav'd up & down, with little dells & hollows, & the pines prettily scattered. We passed from Osterode to Catlenburg, the view of the Amtshause [*Amthaus*: house of the Amtmann – bailiff] on the Hill forming a fine English Prospect – and from hence the prospect was quite English in those counties where many noblemen's Seats with great Woods are …

It would seem that if the Welsh tour 5 years earlier had been undertaken in what Holmes describes as a 'subversive mood',[18] one in which his youthful dissatisfaction with life had led him to adopt a critical tone, this trip to Germany, after a long absence, seemed to warm him to England, the many things about it that he missed; and this mood prepared him for life in the Lakes where he could immerse himself in the scenery 'At Home', as Joseph Palmer had put it, without always looking over his shoulder and longing for the greater sublimity of the European mountains, or an idyllic life on the banks of the Susquehanna river in the Pantisocratic commune.

By 24 June 1799 Coleridge was ready to start his journey back to England. Heading for Brunswick, 'He and [John] Chester made another ascent of the Brocken taking the coach to Clausthal … They reached the summit at sunset on the 24th, but again the 'spectre-hunters' were disappointed; after a night on straw at the Inn, they returned to the peak at dawn, but again without any sightings'. Unimpressed by the tales of witches dancing on the summit at midnight on the first day of May, or their 'Ball-room' on the Blocksberg, which he dismissed as 'nothing particularly wild or romantic',[19] and tired out, he headed home to find the Wordsworths.

4

'Gentleman-poet and Philosopher in a mist': Coleridge in the Lake District: 1799 and 1800

THE 'PIKTERESK TOOR' WITH WILLIAM WORDSWORTH,
OCTOBER–NOVEMBER 1799

Between May and December of 1799, following their return from Germany, the Wordsworths lived with their childhood friends Tom, Mary, Sara, and Joanna Hutchinson on the Hutchinsons' farm at Gallow Hill, Sockburn-on-Tees, and it was here that Coleridge found them in October on his return to England. At this time his future was very unclear, and it was at this moment that Wordsworth decided to introduce him to the Lakes, hoping to induce him to stay in the north with them rather than

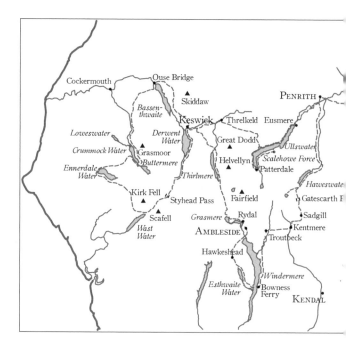

'The Pikteresk Toor', 1799.

72

returning to Nether Stowey and the Quantocks. The resulting walk, named by Coleridge 'the pikteresk Toor', lasted from 27 October to 18 November, and took Wordsworth and Coleridge from Sockburn to Penrith and then all the way round past Haweswater to Windermere, up the tourist route from Ambleside to Keswick, into Borrowdale, and then up round Bassenthwaite and through Lorton Vale to Ennerdale, Wasdale and Buttermere.

While Dorothy was left behind, the pair were initially accompanied by the publisher Joseph Cottle, and then by Wordsworth's younger brother John Wordsworth, who joined them at Temple Sowerby and left them at Grisdale Tarn high up on the Helvellyn ridge on 5 November to return to the Navy. John's naval career meant that he was away for long periods, but when home he spent a great deal of time in the Lakes and became an important member of the group.

Although Coleridge's Notebook record of this walk starts off very much in the same brief, focused style of the later entries of the Harz mountain tour, it soon becomes clear that once they were alone together, with Wordsworth acting as tour guide, pointing things out for Coleridge to notice, the experience unfolded very much on Wordsworth's terms, as a picturesque tour; a situation which reflected the more fundamental change in the basis of their

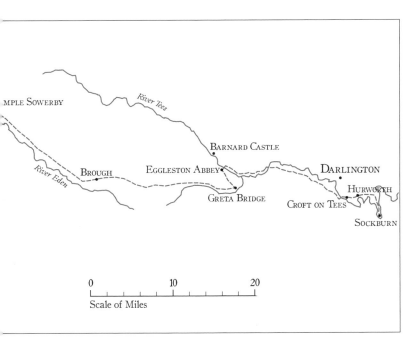

relationship over the past year, which had seen the early equality of their mutual respect for each other replaced by something increasingly one-sided.[1]

Once again, as they set out to walk to the Lakes, Coleridge noticed, as in Germany, the relationships of hamlets and villages to the landscape setting, and typical of this is his description and drawing of the village at Croft-on-Tees. Here he sees the village laid out along the river:

> Mile from Herworth the village of Croft – winding river – House in Trees – picturesque Bridge and high Waggon … We approached it by the foot-path from Herworth on the eastern side of the River – over the river the scene was thus disposed. 1. A Gentleman's House sweetly buried – Major Trotter's – 2. low cottages – 3. The Bridge. 4. the grey flat-roofed church peeping between two Trees – 5 – A neat parsonage house – 6. Meadow – 7. Gentleman's House with an avenue of Trees. 8 – fields – 9 – Curve of the River how elegant – N.B. a seven-arched Bridge.[2]

In addition to scenes like this he began to be consistently aware of the movement of water, especially waterfalls and rapids, and, unlike his water-fall descriptions in Germany, where he was largely focused on the shape of the rocks that formed the falls, he now noticed the dynamic movement, changing shapes and, above all, the sounds of the water. He also started to notice the contrast of these with the still, silent pools and backwater eddies; an altogether more complex appreciation of what he is actually seeing. At Egglestone Abbey, for example, he noticed the ruins, but his attention was immediately caught by the river:

> We arrive at the Abbey – a grey ruin on a slope, the river in wild turns below it … We pass on and come to a bridge … here struck and astonished with the *rush* of sound which came upon the ear at each opening – till at last we look up the river & behold it pouring itself down thro' a steep bed of rocks, with a wall of woods on each – & again over the other wall of the Bridge the same scene in a long visto except here instead of a rapid, a deep-solemn pool of still water, which ends in a rapid only in the far distance …

and he goes on 'the grey ruin faces you on one side – over the other in contrast of this still pool with the soft murmur of the distant rapid'.[3]

The phrase 'struck and astonished' indicates for the first time in his writing the growing impact that such elements of the natural world are beginning to have on him. He initially appreciates this scene both visually, and aurally, comparing the '*rush* of sound', the 'soft' murmur and the silence of the still pool, but then, a few lines later, he uses similar language when, in an intuitive flash, he suddenly felt, at a deeper level, his existence linked with the dynamic energies of the natural world around him:

> Castle – Star over the Tower [of church at Barnard Castle in the distance] Twinkling behind the motionless Fragment ... behind the bridge see half the arch ... the abbey seeming to rise upon the arch ... appearing to float in air – The murmur of the rapids, and again a deep pool motionless as its walls of rock almost ... [The] River Greta falls into the Tees – Shootings of water threads down the slope of a huge green stone – the white Eddy-rose that blossom'd up against the stream in the scallop, by fits and starts, obstinate in resurrection – It *is the life* that we live.

And, as he intuitively became aware of this fundamental connection, in the middle of taking it all in, he suddenly looked down and paused long enough to count the spots of decay on a fallen leaf 'Black round spots from 5 to 18 in the decaying leaf of the Sycamore' – noticing not the great sweeps of landscape grandeur, but the humblest detail of the cycles of life moving on amidst it all.

Cottle left the party at Greta Bridge to return home, but at Temple Sowerby they were joined by John Wordsworth, of whom Coleridge wrote to Dorothy, 'We met your Br. John who accompanied us to Hawes Water, Windermere, Ambleside & the Divine Sisters, Rydal & Grasmere.' This was Coleridge's first meeting with John whom he described as 'a tall, silent, kindly man of deep and inarticulate feeling, passionately devoted to his elder brother and sister ... [he] was on Merchant Navy shore-leave between two East India voyages.'[4] He was to continue to enjoy John's company, particularly on their walks around Grasmere, sensing in him a deep, quiet reflective nature, a quality of calm, almost a ponderousness of thought and reaction, which attracted him, these things being so different from his own character.

Leaving Penrith they walked up to Bampton and Haweswater, and it is at this point that the Notebook starts recording the moment when Coleridge saw the Lake District up close for the first time – 'a world of scenery absolutely new to me' as he was to write later. The walk along Haweswater to the head of the lake is couched by both Coleridge and Wordworth in the language of William Gilpin's picturesque 'rules' of '1st distance', '2nd distance', 'backdrops' and so on, with careful descriptions of the ridges and peaks that define the compositional limits of the views. 'Stations' mark the points at which a new view, complete enough to be a painting, becomes visible, and this style sets the tone for the whole tour.[5]

The first 'reach' of the lake is terminated by Walla Crag [Wallow Crag] when

> Walla's Toes run into the Lake … [and] there are inclosures too from the opposite mountains run into it – & these form that narrow part of the Lake, which as you first approach appears the termination [then] you behold a second reach – where there are no inclosures, but the bare Mountain on the right which alone we see, forms a bay – a beautiful Crescent.

This view has been largely lost due to the subsequent damming of the Lake, but then a third view opened up 'after the chasmy interval the Arm [The Rigg?], the embracement of the enfolding mountain – & another arm, rises again as much higher than this, as this was of the first …' On the left this would have been Branstree, and then above and beyond that, the crags of Harter Fell.

At this point a heavy mist descended, and so, as he writes in the letter they wrote jointly to Dorothy, Wordsworth chose a different route: 'the mists hung so low upon the mountains that we could not go directly to Ambleside, so we went round by Longsleddale to Kentmere.' Their direct route would have been up to High Street, down by Stony Cove Pike to Kirkstone Pass at the Inn, across the road and on down the side road above Stock Ghyll to Ambleside. Instead they had to divert across Gatescarth Pass and on to Sadgill, before following the old cart track over the ridge on the right to Stile End and then Kentmere. From here they crossed the ridge via Garburn Pass to Troutbeck.

Wordsworth continues 'Next to Troutbeck, and thence by Rayrigg to Bowness … [and] on to the Ferry – a cold passage – were much disgusted by the New Erections & objects about Windermere – thence to Hawkshead', where he had been at school as a child. Wordsworth had not seen the Lakes for some five and a half years, and these years had seen the beginning of the great boom in lakeside villa building as the area became increasingly popular, a trend already commented on by Joseph Palmer. Throughout the trip Wordsworth registered his disapproval of the new buildings, particularly those that had been whitewashed, and we sense Wordsworth, familiar with this part of the world, very much leading the way, commenting on what he sees, and the delighted Coleridge listening to him, taking it all in and then, in turn, recounting what they saw in precise detail.

Typical of this is his description of Haweswater: looking up the lake from the now lost narrowest point, it appeared to him as a 'complete River, the simple & tame Beauty of encircled lower Lake, & the wild betongued savage mountained upper Lake – & the pastoral River, on its right bank mirror-smooth enclosed Meadows, the steep mountain on its left Bank – the steep Mountain [Branstree] its one precipitous huge Bank!' Then before heading for Longsleddale, they:

> ascend the Hill [up the path to Small Water] & stand by the waterfall here [looking back down the lake] the upper Lake assumes a character of Beauty … the third compartment running slant down into a Lake in a soft tongue – a most woody promontory [The Rigg] then comes a chasm [Gatescarth Pass], then a hill [Harter Fell] steep as a nose running behind the embracing Giant's arms – with a chasm interposed – then the high black rampart, Mist-covered terminating all.

Leaving Hawkshead the next day they walk on to Rydal and Grasmere, Coleridge noting ahead 'on my left 5 huge jagged mountains, rising one above the other in wild relations of posture' as they pass by Blelham Tarn, and, again, taking a lead from Wordsworth, he roundly condemns the whitewashed new houses 'Head of Wynandermere – Mr Law's White palace – a bitch! …'[6]

Reaching Grasmere and staying at Robert Newton's Inn, they are forced by bad weather to stay a few days, but, while Wordsworth reports that Coleridge is 'much enchanted with Grasmere and Rydal', Coleridge, unlike Palmer seven years before, is not taken with the view of Helm Crag, let alone drawn to climb it 'Embraced round by Hill's arms behind – before us what ridges & on the side of that little spot of Lake. What an aweful mount!' Yet while Helm Crag did not tempt them, they did take on Helvellyn, Wordsworth and Coleridge reaching the summit from Grasmere after parting with John Wordsworth at Grisdale Tarn. Wordsworth briefly records that 'the day was a fine one and we had some grand mountain scenery', but Coleridge, excited by his first experience of a mist-free Lakeland mountaintop view, wrote:

> First the Lake of Grasmere like a sullen Tarn, then the black ridge of mountain – then as upborne among the other mountains the luminous Cunneston Lake – & far away in the Distance & far to the Lake the

glooming Shadow, Wynandermere with its Island – Pass on – the Tarn – & view of the gloomy Ulswater & mountains behind, one black, one blue, & the last one dun. Greisdale Halse – Gowdrell Crag – Tarn Crag – that smoother Eminence on the right is called Fairfield.[7]

It is at this stage that we start to see a change in Coleridge's writing. Previously the descriptions had been in pretty standard picturesque vocabulary striving to describe the construction of the views, and the intellectual pleasure to be gained from the composition of the landscape. Entries from here on, however, become less considered, more intuitive perhaps, as Coleridge jots down fragments that capture the sensation of being there, the immediate effect on the senses, those ephemeral effects of mists, falling water, moving shadows, trees, branches, leaves bending, 'yielding and parting', the 'streaming air', the sudden opening up and closing down of a particular view, the revealing and obscuring of elements of the landscape, mist or wind on the cheek, the sudden chill deep in a gorge when the sun is blocked out, attempts to express what he is actually seeing and feeling moment to moment. In Germany, he had hoped, indeed expected, to find the *genii loci* of the mountains revealed in sensational spectres, apparitions in human form to which one could relate, but the notebook of these early months in the Lakes records his growing conviction that the spirit connected to a place, and the inspiration that may be derived from it, was going to be revealed in much more subtle and mysterious ways:

Churnmilk Force – appearing over the Copse – the steaming air rising above it – the water fall – the rock that stands up & intercepts all but the marges & rims of the lower half – the Copse, whose trees sometimes yielding & parting in the wind make the waterfall beneath the rock visible – the first Bridge from the water fall, one arched – ferny – its parapet or ledge of single stones not unmorter'd yet cemented more by moss & mould … [8]

For Coleridge this was a place of invisible forces moving amongst the visible, steaming air and streaming water, both flowing round immovable rock, everything both hidden and revealed by the movement of the branches, the bridge stones locked together by the living structures of moss and ferns, and, if they refer to the same waterfall, his animated description stands in stark contrast to Wordsworth's brief comment to Dorothy: ' to the upper waterfall at Rydal, and saw it through the gloom, and it was very magnificent.'

It is also at this point that we get a hint of what was to come when Wordsworth writes to Dorothy that 'C. was much struck with Grasmere & its neighbourhood & I have much to say to you, you will think my plan a mad one, but I have thought of building a house there by the Lakeside ... We shall talk of this ...'. He then goes on to report that 'There is a small house at Grasmere empty which perhaps we may take ...'. This was, of course, Dove Cottage, and clearly being back in the Lakes also inspired Wordsworth himself.

In turn, Coleridge continues the letter to Dorothy telling her that 'I cannot express for myself – how deeply I have been impressed by a world of scenery absolutely new to me'. Although he felt 'deep delight' in Grasmere, and though the 'varying views' around Haweswater 'kept my eyes dim with tears', it was when he saw Derwentwater and Keswick and the 'diversity of harmonious features, in the majesty of its beauties & in the Beauty of its majesty ... the Black crags close under the snowy mountains, whose snows were pinkish with the setting sun', that Coleridge, like Gray before him, was captivated by 'the Vale of Elysium in all its verdure' as the latter had called it. 'It was to me a vision of a fair Country. Why were you not with us Dorothy?' It was a good question, and soon enough she was, and his own enthusiasm for these views was to lead him, in turn, to settle in Keswick.

By this time, it would seem, Coleridge had been in the Lake District long enough to feel that this really was a very special place, that this was a place he wanted to get to know much better. The fact that it is at this point in his notebook that he writes out part of Joseph Palmer's poem *Windermere*, which had been published the year before, is perhaps significant. While Palmer's poem took the standard picturesque viewpoint that the Lakes should be seen as 'perfect miniatures' of such grander places as the Alps, it nevertheless emphasizes that many of the qualities found in such places – 'wide-extended Lakes', the 'golden richness of the setting Sun', the 'soften'd Fragrance of the evening air', 'the mighty mountains' – could also be viewed here, 'At Home.'[9] Following his experience of the Harz mountains, Coleridge would seem to have agreed with Palmer, and there is no doubt that as the walk progressed, what he saw around him and the special atmosphere of the places combined to stimulate a rich new element in his writing.

Entries such as his description of 'Churnmilk Force' alert us to this new sensitivity to liminal effects, and it is followed by this extraordinary description of a shower drifting across the landscape: 'Exquisite Network of Film so instinct with gentle motion which, now the Shower only steadies, & now it melts it into such a mistiness as the Breath leaves on a mirror.'[10]

Equally, this description of a waterfall, possibly stimulated by what he had seen at Churnmilk Force a few days before, reflects a new quality of perception and language which took him beyond the stock accounts of 'magnificence' and 'gloom': 'Mist as from a volcano – Waterfall rolled after long looking at like a segment of a Wheel – the rock gleaming through it – Amid the roar a noise as of innumerable grasshoppers or a spinning of wheels.'[11]

On Friday 8 November, Coleridge and Wordsworth continued their walk alone, moving on from Keswick to the foot of Bassenthwaite and to the Inn at Ouse Bridge. Looking back up the lake from a window of the Inn, they were, perhaps, sitting at the same table that Joseph Palmer had used when he stayed at the Inn little more than a year before, after he walked up 'beneath the giant Skiddaw' on his way to see the icicles on Scale Force, and where Thomas Gray had eaten lunch on his trip up the east side of Bassenthwaite in October 1769. Of them all, however, only Coleridge caught the moment and the view:

> From the Inn Window, the whole length of Basenthwaite, a simple majesty of water & mountains – & in the distance the Bank rising like a wedge – & in the second distance the Crags of Derwentwater, what an effect of the Shadows on the water! – On the left the conical Shadow, On the right a square of splendid Black, all the area & intermediate a mirror reflecting dark and sunny Cloud – but in the distance the black Promontory with a circle of melted Silver & a path of silver running from it like a flat Cape in the Lake – The Snowy Borrodale in the far distance – & a ridge, nearer mountains sloping down as it were to the faint Bank of Basenthwaite.[12]

When he described the view they looked at through the frame of the window, it is notable that Coleridge used the full gamut of Gilpin's picturesque vocabulary in his description – 'in the distance ... in the second distance ... On the left ... on the right ... far distance'. This tone permeates his accounts of this walk, but from the following year, as he started walking on his own, a much more original style was to emerge.

The next day, although they do not appear to have actually visited Cockermouth itself, they entered the landscapes of Wordsworth's childhood, and one very much gets the sense that Coleridge was seeing this section

The 'Second View': Grasmoor on the approach to Crummock Water [author].

As Coleridge and Wordsworth proceed up Lorton Vale, 'a most sublime Crag' of Grasmoor comes to dominate the view ahead. Seen here from the road, even among the mists and low cloud, Grasmoor is an impressive sight as it rises beyond the slopes of Whiteside.

of the walk down to Buttermere through Wordsworth's eyes. Walking from Ouse Bridge, they crossed the valley at Embleton and walked along under Ling Fell and Long Fell, the 'fantastic ridge, brown, iron brown', and turned down into Lorton Vale. The long entry describing the walk to Buttermere is entirely focused on five sequential views:[13]

First, they passed Red How Crag set alone in the middle of the Vale, a 'single Hill covered with wood & fantastically shaped … as we pass, its gable a precipice with peeping rocks.'

Second, between Red How and Scale Hill, they became aware of Grasmoor high on their left terminating their view on that side: 'a most sublime Crag, of a violet colour, patched here and there with islands of Heath-plant – & wrinkled and guttered most picturesquely …', an appearance which 'contrasts with the Hills on my Right, which tho' in form ridgy & precipitous,

The 'Third View': Crummock Water from Loweswater [author].

'O God, what a scene', Coleridge's comment still sums up perfectly the complex beauty of the 'Third View', seen here from the road from Scalehill Bridge and the village of Loweswater.

are yet smooth and green.' This attention to the details that made up the view, suggests that Grasmoor and the composition of the landscape on either side of Scale Hill, with the mouth of Crummock Water beyond, may have been something the two actually stopped to discuss.

Third, passing the Inn at Scale Hill, a new view opens up to the right, up into the valley of Loweswater: 'tis a sweet country that opens up before us, Somersetshire Hills, & many a neat scattered House with Trees round of the Estates Men. – The White Houses here beautiful & look at the river & its two-arched Bridges'. Having walked a little way up towards Loweswater, Coleridge turns around and 'O God, what a scene – the fore ground a sloping wood, sloping down to the River & the wood meadows terminated by Melbreak'. Interestingly enough, Coleridge, perhaps speaking for himself, sees the white houses here as 'beautiful'. In all, it is a perfect scene, on a similar scale to Grasmere and its hills, but as his eye roams further on beyond Melbreak, everything changes again:

Scale Force

Scale Force [A. Wainwright, *The Western Fells*].

While Palmer had become 'lost in vacant delights' on seeing this fall, and Coleridge writes to 'the great fall, of which the Height and Depths is sudden & out of all comparison', in his description of Scale Force Wainwright leaves his drawing to speak for itself, commenting only that 'the attraction of this popular route is Lakeland's highest waterfall'.

Fourth, 'At the end of this wall a peep of Crummock Water and in continuation of the Melbreak, after a break [the valley of Scale Force waterfall], but in the same line the snowy Ridges, which seem to curve round, but a huge Gable-Crag starts up in the middle & fronts me – close by my left hand a rocky wooded Hill [Scale Hill], and behind it, half hidden by it, the violet crag of Grasmere visible/the woody Hill leaves only the Top Third of Grasmere visible.'

Walking through the woods he sees 'nothing else', until emerging the other end at which moment 'the whole violet Crag rises & fronts me'. Then rounding the point where Rannerdale Knotts runs steeply down to the water's edge, he saw the seven 'tiny islands' of upper Crummock Water and then, looking further up, Buttermere.

Fifth, 'Buttermere comes upon us, a fragment of it – the view enclosed by a huge Concave Semicircle.' A short enough description but the view is in fact striking, the narrow lake leading the eye up between the high, parallel ridges of Buttermere Fell on the left, and the Red Pike – High Stile – High Crag ridge on the right, before both curve in to meet in the towering concave ridgeline that sweeps round from Honister Crag to Haystacks. [14]

As he took all this in, Coleridge noted some details that caught his eye: the Crag House Crags to their left, and far up to their right 'The hill like a Dolphin so beautiful in the Lines of snow … is named Red Pike – the Ridge that seems to run in behind it is named High Stele.' That night they stayed at the Inn at Buttermere (and were no doubt told all about that 'cheeriest of strangers', Palmer, who had so enjoyed the night of dancing there) before setting out next day to climb to Scale Force and continue over past Floutern Tarn to Ennerdale.

At Scale Force Coleridge was inspired to write one of his detailed descriptions of a waterfall that focused now on the activity of the water itself:

The first fall a thin broad white ribbon from a stupendous height [c. 100ft], uninterrupted, tho' not unimpinged by, the perpendicular Rock down which it falls, or rather parallel with which there is no pool at the bottom, but a common shallow brook over small flattish pebbles – but the chasm thro' which it flows, is stupendous – so wildly wooded that the mosses & wet weeds & and perilous Tree increase the Horror of the rocks which *ledge* only enough to interrupt not stop your fall – and the Tree – O God! to think of a poor Wretch hanging with one arm from it. The lower Fall i.e. the Brook is broader; but very low in comparison & only markworthy as combining admirably.

Scale Force waterfall [Derry Brabbs].
'The first fall a thin broad white ribbon…'

Before the great fall are six falls, each higher than the other, the chasm still gradually deepening, till the great fall, of which the Height and Depths is sudden & out of all comparison ... [15]

The description is an interesting combination of both the scene itself and his reaction to it. One wonders, in fact, whether they had not heard some terrible tale of a stranger getting into difficulties there when they were at the Inn.

From here they walked up over the saddle between Mosedale Fell and Gale Fell, and Coleridge's note 'and have now entered entirely enclosed by Hills, a plashy Plain – My eyes fatigued – walking climbed and a cold, looked at the lovely mosses at feet', gives us a glimpse of him, tiring from the climb, bent forward as the hill steepens, seeing little but the ground in front. Finally, dropping down between Banna Fell and Herdus, he sees Ennerdale Water below him, the end of the lake, 'a circular Bay, like the head of a Battledore ... No house – no Tree & an Unbroken Line of the steep Crag is tremendous – but on the left hand of the Lake, as you ascend up it, the rubbishy Crag with sheep picturesque as Goats & as perilous feeding – on the very Summit two large Yews or Hollies.'

The last section of this entry would appear to relate to their route the next day as they set off up Ennerdale to cross over to Wasdale Head, passing the 'rubbishy Crag' [Bowness Crag?], and the walk is then picked up in the next entry as they passed below the 'Screes – opposite to it Middle Fell', after which they turned up Black Sail Pass, catching sight of Scafell, Great Gavel [Great Gable] and Great Yeaborough [Yewbarrow] as they descend down to Wasdale Head.[16]

After two nights at 'T. Tyson's' in Wasdale Head – a place Coleridge would stay at again on his 1802 solo walk, before his ascent of Scafell – the two proceeded up the old track over Styhead Pass and down into Borrowdale.[17] The brevity of the entries from Scale Force onwards, and the lack of later accounts in letters, suggests that either the pair were tiring, or that they were no longer on quite such easy terms as they had been earlier in the trip. One has the impression of them walking separately, Wordsworth lost in his plans for moving with Dorothy to Grasmere, while Coleridge continued record-ing the details of what they saw; no longer analyzing the composition of the wider views, but absorbed in all the extraordinary variety of sights that caught his eye and searching for the vocabulary to explain them: 'Brooks in their anger – all the Gullies full & white & the Chasms now black, now half hid by the mist, & ever and anon the waterfall in them flashing thro' the mists. On one hill I counted 7 huge Gullies – a dark misty thunder-murmured Scene – Remember all about Sheep & Larches …'

In phrases such as 'a dark misty thunder-murmured Scene' there is a stream of consciousness quality in the writing which catches the experience of passing through this landscape in a way which had not been seen before, and has not often been bettered since.

Having spent the night in Rosthwaite, they passed through Keswick and walked up past Castlerigg Stone Circle, 'A Druidical circle on the right of the Road', to spend the next night in Threlkeld. On the morning of the 16th they 'proceeded over the Hills, a barren moss-peat, to Matterdale', where they are struck by the sight of a small walled enclosure that caught their eye as they passed:

> We noticed one field to our right … the field a small Inclosure of about an acre … Key: 1: a stick with a rimless Hat on it looking like a Bell – 2: another – the Hat sunk down to the Bottom, a bit of the crown remaining on the Top. 3. a single ram.[18]

Although the ram remained, the unfortunate owner of the hat and stick was long gone, hopefully unscathed. After passing Aira Force and the gothic folly called Lyulph's Tower, they reached Ullswater, where they turned right and walked round to Patterdale.

After a night in the Inn in Patterdale they:

> went down the Lake by the opposite shore – the hoar-frost on the ground, the lake calm & would have been mirrorlike but that it had been *breathed* on by the mist … We passed the first *Great* Promontory, & What a scene! Where I stand, on the shore is a triangular Bay, taking in the whole of the water view – on the other shore is a straight deep wall of Mist & one third of the bare mountains stand out from behind it – the top of the wall only in the sun – the rest black – & now it is all one deep wall of vapour, save that black streaks shaped like strange creatures, seem to move in it & down it … & over the forke of the Cliff behind … the sun sent cutting it his thousand silky Hairs of amber & green Light – I step two paces and have lost the Glory …

A wonderful passage that captures the mystery, fleeting and otherworldly effects of light and Coleridge's fascination with what he has witnessed. At this moment the fog 'closed over the Lake', and they continued their walk along the track which follows the shoreline round under Place Fell and Silver Crag.

How far they went is not clear but in the next entry they visit 'Clark's Niagara – one of Nature's originals, horse-shoe in shape', which raises the possibility that their destination was Scalehow Force ['Clark' is their mutual friend Thomas Clarkson who lived at Eusmere in Pooley Bridge]. Once there Coleridge is clearly not that impressed by it, 'but with none but two locum-tenentes of a petty order', and it is here that they appear to have turned around to return to Patterdale.

'Now as we return the fog begins to clear off from the Lake', creating some wonderful effects. The entry ends:

> Lyulph's Tower gleams like a Ghost, dim & shadowy – & the bright Shadow thereof how beautiful it is cut across by that Tongue of *breezy* water – now the Shadow is suddenly gone – and the Tower itself rises emerging out of the mist, two-thirds wholly hidden, the turrets quite clear – & a moment all is snatched away – Realities & Shadows.[19]

'Realities & Shadows', the juxtaposition of the elements of the natural world which so excites Coleridge, the suggestion of worlds, energies, lives moving below the surface of what we actually see.

The subsequent walk from Patterdale round to their friend Clarkson's house at Eusemere is not recorded, but with this the 'Pikteresk Toor' came to an end. On 18 November, while Wordsworth stayed on with the Clarksons for a while longer, perhaps going over the possibilities of leasing the cottage he had noticed in Grasmere, Coleridge left, and at some point around this time he makes the following observation: 'I would make a pilgrimage to the burning sands of Arabia … to find the Man who could explain to me there can be *oneness*, there being infinite Perceptions – yet there must be a *oneness*, not an intense Unity but an Absolute Unity … '[20] As enigmatic an entry as any such, reflecting his brief remark at Egglestone Abbey, 'It *is the life* that we live'. The timing is interesting, suggesting perhaps the deeper drift of Coleridge's thoughts during the course of this walk, his initial experience of the Lake District. It was a theme that we see taken up again the following year once he came to live at Greta Hall, and in the course of the walks which followed.

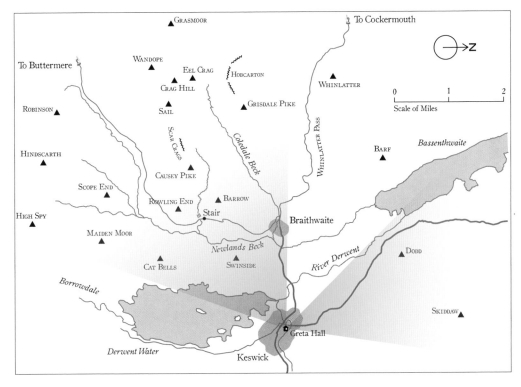

The views from Coleridge's Study at Greta Hall

'At Home': Coleridge at Greta Hall, Keswick, 1800

Coleridge, his wife Sara and their son Hartley arrived at Dove Cottage, Grasmere, on 29 June 1800 from Somerset and stayed with the Wordsworths for the next three weeks while Greta Hall, the house they had leased in Keswick, was prepared for them. They then moved up to Keswick on 23 or 24 July, taking half the house, the other half being occupied by the owner, William Jackson. Coleridge soon established himself in his study, choosing the room because its dual aspect gave him wide views to the south-west, the west and the north.

Almost immediately he became fascinated by these views and recorded himself gazing out and studying the topography of the landscape, catching sudden effects of clouds, rain or mist, in both sunlight and moonlight – all the things which played across the mountains and brought them to life. From his first day of occupation onwards we get a series of descriptions in both his notebook and his letters of these views, which together establish

Above: William Westall, *Fields, River and Greta Hall*, 1850 [courtesy of The Wordsworth Trust, Grasmere].

This historic image of Greta Hall shows the position of the house on top of the open hill and illustrates just how extensive the views were that Coleridge had from his study windows; views which are today largely obscured by trees and buildings, especially to the north.

Facing page, top: Greta Hall today [author].

The house today, seen here beyond its gates, still retains a strong sense of its extraordinary history. The Coleridge wing is seen here on the left of the front door, with the sitting room window on the ground floor, and the window of Coleridge's study (now a bedroom) above it. To the right is the wing subsequently occupied by the Southey family.

Facing page, bottom: View from Greta Hall looking south-west [author].

The growth of trees, and the houses which now fill the slope below the house, make it impossible to see the extent of the views Coleridge saw from his study. However, some idea of his 'camps of giants' tents' can still be glimpsed from the gardens at Greta Hall. In this photograph looking south and south-west, the brown slopes from Cat Bells to Maiden Moor and High Spy run along above Derwent Water to Borrowdale in the left background. Beyond these, the peaks of Dale Head, Hindscarth and Robinson.

the physical parameters of the landscape setting he found himself in, and add up to a sense of the place he felt himself to occupy, a place he then systematically set out to explore.

These descriptions are both interesting and important, since they are part of the background to his creative life in Keswick and to the extraordinary period between July and October 1800 when he was to discover the Lakeland landscape on a series of solo walks. It was also the golden period of his friendship with the Wordsworths when anything and everything seemed possible, a period that can be seen to end in October 1800 with Wordsworth's rejection of Coleridge's poem 'Christabel' for inclusion in the second volume of their collaborative collection of poems, the *Lyrical Ballads*. This event and everything associated with it in turn marked the start of a period of deepening depression and nagging illness that changed his mood completely, and it was to be another two years before he set out walking in the Lakes again in 1802.

In addition, these descriptions are important because they are centred on the place where he actually lived. Whereas previously the places he noticed and described tended to be those he saw on his walks and tours, now they represented places he has the leisure to contemplate and the interest to explore in intimate detail. On his walks over the next few months he climbed up, round or across the fells, peaks and ridgelines, the 'camps of giants' tents' as he described them, that make up these views; and those sections of the letters that concern the views show Coleridge steadily honing his style, his choice of language and vocabulary, as he tried to improve his ability to describe what he saw and how it affected him.

As he sat in his study in Greta Hall, Coleridge described what he saw out of his windows in a series of letters to friends, listing the names of the mountains: straight ahead, through the southwest-facing window, lay the dramatic ridge of Maiden Moor and Cat Bells running the length of Derwent Water on the west side, and beyond it lay Hindscarth and Robinson. Round to the west ran 'a wilderness of mountains' above Swinside and Barrow, the long jagged skyline from 'Rolling End' [Rowling End] to Causey Pike, Sail to Eel Crag, and over Coledale Hause before rising again to the sculpted heights of Grisdale Pike. To the north, a second window looked out along the western ramparts of Skiddaw and provided partial views of Bassenthwaite running north below them, off towards the low fells west of Binsey.[21]

As his descriptions of these various landscapes build up, we get a growing

View from Greta Hall looking west [author].

To the west, as he sat at his desk, Coleridge saw straight before him 'a wilderness of mountains, catching & streaming lights or shadows', a wilderness dominated by the skyline leading off from Rowling End up the ridge to Causey Pike, Sail, Crag Hill and Eel Crag, before dropping into Coledale Hause and ascending again to the dramatic outline of Grisdale Pike. In front of these he identified Swinside and Barrow, all making up a landscape, a great 'encampment' which caught his imagination and initiated his fell-walking adventures.

sense that he felt his desk and study to be located not in a particular house, or on a particular street, or even in Keswick itself (which he rarely mentions by name), but within a place defined by these mountains, lakes and valleys; his 'place', defined, enveloped and protected by these mighty folds of the earth and specifically by the river Greta flowing down from the heights of Skiddaw and Saddleback to encircle the house and study in a wide looping bend.

'The Lake of Bassenthwaite with its simple and majestic *case* of mountains'
[A. Wainwright, *The Northern Fells*].

Wainwright's image of the view from Latrigg gives an indication of Coleridge's
view, now blocked by trees and houses.

One of the first of these letters was written on 24 July to his friend and
patron Josiah Wedgwood, who with his brother Tom had taken an early
interest in Coleridge's career:[22]

This is the first day of my arrival at Keswick – my house is roomy, situated on an eminence a furlong from the Town – before it an *enormous*
Garden more than two thirds of which is rented as a Garden for sale
articles, but the walks &c are ours completely. Behind the house are
shrubberies, & a declivity planted with flourishing trees of 15 years'

growth or so, at the bottom of which is a most delightful shaded walk by the River Greta, a quarter mile in length. The room in which I sit, commands from one window the Basenthwaite Lake, Woods, & Mountains, from the opposite the Derwentwater & fantastic mountains of Borrowdale – straight before me is a wilderness of mountains, catching & streaming lights or shadows at all times – behind the house & entering into all our views is Skiddaw …

From this it is clear that Coleridge is already looking beyond the tourist 'stations' situated at key points along the lakes and valleys, and it would only be a matter of weeks before he explored not just Skiddaw and Borrowdale, but also the 'wilderness of mountains' straight before him, places located around the valley of Coledale Beck above Braithwaite, but which until now were unvisited by the tourists and unknown except to the shepherds, miners and drovers for whom they were the place of work. Clearly though, the picturesque tour was already having a major impact on the area, since Coleridge adds:

It is no small advantage here that for two thirds of the year we are in complete retirement – the other third is alive & swarms with Tourists of all shapes and sizes, & characters …

Just how excited Coleridge was at this time and how much he was enjoying coming to understand the area around Keswick, is illustrated by the light-hearted introduction he included in his next letter, to James Webb Tobin, a friend from his Bristol days, which reads: 'From the leads on the housetop of Greta Hall, Keswick, Cumberland, at the present time in the occupancy and usufruct-possession of S.T. Coleridge, Esq., Gentleman-poet and Philosopher in a mist.'

The letter continues:

the Lake of Bassenthwaite, with its simple and majestic *case* of mountains, on my right hand; on my left, and stretching far away into the fantastic mountains of Borrowdale, the Lake of Derwentwater; straight before me a whole camp of giant's tents, or is it an ocean rushing in, in billows that, even in the serene sky, reach halfway to heaven? [23]

and in one to Samuel Purkis four days later, he repeats and embellishes this description of the scene:

Yes – my dear Sir! here I am – with Skiddaw at my back – on my right hand the Bassenthwaite Water with it's majestic *Case* of Mountains, all of simplest Outline – looking slant, direct over the feather of this infamous Pen, I see the Sun setting – my god! what a scene – ! Right before me is a great *Camp* of single mountains – each in shape resembles a Giant's Tent! – and to my left, but closer to it [by] far than Bassenthwaite Water to my right, is the lake of Keswick, with it's Islands and white sails, & glossy Lights of Evening – *crowned* with green meadows, but the three remaining sides are encircled by the most fantastic mountains, that ever Earthquakes made in sport; as fantastic, as if Nature had *laughed* herself into the convulsion, in which they are made. – Close behind me at the foot of Skiddaw flows the Greta, I hear its murmuring distinctly – then it curves round almost in a semicircle, & is now catching the purple Lights of the scattered Clouds above it directly before me … now I am enjoying the Godlikeness of the Place, in which I am settled …[24]

In these letters, both the descriptions and the drawing of the location of the house take us back to those of Poele, Neuhof and Rubelleland from the walk in the Harz mountains, only *now* he is identifying those elements that make this place home for *him*.

As these descriptions tumble out in letter after letter, their ever-shifting emphasis and each additional detail all reflect Coleridge's deepening awareness of what he is actually seeing. To Thomas Poole in Nether Stowey he writes in mid-August: 'Our house is a delightful residence … It commands both [the Lake of Keswick], & the Lake Bassenthwaite – Skiddaw is behind us – to the left, the right, & in front, Mountains of all shapes and sizes – the waterfall of Lodore is distinctly visible – In the gardens, etc we are uncommonly well off, & our Landlord who resides next door in the twofold House, is already much attached to us',[25] while, a month later, writing to the philosopher and novelist William Godwin, he repeats much the same description, but this time emphasized not so much the shapes of the mountains around, but the relationship of the house to the various features:

Our House is situated on rising Ground, not two furlongs from Keswick, about as much from the Lake, Derwentwater, & about two miles or so from the Lake, Bassenthwaite – both lakes & their mountains we command – the River Greta runs behind our house, & before it too – & Skiddaw is behind us, not half a mile distant – indeed just distant enough, to enable us to view it as a whole. The Garden, Orchard, Fields, & *immediate* country, all delightful.[26]

By the end of the year there is a distinct change in tone, as he became increasingly familiar with the views and increasingly able to stand back from them and understand the relationship he has developed with them. This becomes clear in a letter of 1 November to Josiah Wedgwood:

> Everything I promised myself in this country, has answered far beyond my expectations. The room in which I write commands six distinct Landscapes – the two Lakes, the Vale, River, & mountains, & mists, & Clouds, & Sunshine make endless combinations, as if heaven & Earth were for ever talking to each other – Often when in a deep Study I have walked to the window & remained there, *looking without seeing*, all at once the Lake of Keswick & the fantastic mountains of Borrodale at the head of it have entered into my mind with a suddenness, as if I had been snatched out of Cheapside & placed for the first time on the spot where I stood. – And that is a delightful Feeling – these Fits and Trances of Novelty received from a long known Object. The river Greta flows behind our house, roaring like an untamed Son of the Hills, then winds round, & *glides* away in the front – so that we live in a peninsula …[27]

It was from this clearly defined place amidst these 'six distinct landscapes', embraced by the river Greta flowing, winding and gliding around it, and with Skiddaw guarding its back, that Coleridge was to set forth on walks that radiated from his central location; walks on which he hoped not only to discover the physical realities of this great 'encampment' of mountains, but also, if possible, to listen in on, understand and perhaps even participate in, that endless conversation between heaven & Earth 'talking to each other' that he sensed happening all around him. He also felt he understood now how to participate in this world, how to allow himself to experience it through his intuitive self rather than his intellect, to 'look without seeing'.

In a letter to the playwright William Sotheby two years later, after his great adventures in these landscapes, he described the views again, this time in a way that seems to suggest that he had succeeded in achieving that, as he describes it, 'transfiguring' experience:

> O that you were now in my study, & saw what is now before the window,

at which I am writing, that rich mulberry purple which a floating Cloud
has thrown on the Lake – & that quiet Boat making its way thro' it to the
Shore! ... but showery weather is no evil to us – & even that most oppressive of all weathers, hot small Drizzle, exhibits the Mountains the best of
any. It produced such new combinations of Ridges in the Lodore and
Borrodale Mountains ... wild, & transfiguring, yet enchantingly lovely ...
Wordsworth, who has walked thro' Switzerland, declared that he never saw
anything superior – perhaps nothing equal – in the Alps.[28]

Throughout his life, Coleridge had been aware of those moments when he
suddenly identified the specific place he was occupying and the nature of
what it was that created the 'structure' of that place, and in later life, looking
back, he remembered the place to which he had instinctively fled as a child of
seven, running from his home in Ottery St Mary after a family argument. As
he had recounted in a letter to Thomas Poole in 1797, fearing a beating from
his mother, he 'ran away, to a hill at the bottom of which the Otter flows', the
river and such places along its banks which were central to his childhood. He
went on, 'There I stayed; my rage died away ... [and] I distinctly remember
my feelings when I saw Mr Vaughan pass over the Bridge ... and how I saw
the Calves in the fields beyond the river. It grew dark & I fell asleep ... and
[feeling] cold in my sleep, I dreamt I was pulling the blanket over me, & actually pulled over me a dry thorn bush.[29]

He was eventually found next morning, but he seems never to have forgotten this 'place' where he stopped running, where he 'stayed', where his
'rage died away', and it was not simply an undefined open space on a hillside,
he remembered specifically the river, the bridge, a neighbour, the calves, and,
above all, the dry thorn bush he crawled under; all these things came together
to create the specific place he sought out for protection, where he could stop
and be safe enough to fall asleep.

Something very similar also emerged when he married Sara in Bristol
and the couple moved into a small cottage near Clevedon. It was a place he
called 'our pretty Cot', and he referred to it specifically in a poem he called
Reflections on having left a place of Retirement, written 1795:

> Low was our pretty cot! our tallest rose
> Peeped at the chamber-window. We could hear
> At silent noon, and eve, and early morn,
> The sea's faint murmur. In the open air

> Our myrtles blossomed; and across the porch
> Thick jasmines twined: the little landscape round
> Was green and woody and refreshes the eye.
> It was a spot, you might aptly call
> The Valley of Seclusion

For Coleridge, although it was not to last, this 'cot', defined by the roses, myrtles and 'thick jasmines', and surrounded by the little 'green and woody' landscape, represented the ideal location for his marital bliss; like the branch of brushwood pulled over him, and later the house in Keswick, defined by the encampments of mountains and the Greta river, the cot represented a psychological space as much as a physical location. His place within the materials of the natural world.

Similarly, in the summer of 1797 at Nether Stowey, as he is 'sitting in the arbour of T[homes] Poole's garden', having spent the afternoon missing William, Dorothy and his friend from his school days, Charles Lamb, who were out walking on the hills, he once again becomes aware of another such space he was occupying. In the words of the poem he wrote inspired by this, 'The Lime-Tree Bower', we see this place emerge not as a built structure, but as a place created by light, and due to this revelation the 'bower' is no longer the 'prison' he had superficially felt it to be, but a reminder from Nature about the abundance of the life that is always around us:

> This little lime-tree bower, have I not marked
> Much that has soothed me. Pale beneath the blaze
> Hung the transparent foliage; and I watched
> Some broad and sunny leaf, and loved to see
> That shadow of the leaf and stem above
> Dappling its sunshine! And that walnut-tree
> Was richly tinged, and a deep radiance lay
> Full on the ancient ivy, which usurps
> Those fronting elms, and now, with blackest mass
> Makes their dark branches gleam a lighter hue
> Though the late twilight and though now the bat
> Wheels silent by, and not a swallow twitters,
> Yet still the solitary humble-bee
> Sings in the bean flower! Henceforth I shall know
> That Nature ne'er deserts the wise and pure

Towards the end of that long afternoon, as the sun 'sink[s] slowly behind the western ridge' he was 'struck with joy's deepest calm', and rather than wishing he was with the others out on the hills, he suddenly becomes aware, as the twilight deepens and reality starts to drift, of a place defined by the changing light; defined by the sunlight on 'each broad transparent Leaf', by the broken 'shadows of the Leaf or Stem', by the 'richly ting'd Wall-nut Tree', the 'deep radiance' lying 'Full on the ancient ivy', and by the 'blackest mass' which makes the … dark foliage gleam a lighter hue / Thro' the last twilight'. Coming out of his daydream he tells himself that 'Henceforth I shall know / That nature ne'er deserts the wise and pure …'.[30]

Against this background, we realize that the significance of the place he discovered for himself at Greta Hall is that this time, rather than being a place of childhood intuition, of idealized marital bliss or a liminal place of light, this time the things that defined it were physically there. Having spent his life to this point in a world of increasingly familiar and, in a sense, comfortable 'early visions', as Holmes terms it, he now had something tangible to help him move beyond the comfortingly familiar; the normally gregarious Coleridge would explore these new places on his own.

In March 1798, following a visit to his childhood home in Ottery, Coleridge had written a letter to his brother George from Nether Stowey which contained the line 'I love fields & woods & mountains with an almost visionary fondness'.[31] The walks he was about to undertake from Greta Hall some two years later were to explore that sense of the visionary, and enable him to understand the real nature of that fondness and what it meant, and it was the experience he gained of existence by leaving the world of fields and woods, the familiar, and entering the world of the mountains, the unfamiliar, which was to make this possible.

'O Joy for me!':
Coleridge's Lake District Walks, 1800

DUNGEON GHYLL FORCE

> Bell thro' a mist in Langdale vale …
> what a simile for a melancholy[1]

K athleen Coburn suggests that this poetic image of the 'melancholy' sound of a church bell emanating from the mist represents 'the first entry after Coleridge has settled down in the Lakes, no longer a tourist, but with time to examine at leisure,' and it will have been one of the things that caught his attention on his walk up Langdale as far as Dungeon Ghyll Force in June or July 1800. If, as seems likely, he had read Palmer's account of his 1797 outing to the Langdale Pikes, Coleridge may well have been curious to see the waterfall at Dungeon Ghyll and its dramatic setting, the 'chasm, where a tremendous stream roared into it'. Here 'the mind was actively employed', as Palmer had written, and Coleridge made it one of his first destinations beyond the immediate environs of Grasmere and Rydal Water, places he had been exploring with the Wordsworths. His account of what he found concentrates entirely on the fall, and is full of his growing sense of the 'connections' within the world of nature, a sense which was soon to widen to include himself:

> Dungeon Gill Force. Stand to the right hand close, by the bellying rock, so as to see the top of the waterfall only by the Daylight on the wet rock – the arch right above the little *imitation* of the great waterfall, connections in nature, between the arch & the great Waterfall an arch of Trees … the Stream widens from a foot to a yard and a half, as it widens, varying from a vivid white to a blue thro' all the intermediate shades – the second divided from the first by a huge [boulder?] contiguated to the two

sides by rocks small and pendulous – plumy ferns on the side … Going up to the force notice a Sheepfold … and the fold inclosed a curve of the path of a mountain [beck].[2]

Interestingly enough, it is also at this time that Coleridge records seeing 'Ladies reading Gilpin' and comments on their 'passing by the places instead of looking at the places,' a remark which seems to sum up the difference in how Coleridge sought to experience the landscape, as illustrated in his detailed account of Dungeon Ghyll, and the contemporary expectations of the picturesque tourists. It is this difference, this desire to 'look at places' instead of passing them, that comes to dominate Coleridge's notes as he began to record his series of walks undertaken to explore the landscape between August and October of 1800.

ASCENT OF SKIDDAW, JUNE

Perhaps inevitably, due to its dominant presence above Greta Hall, Coleridge's first major walk that summer was to the summit of Skiddaw. There are no details of the walk itself in the Notebooks, just a description of an incident which occurred on the summit in a letter to Thomas Poole: 'I was standing on the very top of Skiddaw by a little Shed of Slatestones on which I had scribbled with a bit of slate my name among the other names – a lean expressive faced Man came up the hill, stood beside me, a little while, then running over the names, exclaimed *Coleridge! I lay my life, that is the Poet Coleridge.*'[3]

Coleridge makes no further comment about this – except to say that he did not reply – or about the walk itself, but it was clearly an important starting point for him, since it gave him panoramic views of the ridges and summits that surrounded the vale of Keswick and which he had been noting through his study windows. From the top, the massive mound of Saddleback nearby would have dominated the view east, and a little further round to the south his eye would have picked up Clough Head, the first of the peaks ranged along the Helvellyn ridge, the dominant feature of the landscape leading away to the south-east and towards Grasmere. It was these two features, Saddleback and area around it, and the Helvellyn range, that became his next destinations.

SADDLEBACK, JULY/AUGUST, AND BANNERDALE CRAGS, AUGUST

Coleridge set off on what he calls a 'tour up Saddleback', probably soon after 17th August.[4] Leaving Keswick, he followed the 'meandering' Greta river upstream below Windy Brow and turned to follow Glenderaterra Beck up between Lonscale [Longscale] and Blease Fells.

Glenderaterra Valley and Saddleback [author].

The route of Coleridge's 'tour of Saddleback' led him up the valley of the Glenderaterra Beck, seen here on the left, before heading up the smooth slopes of Blease Fell to the rugged 'precipices' of the summit.

As he then made his way up to the Saddleback ridge the views start to dramatically open up: 'mount, mount, mount, the vale now fronting me as I stand – lay down, beautiful effect of the vale of St John's with Withburne Water [Thirlmere] on the right in the distance, endless squares of Land, whose multiplicity by multitude acquires unity.' He continues, 'Now at length come to Saddleback ... & see beneath me those precipices & ridges,' and he paused to take in the wide landscape, before he turned north and walked down across the saddle towards Foule Crag. Passing along the top of Tarn Crags, he stopped to 'look at the place', and the entry switches from recording the 'endless squares of land' and becomes an intensely focused description of a tiny part of the 'place' below him:

Descend Northward, and ascend, & thence see the Tarn [Scales Tarn], a round bason of vast depth, to the west an almost perpendic precipice of naked shelving crags (each crag a precipice with a small shelf) – to the East the outlet [Scales Beck] – North west between a narrow chasm a little sike, wound down over very green mossy, and at every fall the water fell off in little liquid Icicles, from the points of Moss Jelly bags – in one place a semiround stone, with 16 of these Moss Jelly-Bag-shaped. The tarn oval ... no ... no noise but that of the loose stones rolling away from the feet of the Sheep, that move slowly along these perilous ledges.

There is no further description of his route after this, but something of his mood at this time is reflected in these early notebook entries. The entries are not a full account of the whole walk, or the route he took, but rather, scribbling rapidly and sketching little details, Coleridge sought to record the experience and sensations of being there, the things that catch his eye as they happen, and his reaction to them; one moment he is taking in the wide views; the next some small detail, such as the 'little liquid icicles', catches his attention. Indeed, in the case of this walk, the only other thing he noted was that: 'An eminently beautiful object is Fern [Bracken], on a hillside, scattered thick

Saddleback and Bannerdale Crags.

but growing single – and all shaking themselves in the wind.'[5] As the entries start to build up, however, we see consistent references to the weather, clouds, and the changing colours at different times of day, and above all we get a sense of Coleridge's sheer excitement at what he is seeing, so much more dramatic than what he had seen in Somerset, an excitement captured in short descriptive passages: 'As I sate on the side of Skiddaw at 1 o'clock in the noon of this day saw the shore of the Lake & those of the islands hemmed with silver in the misty, cloudy, rain-spatter'd Lake.'[6]

'Hemmed with silver in the misty, cloudy, rain-spatter'd Lake'; alongside the mountains themselves, he is also exploring a new kind of descriptive prose.

BANNERDALE CRAGS

Eager perhaps to explore further into the area beyond Saddleback, Coleridge returned a few weeks later.[7] By 27 August he was staying with Isaac Todd, a friend of William Jackson, Coleridge's landlord at Greta Hall. Todd lived in Mungrisdale and Coburn suggests that it was from him that Coleridge collected both local stories and some knowledge of the local topography, which he then set out to discover.[8]

An entry dated 28 August would seem to indicate that he spent his first day scrambling up through the crags, becks and falls associated with the Glenderamackin beck, following it up below Souther Fell and soon coming to the point where 'another beck joined my fellow-traveller'.[3] Clambering up beside this new beck, probably Bannerdale Beck, he suddenly looked up 'into a magnificent embracement of cliff, an embracement two thirds of an oval [and] another tarn! another tarn! I cried – I ran, and ran, as I approached, psha! said I – where are my wits – 'tis the same as I before visited [Scales Tarn]'. But, as he approached, he realized that, in fact, there was no tarn there at all, just the encircling cliffs of Bannerdale Crags that he had mistaken for Foule Crag. It was, however, 'A far more magnificent embrace – the ascent in its central part more bulged and step-like – the Crag that imitated Foule Crag not so fantastic or terrible, but far far more majestic … What a noise of kites!' Looking up at the long, ragged line of Bannerdale Crags, he was drawn to explore further, and decided to return the next day.

He retraced his steps to Mungrisdale, and after a another night with Isaac Todd, no doubt spent listening to more stories and planning his route, Coleridge set off for a second walk up to the Crags the next day. In this notebook entry we can follow his progress north along the road below Raven

Crag to Bowscale village, where he turned left and followed the River Caldew up between Bowscale Fell on one side and Carrock Fell to the north. Reaching Bowscale Tarn, he wrote another highly detailed description of its setting (similar to that of Scales Tarn), almost as though he is trying to explain to himself what it is he finds so impressive about these upland elevation pools:

> I now wound along up to the Tarn ... something of this form A.A.A.A ... its shores are a craggy precipice, bulging out [at intervals] ... then at the very edge & with floating reflections of Green, hang a few dwarf trees ... [the other shore] rises up into a round low Hill of gradual ascent ...

Reaching the Fell above the Tarn he reels off a list of names that Todd had told him to look out for, locating the surrounding peaks in all directions: 'Skiddaw fronting me, Carrock, Westfell, Brandelhead Gill, Cokelakes, Snab, & [?Cawvey] which is part of Caldbeck Fells – Skiddaw ends in Littledaw Crag – on my left the eminences, into which the Grand island rises up, are Tarn Crag, & Scaknot ...'

He then 'mounted Scaknot' and walked on along the ridge to the top of Bannerdale Crags, where 'on top of the cliff', he found 'an erection of stones' [the summit cairn] near the edge of what Wainwright describes as 'the great downfall into Bannerdale, [where] the crater-like rim in view to the north is magnificent.'[9]

BOWSCALE FELL

The Summit of Bannerdale [A. Wainwright, *The Northern Fells*].

After admiring the view down into Bannerdale, 'My God! What a thing a Lake would make that place!', he followed the River Glenderamackin down below 'my Tarn', to the extant sheepfold, and on down the side of Scales Fell 'almost to Souther Fell', before arriving at the White Horse Inn, Scales. He then had a five mile walk back to Keswick.

HELVELLYN RIDGE TO GRASMERE, AUGUST

By this time Coleridge seems to feel entirely at home scrambling amongst these wilder parts of the landscape, revelling in the names of the features he sees, as though knowing them made him feel more at home, civilizing the landscape. He is also thoroughly energized by his experiences, and after a night at home in Keswick, he started out again the next morning, 31wv August, this time heading for his friends in Grasmere. This walk is particularly interesting because in his descriptions and comments about it we start to get a real sense of his growing exhilaration with the things he was seeing and experiencing, the sheer joy he feels at his sense of immersion in this extraordinary landscape, with new feasts for the eyes and challenges to his imagination at every turn; a moment when anything and everything must have seemed possible.[10] During this time Coleridge was working with Wordsworth on the content for the second volume of the *Lyrical Ballads*, the poems for the first volume having been largely written during their time at Nether Stowey, and he not only had his next proposal, the poem 'Christabel', in his pocket, but was also full of ideas for the preface. In spite of his eagerness to see the Wordsworths, however, rather than taking the direct route along the road from Keswick, past Thirlmere and on over Dunmail Raise to Grasmere, he opts for the greatest adventure so far. From Saddleback some days before, he had seen the great ridgeline running south towards Helvellyn, and he may well have determined at that moment that this would form his route.

He left Greta Hall, walked up to Threlkeld, crossed the river and, following the Old Coach Road to Dockray, made his way up onto Threlkeld Common before ascending 'straight up' to White Pike and Clough Head. Coburn suggests that 'The slips of the pen [confusing left & right etc] suggest the weariness and excitement of the ascent,' and nothing can hide his excitement on seeing the panoramic view which rewarded his climb: 'O! how glad I was to see the blue sky on the other side. Walked by a more leisurely ascent to the very summit of Whitepike – In front Saddleback stretching away on my left into Skiddaw, Bassenthwaite, and the mountains on the other side of Bassenthwaite'.

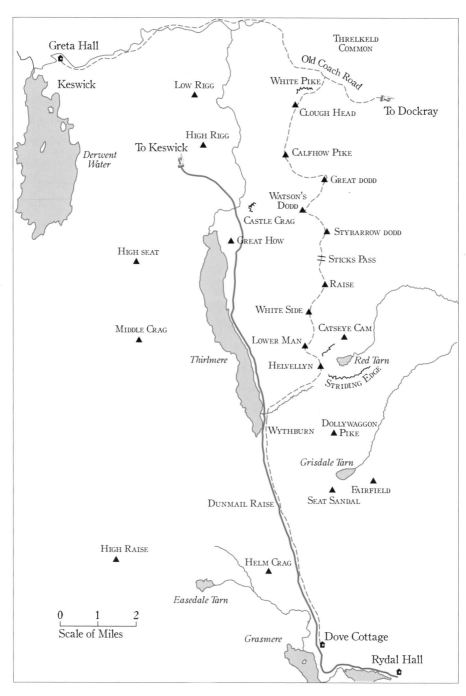

The Helvellyn Range.

His list of names is already impressive and only now and then he needs to ask himself 'What is the name of that with the sheepfold?' or 'What are the names of the ridges that divide St John's and Wanthwaite?' or 'What is the name of that high round hill …?'

He paused to take in the atmosphere of the scene spread out in front of him '*between* the Mountains & the clouds, & slanting adown the clouds, and adown the Mountains, are columns or arches of misty light!' before dividing it up into picture-sized scenes:

> From the utmost points beyond the great Gabel to the head of Derwent water [the peaks] extend – I count 25 of them. What a view of mountains, looking over into the Buttermere Country I count 7 great Mountains, one behind another – and I can look in no direction from Langdale to Whinlatter but there are 4 distances ; in one direction I count 9 – yea 10 …

Setting off again, he made his way along the ridge above St John's Vale, reaching the first of what he refers to as 'two summits', Calfhow Pike, before following the curving ridgeline up to the second summit, Great Dodd (which at 856m dominates this northern end of the ridge):

> When I had wound round so as to come at the very head of the Gill I determined to wind up to the very top, tho' it led at least 3 furlongs back toward Threlkeld – I went, my face still toward Wasdale, Ennerdale, Buttermere, & till I reached the very top, then, & not til I then turned my face, and beheld (O Joy for me!) Patterdale & Ullswater … & then just a turn of my Head and lo! Bassenthwaite in the shape of a wedge – & Derwentwater (the higher third of it) … This Mountain has two summits, on that which I reached first is a great Heap of stones …

Commenting on Coleridge's phrase 'O Joy for me', Coburn rightly notes that 'the use of the word 'Joy' gives a very special sense of Coleridge's exuberance and creative mood', and the text here is accompanied by a series of quickly sketched lines, capturing the 'bow', 'two bows', and 'two bows laid back to back' that he sees in the layout of the ridge-line ahead, adding to the sense of Coleridge attempting to capture every detail of this exhilarating experience.

After noting these rhythmically sinuous windings of the path ahead up to Helvellyn, like 'bends in a bow', he detoured slightly off the path to walk to the summit of Watson's Dodd, 'that sugarloaf on the Mountain that looks

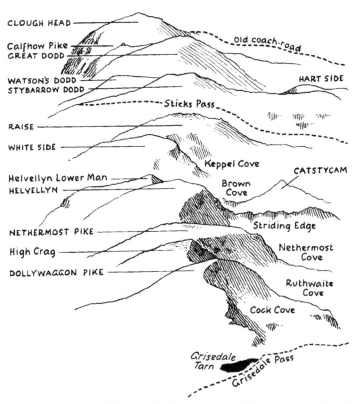

Wainwright's drawing of the Helvellyn Range [A. Wainwright, *The Eastern Fells*].

down on Wythburn', with 'an uncommonly well built *Cone* of Stones.' Here he discovered that 'the view it commands is divine', and looking down on Thirlmere and St John's Vale, he paused to sketch St John's Vale (with Yew Crag and High Rigg dividing it from the vale leading over to Keswick, the route of the stream winding round the bulk of Great How from Thirlmere).

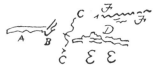

A   the lake
B   that noble single Hill [Great How]
C   the river
D   the ridge that divides these vales [High Rigg to Low Rigg]
E E St John's & Wanthwaite [St John's in the Vale]
F F that Keswickwards [Naddle]

Of the lake itself he says: 'Thirelemeer … its shores running ever in crescent bays – but (O God) the river that runs across the vales, and that beauteous bridge just seen over the bottom of the ridge that divides the vales of St John's & that Keswickward – it's one arch!' capturing in a flash the things, shapes and relationships that have caught his eye.

110

After noting 'that vale which I look into over the opposite Thirelemere Cliffs what is it – Ennerdale or Wasdale?', and Castle Rock 'the single noble Hill which blocks up this Hollow or Vale' below him, he then walked on to Stybarrow Dodd, before descending into the pass of 'Styx top'.[11] The pass itself is 'a perilous morassy bit of Level, unpassable certainly in less dry Weather', and the ascent up to Raise presented 'a scene of horrible desolateness … so scarified with peat holes, on its left running down with white cliffs – Whiteside I suppose'. Reaching Raise he saw 'the ragged stones on the top, scorious as the dross of a smelting House', but since 'the Evening was now lating, I had resolves to pass it; but Nature twitched me at the heart strings – I ascended it – thanks to her! Thanks to her – What a scene! nothing behind me!' He was particularly taken with the view of Ullswater: 'two complete reaches, then a noble Tongue of a Hill [Stang] intercepts me, and then I see it again, about half of the Patterdale reach', but he was drawn on again by the sight of the 'precipices stained with green amid their nakedness, & ridges, tents, embracing semi-circles … and a narrow ridge between them' beyond White Side. Descending the summit of Raise, he 'bounded down [and] noticed the moving stones under the soft moss, hurting my feet'. He passed White Side before ascending Helvellyn itself, where he was entranced by the complex views, both in the distances and immediately in front of him to the east; Swirral Edge and Striding Edge, 'that prodigious Precipice of grey stone with deep Wrinkles', the Tarns below, the deep, sharp, folds stretching away in every direction, and the water of Grasmere 'the most beautiful, in a flat meadow', at last visible.

All this was seen in the fading light of the late summer evening and as the moonlight takes over, 'travelling along the ridge' he left the summit of Helvellyn, and came:

> to the other side of those precipices and down below me on my left – no – no! no words can convey any idea of this prodigious wildness, that precipice fine on this side was but its ridge, sharp as a jagged knife, level so long, and then ascending boldly – what a frightful bulgy precipice I stand on and to my right how the crag corresponds to the other, and how it plunges down, like a waterfall, reaches a level steepness, and again plunges!

This description suggests that he left the summit heading south and in the twilight stared down into the depths of Nethermost cove below Striding Edge. It was now perhaps 9pm and he needed to descend rapidly:

The Moon is above Fairfield almost at the full! – [I] now descended over a perilous peat-moss then down a hill of stones all dark, and darkling, I climbed stone after stone down a half dry Torrent and came out at the Raise Gap / And O! my God! how did that opposite precipice look – in the moonshine – its name Stile Crags [Steel Fell].

Clambering down a stream bed for at least a portion of this descent,[12] his route seems to have been almost directly off the top of Helvellyn and down Whelpside Gill to Wythburn.

We know from Dorothy's *Journal* how and when Coleridge finally arrived at Dove Cottage and how this momentous day ended. She wrote 'At eleven o'clock Coleridge came, when I was walking in the still clear moonshine in the garden …'[13]

If we assume that Coleridge had left no later than 10am, that means his walk took at least 13 hours, and if he left earlier then it was an even longer day. He had no special equipment; it was to be another two years before we have any record of Coleridge making any serious preparations for these walks, when he was to kit himself out with studded boots, a sketch-map of his intended route, 'a converted besom-stick or broom handle as his staff' and a knapsack for his 9-day walk in August 1802. On this occasion he had simply set off, bounding and scrambling his way along the high, exposed Helvellyn ridge. And when he arrived, he still had the energy to read 'Christabel' to the Wordsworths, and then talk until half past three in the morning, 'about the mountains'.

The next day was one of rest and recovery after their late night. Dorothy recorded that:

We walked in the wood by the lake. Wm. read *Joanna* and the *Firgrove* to Coleridge. They bathed. The morning was delightful, with somewhat of an autumnal freshness. After dinner Coleridge discovered a rock-seat in the orchard. Cleared away the brambles …[14]

and, at some point during the day, perhaps when sitting on the newly discovered seat looking out past the cottage over the lake, Coleridge saw and noted down the following dreamlike vision: 'the beards of Thistle & dandelions flying above the lonely mountains like life, & I saw them thro' the Trees skimming the lake like Swallows.'[15]

His descriptive prose now matched any similar line of his poetry and, indeed, almost anything that has been written since.

In turn, Dorothy's *Journal* entry very much reflects the easy intimacy of their relationships at this time, sharing an enjoyment of each other, each other's work, company and interests. It was the great moment of their relationship. For Coleridge, discovering the rock-seat in the garden of Dove Cottage must have been an exciting moment; these were exactly the places he was looking for: bowers, little places where they could sit together at ease amidst the fabric of the landscape, and, for him personally, amidst the Wordsworth's world at the cottage. It seems too that discovery of the rock-seat, something created in the past and long forgotten, was a seminal moment for him in another way, since it suddenly opened up a link to the past of this place. His openness to experience had led him to a certain spot and, probably unaware of what he was doing, he had started to pull aside brambles, brush off deep piles of damp leaf mould, and, with growing excitement exposed a rock-seat carefully placed by unknown hands at an unknown time in the cottage's past; and sitting on it, sharing a view unappreciated for years, he was no longer just a visitor here.

The next day, once Coleridge was a little recovered, they set off for Langdale, up Red Bank and round by the road past Chapel Stile, and 'climbed up by the Knots to the Tarn' [probably via Millbeck and Miller Crag, to Stickle Tarn]. At the tarn, with 'Langdale Pike at the side nearest the vale', Coleridge notes 'fronting me a stupend … [a] Perpendicular Crag'. For Wainwright, this 'stupend', the cliffs of Pavey Ark, represents 'one of the finest scenes in Lakeland',[16] but Coleridge records nothing more than to say 'ascend that – meet rocks overgrown with limpets, exact Pyramids – see from this place Helterwater, Loughrigg Tarn, Wynder & Esthwaite, & the Sea'. Coleridge unfortunately gives us no further hint as to what route they took, whether straight up or round the crags of Pavey Ark, or about what they did next, whether they walked on to Harrison Stickle and looked across to Loft Crag, where Joseph Palmer had sat with Paul Postlethwaite only four years before. The only other observation he makes in this entry is of another Bower, this one in the garden of one of the houses they passed, 'all flower-gem'd with Honeysuckles in the garden of the Cottage'. But one thing is certain: unlike Palmer, they would not have hired a guide, Coleridge, at least, over the past few weeks, having set a new precedent for the self-discovery of the landscape.

By 3 September, they are ready for another challenge, and Coleridge, no doubt anxious to share his experience of three days before, set off with

Wordsworth and his brother John to climb Helvellyn. Dorothy walked with them as far as the blacksmith's, just by the Mill Bridge on the Dunmail Raise road, and, after collecting Mr Simpson, the Wordsworth's friend and neighbour from Broadrain, they climbed the path up from the bridge on one side or the other of Great Tongue to Grisdale Hause, from where they followed the ridge up to the summit. From the top, Coleridge records the view, the 'Range of Hills, Coniston Fells & Old Man, Langdale Mountains, to Bowfell, Bowfell to Scafell, to Great Gavel … The whole prospect in one huge sunny mist.' He also notices 'Harrop Tarn just opposite the Cherry Tree', the small tarn tucked in below the Tarn Crags on the west side of Thirlmere, and along the way home he notes 'Tarn Bank, Stoney rigg, Burset, Whelpside, & then Helvellyn – Green Crag [Castle Crag] at the head of St John's – Wren Crag'. From Thirlmere Coleridge carried on to Keswick, while Wordsworth, John and Mr Simpson returned to Dove Cottage at 10pm; another long day for everyone.

If Coleridge's account of his initial walk along the Helvellyn ridge appears to mark what was, perhaps, one of the most magical moments in his experience of the Lakes, it also marks the last days of real closeness with the inhabitants of Dove Cottage. Compared to the notebook entries for the earlier walks, those for the Langdale and Helvellyn walks with the Wordsworths are noticeable for their brevity and their subdued tone. Gone is the exuberant language, the sudden outbursts of joy, and the rich description of light and atmosphere. It is as though Coleridge's imagination suddenly lacks the freedom he had discovered walking on his own, as though the company of others, and particularly the dominant presence of Wordsworth, inhibited his reactions and broke his concentration. This, in turn, is perhaps an early indication of the growing tension in Coleridge's relationship with Wordsworth, as the latter sought to exercise increasing control over the content of the *Lyrical Ballads*.

As early as 15 September, we get an indication that Wordsworth is not happy with 'Christabel', when he writes to Biggs & Cottle [the printers] that 'I had no notion that the printing of "Christabel" would be begun till you had received further intelligence from Mr Coleridge', and, in spite of Dorothy noting that they were 'Exceedingly delighted with the second part of "Christabel" on 5th October, by the next day she reports: 'Determined not to print "Christabel" with the L.B'. Within two days of this, Wordsworth informs Biggs & Cottle: 'It is my wish and determination that (whatever the expense may be, which I hereby take upon myself) such pages of the Poem of Christabel as have been printed (if such there be) be cancelled'. Some indication of what had happened was later given by Wordsworth himself in a letter of 18th December to Longman & Rees, the book's sellers: 'I found that the Style of the Poem was so discordant from my own that it could not be printed along with my poems.'[17] Coleridge did not record his response to this news, but it was to become clear that this decision proved devastating to his confidence as a poet.

By early October, Wordsworth had both rejected 'Christabel' for inclusion and decided to write the preface himself, and the changing nature of their relationship meant that the companionable atmosphere of their earlier walks in Somerset, on the 'Pikteresk toor', and their walks 'in the wood by the lake' had dissipated; in the event, their walk up Helvellyn was to be their last shared experience until April 1802.

COLEDALE FELLS, SEPTEMBER

Having climbed Skiddaw, Saddleback and the fells beyond it, walked the length of the Helvellyn ridge, climbed Pavey Ark and revisited the summit of Helvellyn, after a few days at home Coleridge now set off into the mountains he could see away to the west of the house.[18] On 9 September, he embarked on what Coburn describes as 'a preparatory walk' for the one that he was to undertake three days later on the 12th.

Leaving Greta Hall, Coleridge crossed the river, skirted round Portinscale and Swinside and walked up the 'vale of Newlands' to Stair, noticing on the left Skelgill, Cat Bells, High Crags, Maiden Moor, and to the right Barrow, Rolling end [Rowling End], and Causey Pike. Delighted with his surroundings, he writes 'The vale of Newlands ... is so arborous as to look almost like a Somersetshire vale – the winding river with one of its arched bridges ... lovely ...'

After crossing the river to Stair he 'went down the Lane, stopped at the gate, saw a beautiful Bassenthwaite thro' an inverted Arch – the round Hill Binsey terminated the view', before crossing the 'lovely Bridge', and climbing 'straight up a Field till I came to Barrow Gill [Stoneycroft Gill] ... followed this gill ... winding along with Casuey Pike on my left, & on my Right one point of Barrow.' He climbed up the little valley as far as High Moss, and once there he admired the sweeping views and the red colours of the screes under Sail, although dense mist obscured the higher peaks.

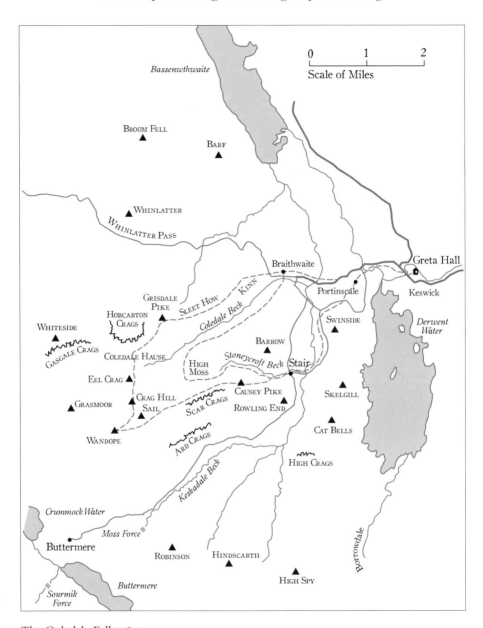

The Coledale Fells, 1800.

Catching sight of some shepherds 'running down the hill in the mist', he quickly followed and, catching up with them by a sheepfold, gathered as much information about the surrounding fells and features as he could: 'the narrow Bottom is called Cowdale – over Force Crag is Cowdale Haws which leads to Buttermere – on the left of Cowdale runs Grysdale Pike, standing on Long ridge which descends into a Tongue End called Heavyters and undivided descends into Keenbrow …' As no doubt happened on a number of such occasions, listening to the shepherd's local accent, Coleridge seems to have misheard 'Coledale' as 'Cowdale', but armed with this all information, and with a route in mind for a lengthier walk, he followed the Coledale Beck down to Braithwaite and returned to Keswick.

Before he could set out on this second walk, however, Wordsworth arrived to discuss Coleridge's proposal for the Preface for the new edition of the *Lyrical Ballads*. During what must have been a very uncomfortable meeting for Coleridge, it will have become clear that Wordsworth, unhappy with what Coleridge had written, intended to write the Preface himself, and, indeed, on 20th September, Wordsworth sent a new version of it to Cottle, written by himself, remarking only that it had been written with 'the assistance of a friend who contributed largely to the first volume'.[19] Coleridge does not record the impact of this meeting on himself, but, in the event, it was to be another three days before he set out for the Coledale Fells again, starting this time with the ascent of Grisedale Pike. It is not entirely clear which path he took, but he seems to have followed the direct route up from Braithwaite between Kinn and Heavy Sides, and then up the ridge of Sleet How and on to the summit. On the way up, once he reached the ridge, the steep valleys on the north eastern side would have been visible, particularly that of Grisedale itself down which Grisedale Gill flows out towards the road over Whinlatter pass, the 'turnpike road' Coleridge mentions several times. At this point he notes that the 'slope of Grysdale on the other [northern?] side of that bottom is prodigious steep, and covered with heath so as to almost look like Rappee' (a word defined by the *Oxford English Dictionary* as 'A coarse kind of snuff made from the darker and ranker tobacco leaves, and originally obtained by rasping a piece of tobacco'), and the slopes above the Gill still have this covering today.

Reaching the summit of Grisedale Pike he stared down into:

another & broader bottom [Hobcarton with Hobcarton Gill running down it], a wondrous precipice, bulgy, & stained with green which descends

& rises again to another Pike. From the end of the Long ridge looking down on the Turnpike, going round that Pike which likewise slopes down into the Road, you will have described a perfect Horse-shoe.'

A   Grysdale
B   a second pike
C   the precipice pike
D   That which slopes
      down to the road

Walking round the horse-shoe [Hobcarton Crag], he reached the subsidiary summit of Grisedale Pike from which he descended to Coledale Hause 'a small level, nearly over Force Crag', and from here he set off along the line of summits from Eel Crag (which he mistakes for Sail) to Causey Pike. Reaching Scar Crag, and looking down the long Wandope ridge towards Crummock Water, he writes, 'another bottom, and as I front, on my right hand a long ridge led directly down to Crummock Water, which I saw at the bottom of the bottom, this ridge is a precipice, the chasms of which are so deep, so continuous, & so regular, as to give the appearance of a huge black rampart walls running halfway down the Steep – I counted 23 of these walls.' He also notes 'Buttermere & Scale Force with its prodigious length of silver *Lock*, or Twist'[20] below.

Walking along the ridge to Causey Pike he passed Sail and Scar Crags [which he calls Long Comb Fells] with Coledale Beck below to his left, and stretching away to his right the 'Comb-making Ridges in all directions' laid out towards Dale Head on the Derwent Fells. Reaching Causey Pike, he turned to look north towards Grisedale Pike. Below to his right, the view drops away passed Stile End and out over Braithwaite towards Bassenthwaite, while to his left he looked over to Force Crag and, to its left, Coledale Hause, the 'green ascent, making an inverted Arch at its summit', beyond which he glimpsed the '*wall*-crags' of Gasgale Crags below Whiteside.

He then turned around, continuing: 'On my left is Derwentwater & on my right Hill Crags and Sail – in front Coombes – that immediately fronting is a Ness quite grey-white and naked – under my feet a precipice walled as deeply & strikingly as that leading to Crummock Water'. The 'grey-white and naked Ness' was probably Aikin Knott, and the 'precipice' under his feet was the deep valley of Rigg Beck. Looking further south in the middle distance he saw Gable Crag, Dale Head and Hindscarth and, beyond these, the long skyline of peaks running round from Glaramara, past Bowfell, Esk Pike, Broad Crag, Scafell Pike, Great Gable, and on round to the south-west, Haystacks, High Crag, High Stile, Red Pike and Starling Dodd, before the long view is blocked to the west by Whiteless Pike and the Eel Crag ridge.

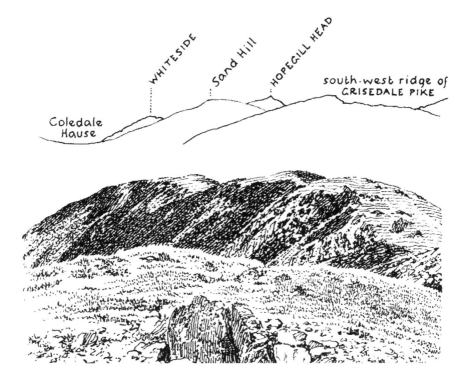

The 'ridge west from Causey Pike' towards Sail [A. Wainwright, *The North Western Fells*].

Once again, in this resumption of solo walks, we have Coleridge absolutely focused on and absorbed in the landscapes around him, writing down every view and wrinkle, as if determined to capture both the setting and his ongoing reaction to it; an unedited record of the natural world as it actually was, such as had been rarely, if ever, recorded before. This panoramic view would have been quite a reward for his long walk, and it is quite possible that Coleridge had long been fascinated by Causey Pike. This has such a dramatic and unusual profile when seen from Swinside or Portinscale, and indeed from Derwentwater itself, that climbing it was the real aim of his walk. It was a walk which had also tied together his experiences of the last month, and more or less completed the circuit of the central lakes that he had started with Wordsworth in 1799. Now that he had visited most of the landscapes and notable peaks that he could see either from Greta Hall or on his walks to Grasmere, he probably felt that he understood and had experienced the basic geography of the central Lakes.

The time between this walk and the next marks a further change in Coleridge's mood. After the visit to Grasmere which had ended on the 3rd September on such a high note, and his second ascent of Helvellyn three days later, he did not visit Grasmere again for over a month. Kathleen Coburn comments that October 'had seen the decision to send the second edition of the *Lyrical Ballads* off without 'Christabel' and the Preface by Wordsworth instead of Coleridge; in short it brought a growing sense of failure beside Wordsworth [and] the falling off in Coleridge's trips to Grasmere ... suggests unhappiness in this situation for him ...'[21]

In addition to his struggling to come to terms with this sudden end of the shared dream of a new poetry, the intimacy of the tight-knit group of Coleridge and the Wordsworths which had been brought together in Grasmere from July 1800, and maintained through the early part of August by frequent visits from Keswick, slowly began to unravel. It had been a period during which Coleridge really, and perhaps for the first time, rejoiced in the sense that he had found a place at the heart of the Wordsworths'r inner circle. But, between 3rd September and 22nd October, Coleridge was only to make one visit to Grasmere, during which he was told of Wordsworth's decision not to print 'Christabel'. It is, therefore, perhaps not surprising that, given the tensions building up in his life, Coleridge's final expedition of the year should bring these months of walks to a suitably dramatic finale.

'BACK O'SKIDDA' AND CARROCK FELL, OCTOBER

After the difficulties of his meetings with Wordsworth, there is a three-day lull following his visit to the Coledale Fells, during which Coleridge wrote an interestingly other-worldly account of the effects of moonlight on the landscape around Derwent water: 'Moonlight with no moon visible – Brandelhow & all the mountains on the side of the Castle black – but the Castle ... & all Borrodale, in a white shroud'. But there is no other suggestion of what is to come, until, on 10 October, he suddenly set off on a two-day walk that he would later refer to as a tour round the 'back o'Skidda'. It was a walk that would take him away from the central fells and lakes, and all his recent disappointments, to the remote fells of the north-east, ranges of hills he had seen from Skiddaw, Saddleback and the Bannerdale Crags, places where he could, perhaps, listen in on the conversations between the mountains and the skies; and, if his friends had disappointed him, nature would not, because it was on this walk, caught in a ferocious storm on the summit of Carrock Fell,

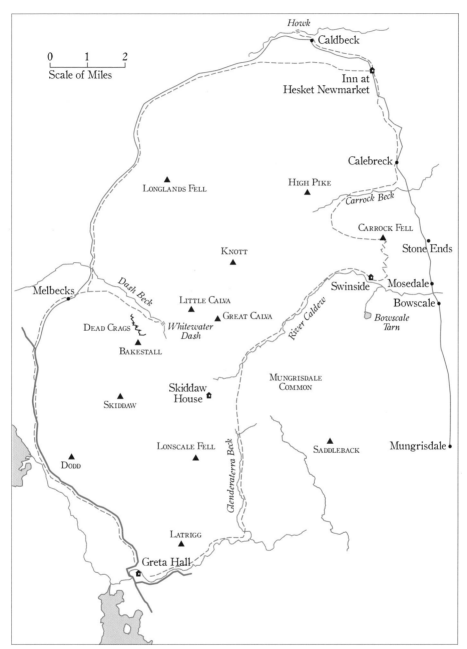

Howk

Caldbeck

Inn at
Hesket Newmarket

0   1   2
Scale of Miles

Calebreck

HIGH PIKE ▲

LONGLANDS FELL ▲

Carrock Beck

CARROCK FELL ▲

Stone Ends

KNOTT ▲

Dash Beck

Melbecks

Swinside

Mosedale

LITTLE CALVA ▲

▲ GREAT CALVA

River Caldew

Bowscale

DEAD CRAGS ▲

*Whitewater
Dash*

*Bowscale
Tarn*

BAKESTALL ▲

MUNGRISDALE
COMMON

Skiddaw
House ⌂

SKIDDAW ▲

LONSCALE FELL ▲

Glenderaterra Beck

SADDLEBACK ▲

Mungrisdale

DODD ▲

LATRIGG ▲

Greta Hall ⌂

'back o'Skidda' and Carrock Fell, 1800.

Above: Whitewater Dash Falls: the 'strange and silent crater' [author].

Coleridge's 'Horse shoe valley' is formed in part by this brooding line of cliffs which run off to the right and is known as Dead Crags. This description is echoed by Wainwright's, 'a rising horseshoe of cliffs half a mile in length'.

Facing page: Whitewater Dash: the falls [author].

'The fall assumes a variety & complexity – parts rushing in wheels, other parts perpendicular, some in white horse-tails'; Coleridge's description of the falls captures the full drama of this complex succession.

that Coleridge suddenly found himself participating in those conversations 'between heaven and earth'.

The notebook entry for the first day of this walk would seem to suggest that he set off walking from Greta Hall up the road along the east side of Bassenthwaite Water, round below Skiddaw, turning right to pass 'Melbrecks', before following the Dash Beck up to the Whitewater Dash waterfalls at the head of the valley.[22] Beyond the falls the beck runs on up into Skiddaw Forest.

Drawn steadily up the valley by the sounds of falling water amplified by the steep sides of the valley, he described the fall itself from four different viewpoints, each one delivering a view of some new aspect of this complex site. The setting of the fall is dominated on one side by the sharp, jagged lines

of the Dead Crags, described by Wainwright as a 'a rising horseshoe of cliffs half-a-mile in length … a dark yet colourful rampart of buttresses and jutting aretes … [a] strange and silent crater',[23] and on the other by the steep rock outcrops at the base of Little Calva. Although Coleridge mentions in this entry both Churn Milk Force [Sour Milk Gill] in Easedale and the falls below Helvellyn at Wythburn, he concludes that at Whitewater Dash 'are the finest Water furies, I ever beheld'.

Walking up into the 'crater', he found:

White Water Dash, at the top of a Horse shoe valley. The Dash itself by no means equal to the Churn Milk at East dale,

a. The Dash a precipice of white rock & purple screes – b.b.b. A semi-circular Bason of craggy rock or the Wythburn Fall – this I wrote standing under the precipice & seeing the whole Dash – but when I went over and descended to the bottom, there I only saw the real *Fall*, & the Curve of the steep slope and retracted – It is indeed so seen a fine thing – it falls parallel with a fine black rock for 30 feet, & is more shattered, more completely atomized & white than any I have ever seen – the pool likewise is formed by a few large stones … as white as the fall itself … the Fall of the Dash is in a Horse-shoe Bason of its own wildly peopled with small ashes standing out of the rocks.

Crossed the stream close by the white pool, stood on the other side, in a complete Spray-*rain* – Here it assumes, I think, a still finer appearance – You see the vast ruggedness & angular points & upright Cones of the black rock – the fall assumes a variety & complexity – parts rushing in wheels, other parts perpendicular, some in white horse-tails – white towards the right edge of the black two or three leisurely Fillets have escaped out of the Turmoil … In short go *close* to it and tis worth seeing.

He continues, 'About 20 yards the Beck forms two other Waterfalls, both pleasing, & both singular'. Further up above all these falls, 'yet another far finer, & above another, they are the finest Water furies, I ever beheld.'

In these entries we get a glimpse of the challenge Coleridge faced as he tried to describe coherently what he was seeing, to capture the impact of the water tumbling through this wild place, with few literary precedents to draw on. This was asking grammar and vocabulary to do something new, to create a meaningful image in itself, rather than simply note-taking.

Coleridge's judgement, that the falls that make up the Dash 'are the finest Water furies, I ever beheld', was echoed 150 years later when Wainwright in turn concluded that 'there are many finer individual waterfalls in Lakeland, but for a succession of falls the first place must undoubtedly be given to Dash Falls'[24] It is also interesting to compare the complexity of this description of the interaction between water and rock that makes the falls here so special, with his earlier, more simple observations of the 'cascade' and 'strange' rocks at the outlet of the Oder Teich just a year before in Germany. It is an indication of just how far his observations, and his ability to describe them, had come.

Coleridge did not record what route he took from the Dash Falls, but he spent the night of 10 October in the Inn at Hesket Newmarket, and in the morning, after visiting the caverns linked to a series of waterfalls on the beck

Carrock Fell from the road at Mosedale [author].

The steep and challenging scree slopes on the south face of Carrock Fell. Coleridge described his descent here as follows: 'I descended by the side of a Torrent, & passed or rather crawled (for I was forced to descend on all fours) … till fatigued & hungry (& with one finger almost broken, & which swelled to the size of two Fingers) I reached the narrow vale'.

at Caldbeck 'near the Howk', he walked south and ascended Carrock Fell. His ascent may have started in Calebreck, leading up the Carrock Beck valley, or he may have gone further south on the road and ascended straight up from Stone Ends (the most direct ascent), but the next entry hints at the nature of what occurred that day:

> 'Climbed Carrock – descended just over the last house in Swinside & almost broke my neck.'[25]

Other than this remark there is no indication in the Notebook entry of the very real drama of this visit, during which he was caught on the summit during a tremendous storm. The fuller description came later in a letter. Finding shelter amongst the rocks, he survived the storm only to almost come to grief during a rapid descent through the steep screes, far off any recognized track.

The Caldew Valley from the summit of Carrock Fell [author].

As another storm closes in over Carrock Fell, the last rays of sun pick out the route of Coleridge's walk home up the Caldew Valley. Mungrisdale Fell on the left faces the steep slopes of Snab to the right as the river flows down from the Lonscale Fell and Skiddaw range. Beyond this backdrop, 'Garamara & Great Gavel' retain what Coleridge described as their 'deepest sablest Blue'.

After getting some refreshment from the farmer's wife in Swinside, he walked on up the Caldew valley and over between Lonscale Fell and Saddleback along a 'splashy mossy path'. The path eventually brought him down to the Keswick road, but, even though he was tired, wet and in a hurry, he had the time to notice and think about a small, insignificant thing he saw on the ground, when he noticed amongst the *Tremella* (a gelatinous fungi still much in evidence on these fells) 'either a Mouse's or a Mole's Leg'. Maybe the drama of what had happened still had not sunk in, but he was more interested in recording this in his notebook than the descent from the Fell.

This was an epic day, and although the Notebook sheds little further light on it, his description of the walk in a letter eight days later to his friend, the chemist Humphry Davy, seems to confirm that he had experienced something quite extraordinary, a moment of 'out of body' peace, communion and comfort amidst the desperate situation his 'wandering' had got him into:

Our Mountains Northward end in the Mountain Carrock – one huge steep enormous Bulk of Stones, desolately variegated with the heath-plant – at its foot runs the river Calder, & a narrow vale between it & the Mountain Bowscale – so narrow, that in its greatest width it is not more than a Furlong. But that narrow vale is *so* green, *so* beautiful! there are moods, in which a man would weep to look at it. On this mountain Carrock, at the summit of which are the remains of a vast Druid Circle of Stones, I was wandering – when a thick cloud came on, and wrapped me in such Darkness that I could not see ten yards before me – and with the cloud a storm of Wind & Hail, the like of which I had never before seen or felt. At the very summit is a cone of Stones, built by the Shepherds, & called Carrock Man – Such Cones are on the Tops of almost all our Mountains, and they are all called *Men*. At the bottom of this Carrock Man I seated myself for shelter; but the wind became so fearful & tyrannous that I was apprehensive some of the stones might topple down upon me. So I groped my way further down, and came to 3 Rocks, placed this wise each supported by the other like a Child's House of Cards, & in the Hollow & Screen which they made I sate for a long while sheltered as if I had been in my own Study, in which I am now writing – Here I sate, with a total feeling worshipping the power & 'eternal Link' of Energy. The Darkness vanished, as by enchantment – : far off, far far off, to the South the mountains of Glaramara & Great Gavel, and their Family, appeared distinct, in the deepest sablest *Blue* – I rose, & behind me was a Rainbow bright as the brightest. – I descended by the side of a Torrent, & passed or rather crawled (for I was forced to descend on all fours) by many a naked Waterfall, till fatigued & hungry (& with one finger almost broken, & which swelled to the size of two Fingers) I reached the narrow vale, & the single House nested in Ashes and Sycamores …[26]

Here in spite of 'dirt and every appearance of misery', he was fed in the most matter-of-fact manner by a 'pale woman' more concerned with a cure for her rheumatism than Coleridge's predicament.

These extensive explorations between August and October left only Scafell and the fells beyond to the south and west to be discovered. However, it was not until 1802 that Coleridge was able to undertake this last great walk, as ill health and other concerns intervened. As his walks of 1800 came to an end, and he tried to pick up the threads of his career after the excitement of the summer and autumn, Coleridge had reached an interesting impasse. On 30 October 1800, clearly speaking about himself, he writes 'He knew not what to do – something he felt must be done – he rose, drew his writing desk suddenly before him – sate down, took a pen – & found that he knew not what to do.'[27]

Most seriously, perhaps, his confidence in his ability to write poetry had collapsed. Throughout the whole summer, as Holmes points out, his 'chief effort was concentrated on finishing "Christabel" … [something] which caused him endless struggles' – Coleridge had written: 'every line has been produced by me with labour-pangs' – indeed, it was never actually fully completed, and, on top of this, its rejection by Wordsworth 'seems to have been a wholly unexpected blow'.[28] Five months later he was to write to William Godwin, 'The poet is dead in me – my imagination (or rather the somewhat that had been imaginative) lies, like a Cold Snuff on the circular Rim of a Brass Candle-stick, without even a stink of Tallow to remind you that it was once cloathed & mitred with Flame …'[29]

And so, even though Coleridge had spent the summer busily writing in his notebooks, and expanding on the notes in letters, when he sat down at his desk at the end of the month he 'found that he knew not what to do', what or how to write. As a writer, even though he had just had some of the most stimulating experiences of his life, he could see no way forward and turned once again to journalism.

Suddenly, it seemed, Coleridge was unable to find a medium in which he could express the nature of the place that his instinctive reaction to the landscape had led him to, or through which he could explore the sensations of pure 'Joy' that had accompanied his walks earlier that summer. Discussing 'Christabel' when it was finally published in 1816, Coleridge said, 'I had the whole present to my mind, with the wholeness, no less than with the loveliness, of a vision.'[30] and the glimpses of the Lakeland scenery that he used in Part II of the poem, written in 1800, came not in the direct language of the Notebook, but wrapped in layers of the mist and magic of that vision:

And hence the custom and law began,
That still at dawn the sacristan,
Who duly pulls the heavy bell,
Five and forty beads must tell
Between each stroke – a warning knell,
Which not a soul can choose but hear
From Bratha Head to Wyndermere.

Saith Bracy the bard, So let it knell!
and let the drowsy sacristan
Still count as slowly as he can!
There is no lack of such, I ween
As well fill up the space between.
In Langdale Pike and Witch's Lair,
And Dungeon-ghyll so foully rent,
With ropes of rock and bells of air
Three sinful sextons' ghosts are pent,
Who all give back, one after t'other,
The death-note to their living brother …
The devil mocks the doleful tale
With a merry peal from Borrowdale.

['Part the Second', l.7–24]

In comparing the 'most deliberately invented, [and] the most magically con-trived' subject matter of the 'Christabel' poem with the startlingly clear-eyed immediacy of his responses to the natural world during those walks, Holmes points up part of the problem. This new source of inspiration seemed to require a new form of expression. Coleridge 'had outgrown the naïve, dream-like ballad form of "Christabel",'[31] and for the moment, poetry as the vehicle of expression. He was recording his new experiences that summer in the prose of his notebook and letters. But there was a problem: not one of this circle of friends considered such prose descriptions to have merit beyond an everyday conveyance of information; it lacked the gravitas and potential for cultural transmission that poetry was seen to have. The words recorded in the notebook and letters were there so the vision was not forgotten, to remain there until a moment of inspiration plucked them out and worked them up into poetic form, or he finally found the time to sift the contents and publish a selection, something that he certainly contemplated but never achieved:

When shall I find time & *ease* to reduce my Pocket-books and Memorandums to an *Index* …? If – aye! And alas! If – if I could see … my Assertio Fidei Christianæ … my Elements of Discourse, Logic, Dialectic, & Noetic, or Canon, Criterion, & Organon, with the philosophic Glossary – in one printed volume, & the Exercises in Reasoning as another … Why, then I would publish all that remained unused, Travels & all; under the Title – of Excursions abroad & at Home.[32]

Similarly, with Dorothy Wordsworth's *Journals*, in spite of reading them avidly and taking inspiration, ideas, images, and even whole passages from their pages, neither Wordsworth nor Coleridge seem to have seen the *Journals* for what they were. No one seems to have stepped back long or far enough to see that her accounts of her interaction with and responses to the life of the landscapes around her, dismissed by Dorothy herself as a poor substitute for the poetic form, and all mixed up with the daily concerns of home, village and family life, actually signalled, with Coleridge's accounts of his walks, the arrival of new form of writing; direct description of the natural world. Equally, Coleridge does not appear for a moment to have considered his notebook entries as anything other than jottings, recording images to be later worked up in the language of poetry. And yet reading both the notebooks and the journals, we see something new taking shape, as both writers struggle to use received vocabulary and style to express what they actually saw and felt, and making up new forms of both as they go along, helping to create the prototype for a new form of prose writing about the natural world.

It seems clear, however, that neither of them realized that they were breaking new ground in terms of the kind of walks they were taking, walking out of the confines of the picturesque vision of tourism and into the modern world of fell-walking. Overall, the changes in the types of walk, and the language in which he described them, that had occurred for Coleridge between August and October of 1800, are clear from the comparison of our poetic starting line: 'Bell thro' a mist in Langdale vale … what a simile for a melancholy', and that last entry concerning his ascent of Carrock Fell, in itself, no doubt, another first for a 'stranger': 'Climbed Carrock … & almost broke my neck'.

On Carrock Fell, Coleridge had come to understand that it was not the activity of the poetic imagination, but direct experience of the reality of these places that was the key to participation in the ongoing conversations between heaven and earth.

6

'To wander & wander for ever and ever': Coleridge's Lake District Walks April–July 1802

After the sheer joy of his transcendental walking experiences between August and October of 1800, the year had ended on a very different note for the 28-year old Coleridge, and Dorothy Wordsworth's brief and sad journal entry for 20 December seems to sum everything up: 'Saturday. Coleridge came. Very ill, rheumatic, feverish. Rain incessantly.' As we have already seen, his relationship with Wordsworth had cooled, and although they were still close, it was now as old friends rather than as poets and collaborators, Coleridge no longer a co-contributor, but rather an advisor. It is clear too that Coleridge's confidence as a poet had taken a severe knock with his exclusion from the new edition of the *Lyrical Ballads*, and he had no idea what use he could possibly make of all his new notebook entries, the story of the past few months. In addition to these issues, there were new strains on his marriage, caused largely by money problems due to his lack of a steady income, but also from Sara's sense of isolation at Keswick. Far from her family and friends in Somerset, Sara was left much on her own and largely excluded from her husband's friendship with the Wordsworths. Furthermore, there was the loss of their second son Berkeley the year before, and the persistent ill-health of a new baby, Derwent, who was born in 1800 but who died two years later.

As all these things came together and Coleridge made the decision to turn once again to journalism, we get a strong sense of his world dissolving around him, the excitement and optimism of their new life in the Lakes slipping away, his mood caught perhaps in a notebook entry from 19 December: 'The thin scattered rain-clouds were scudding along the Sky, above them with a visible interspace the crescent Moon hung, and partook not of the motion – her own hazy Light fill'd up the concave, as if it had been painted & the colours had run'.[1]

The vibrant, sharp clarity of his summer visions have blurred and lost their radiance, the inspirational colours of life have run. It would, in fact, be June of 1801 before two notebook entries suggest he had actually left Greta Hall and ventured onto the fells again, this time on a visit to Grasmere, but how different these entries are from what had come before: the first, 'scenes in Easedale, rocks & woods, & trees starting up around Rocks and out of Rocks – where under the boughs & through the Boughs you have the glimmering Lake, & Church Tower… … To wander & wander for ever and ever'; and the second: 'A Hollow place in the Rock like a coffin – a Sycamore Bush at the head, enough to give a shadow for my face, and just at the foot one tall Foxglove – exactly my own Length – there I lay and slept. it was quite soft'.[2]

Both of these dreamlike entries seem to speak for themselves. There seemed to be nothing left for him in the Lakes.

In November 1801, however, he was offered a contract to work for the *Morning Post* in London, too good an offer to turn down, and one which provided an opportunity to escape the oppressive situation in Keswick; he was soon on his way. A few weeks later, once he had agreed terms and found lodgings, he was joined by Sara and Hartley, and it was not until March 1802 that he reappeared at Greta Hall. A month or so after he arrived back, however, his spirits and health seem to have revived enough to take a walk up Walla Crag, a line of cliffs which dominates the view on the east side of Derwent Water just outside Keswick. His account seems to show that his senses, imagination, writing and sense of joy are slowly re-awakening. His mood may have been helped by the weather that day, which Dorothy describes as a day of spring calm after snow and rain: 'The sun shone, the wind had passed away, the hills looked cheerful, the river was very bright', indeed this may be the reason he went out at all.

Walla Crag, April

Wainwright describes the crag as 'steep, romantic, challenging', while Coleridge seems to have come upon it walking up from the Rakefoot side, perhaps off the Keswick to Thirlmere road, and to have reached the summit cairn, 'the Man of Stones', before he was even aware of how close he was to the steep cliffs below. Initially, he was lost in assessing the wider views:

From the summit above Walla Crag Skiddaw & Saddleback form one beautiful Ellipse – the vales of Threlkeld & Hutton … become one with

Wainwright's drawing of
Walla Crag from Rakefoot
[A. Wainwright, *The Central Fells*].

'[T]remendous indeed, there is
nothing on Helvellyn so terrible,
it is absolutely & strictly perpendicular on all Side': Coleridge's
description of the cliffs shown in
Wainwright's drawing.

from near Rakefoot

Keswick – the islands in the Lake more dishy than ever – the mountains
from Borrodale inclusive to Grysdale Pike more than any where a rude
Jumble – After I had written this I descended from the Man of Stones – &
came all unawares on Walla Crag – tremendous indeed, there is nothing on
Helvellyn so terrible, it is absolutely & strictly perpendicular on all Side
… Come in a few yards to a noble ravine, one side rough and treeless rock
– the other mossy, & shrubby green. In a 100 yards more to a grand slope,
and one *leaning* Tower – on its top a green shorn *Poll* or crown of Head,
railed off with wooden rails & above the ravine another small Precipice –
and here too is one of the noblest Ravines ever seen. Rock on both sides,
grey with white Lichens.

The long Bracken, unreapt, wet, & rotting, Lying, strait dangling, from
the mossy stone-hillocks like an unkempt brown Hair …[3]

Clearly invigorated by the spring weather,[4] the resumption of his walks, and
working on a new poem, *Dejection: An Ode*, some six days later, Coleridge
walked over to Grasmere and spent four days with the Wordsworths. It
was during this visit that Wordsworth and Coleridge walked into Easedale,
seemingly as far as the waterfalls on Sour Milk Gill, while Dorothy reports
she 'was tired and sate under the shade of a holly tree', continuing, 'I sate
there and looked down the stream. I then went to the single holly behind
that single rock in the field, and sate upon the grass till they came down
from the waterfall.'[5] They were then driven home by heavy rain.

Although it would appear from these accounts that the three of them
picked up their friendship where they had left off, things had in fact been

subtly changed by their mutual friendship with two sisters, Mary and Sara Hutchinson. Following the death of her mother in 1778, while her brothers remained at home in Cockermouth attending school, the 8-year-old Dorothy had been sent to live with relatives, first in Halifax and then, in 1787, in Penrith. She was never to return home and never saw her father again, but while in Penrith she became close to the Hutchinsons, seven brothers and sisters who were also orphans living with older relatives. Dorothy became particularly close to the eldest sister Mary, who was much the same age, forming a lifelong friendship which was soon widened to include Dorothy's brother William, who first met Mary on a visit to see Dorothy in 1788 whilst still at Cambridge; over the next decade or so William and Mary steadily formed an 'attachment'.

Details of the developing relationship are scarce, but it is clear that by 1796, when William and Dorothy were living in Dorset, the attachment had grown to the point where Mary spent seven months staying with them. In the event, however, things did not progress much further until May of 1799 when the Wordsworths returned from Germany and joined Mary who was by then living with her siblings on the farm at Gallow Hill, Sockburn-on-Tees. From here their relationship quietly continued and in July 1802 the couple finally married at Gallow Hill, before returning with Dorothy to live at Dove Cottage; by this time, however, the Wordsworth/Hutchinson friendship had widened further to include Coleridge.

Coleridge first met the Hutchinsons on his return from Germany in October of 1799, when Wordsworth, hoping to persuade him to join them in the north rather than returning permanently to Somerset, invited him up to Gallow Hill with the idea of taking him on a walk to introduce him to the Lake District for the first time. The walk to the Lakes, what became the 'pikteresk toor', duly went ahead, but not before Coleridge had become enamoured with the Hutchinsons and their warm family circle. Over the next two years, Coleridge became increasingly attached to Mary's younger sister Sara, particularly when she came to stay with the Wordsworths at Dove Cottage over the winter of 1800 – 1801, and, by the end of 1801, as he left for London, had fallen deeply, and hopelessly, in love with her, adding another layer of complexity to his already complicated life.

Thus, when they met up again in the spring of 1802, the relationship between Coleridge and the Wordsworths now had to adapt to accommodate his doomed but continuing obsession with Sara and the fact that Wordsworth was about to marry Mary.

Nab Scar, April

It was against this complex emotional background that, the day after his walk to Walla Crag, Coleridge joined the Wordsworths and they set off, on a beautiful morning, to walk to Nab Scar. Coleridge left only the briefest notes about this walk, but fortunately for us, Dorothy left a full account, reflecting, it seems, just how much the three of them had enjoyed themselves. Her account is particularly interesting because it gives us not only a priceless glimpse into the interaction and differences between them, but it also records what was to be the last shared walk of just the three of them, of the Dove Cottage phase of their relationship.

Coleridge records only that on 'Friday, April 23rd, 1802. discovered the Double-Bower among Rydal Rocks [Nab Scar] – Ivy, Oak, Hawthorn, Mountain Ash, common ash – Holly, Yews, Fern & Wild Sage, Juniper, &c. Carpet of Moss – & Rocks',[6] and so we turn to Dorothy's account:

'It was a beautiful morning and we set off at 11 o'clock, intending to stay out of doors all the morning. We went towards Rydale … and determined to go under Nab Scar …' Although there is a relaxed air to Dorothy's account of the day, some underlying tension is also clear, 'Coleridge pitched upon several places to sit down upon, but we could not be all of one mind respecting sun and shade, so we pushed on to the foot of the Scar. It was very grand when we looked up, very stony, here and there a budding tree.' She goes on, 'Coleridge and I pushed on before. We left William sitting on the stones, feasting with silence; C. and I sat down upon a rocky seat.' Here they sat 'lingered long, looking into the vales … Ambleside vale … Rydale, the lake all alive and glittering … and our own dear Grasmere … a little round lake of nature's own, with never a house, never a green field, but the copses and the bare hills enclosing it.' Beyond these 'rose the Coniston Fells, in their own shape and colour – not man's hills, but all of themselves, the sky and the clouds, and a few wild creatures.'

Dorothy then records that Coleridge, ever active, has already moved on:

in search of something new. We saw him climbing up towards a rock. He called us, and we found him in a bower – the sweetest that was ever seen.

The rock on one side is very high, and all covered with ivy ... On the other side it was higher than my head ... About this bower there is moun-tain-ash, common-ash, yew-tree, ivy, holly, hawthorn, mosses, and flowers, and a carpet of moss. Above, at the top of the rock, there is another spot – it is scarce a bower, a little parlour only, not *enclosed* by walls, but shaped out for a resting-place by the rocks and the ground rising above it. It had a sweet carpet of moss. We resolved to go and plant flowers in both places to-morrow.[7]

Once again, the shared experience of finding these private places, the seats and bowers, seems to bring them closer together, but they never returned to plant the flowers. For Coleridge this was to be the last of those places they found together, the places where they marked their presence within the vale of Grasmere, that indicated, as other 'seats', stones carved with their initials, sheepfolds and rocks did, their occupation of the landscape. For the Wordsworths, however, the discovery of this place seems also to have initiated a burst of work on their own garden, where they went on to create a new bower of their own. A hint of what they were planning comes in Dorothy's Journal for 1 May where she writes 'We went and sate in the orchard till dinner time. It was very hot ... We planned a shed, for the sun was too much for us,' and then on 6 May she tells us 'here we are sitting in the orchard ... upon a seat under the wall, which I found my brother building up, when I came to him with his apple.' Dorothy goes on to note in May that William completed the steps in the orchard, while she was busy planting, and finally we hear of the completed 'Moss hut', when she notes at the beginning of the manuscript for her *Recollections of a Tour made in Scotland 1803,* that she 'Finished copying this Journal May 31st, 1805, in the Moss hut at the top of the orchard – DW.'[8]

An echo of the walk the three of them took to Nab Scar can be found in Wainwright, who describes it as known for 'its associations with the Lake poets, who came to dwell at the foot of its wooded slopes [and] have invested it with romance', yet his description of the same view determinedly avoids any suggestion of that romance, or indeed, the bower from which they admired the view: 'Lakes and tarns are a very special feature of the delightful prospect to south and west and the grouping of the Coniston and Langdale fells is quite attractive.'[9]

Nine-day Walk to the Coast and Back, via the summit of Scafell, 1–10 August 1802

In July 1802, the Wordsworths left Grasmere to meet Mary Hutchinson at Gallow Hill, and then to visit France to settle matters with Annette Vallon, the mother of Wordsworth's daughter Caroline, before returning to Gallow Hill for his wedding to Mary on 4th October and arriving back at Dove Cottage on 6th October. During this time, left to his own devices again, Coleridge planned his most ambitious walk to date.

By late July, Coleridge's plans for an excursion walk to St Bees, 'wither I mean to walk tomorrow & spend 5 or 6 days, for Bathing', as he told Robert Southey, were well under way. Perusing his copy of William Hutchinson's *The History of the County of Cumberland*,[10] Coleridge not only planned his route, using Hutchinson's map, but also noted down historical stories and anecdotes of places of interest along the way, some of which he would go to great lengths to find. His stated aim may have been to reach St Bees for some bathing, but the excursion was to be very much more than this: a nine day walk on his own over some of the most remote and unknown mountain landscapes, the route, much of it far from the regular tourist routes, taking on, rather than skirting round, the central massif of Scafell.

Typical of the features he noticed from the map, and planned to seek out, possibly from the map in West's Guide (see pp. 26–7), was the pattern formed by the rivers Irt, Mite (in conjunction with Muncaster Fell), and Esk, which appeared to him as the 'prongs' of a trident.

He was clearly looking forward to finding a high vantage point from which he would be able to see it, and although in the end this turned out to be Scafell, he was pinning his hopes on Muncaster Fell.

The first section of his planned route is not detailed, perhaps because he already knew the way he would take up Newlands to Newland Hause via Kescadale. From here he would descend to Buttermere for the night, and next day find his way up past the Scale Force falls and over to Ennerdale, as he had done three years earlier with Wordsworth. Here he would spend the second night at Long Moor.

From Long Moor his plan was to follow the roads out from Ennerdale to the coast at St Bees, but the desire to bathe, let alone spend six days there,

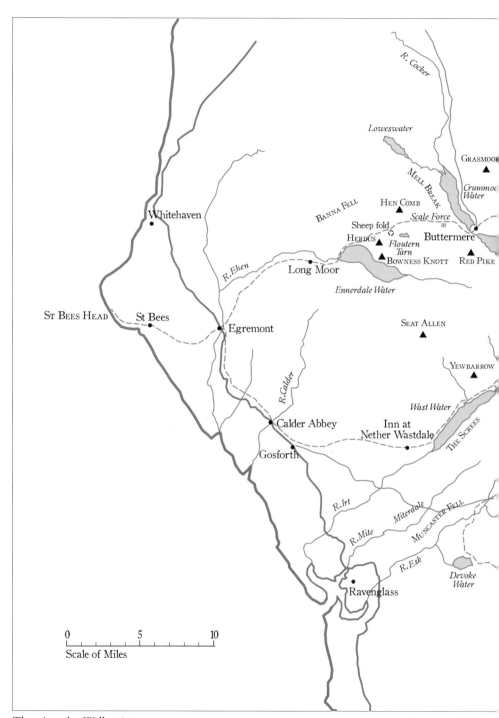

The nine-day Walk, 1802.

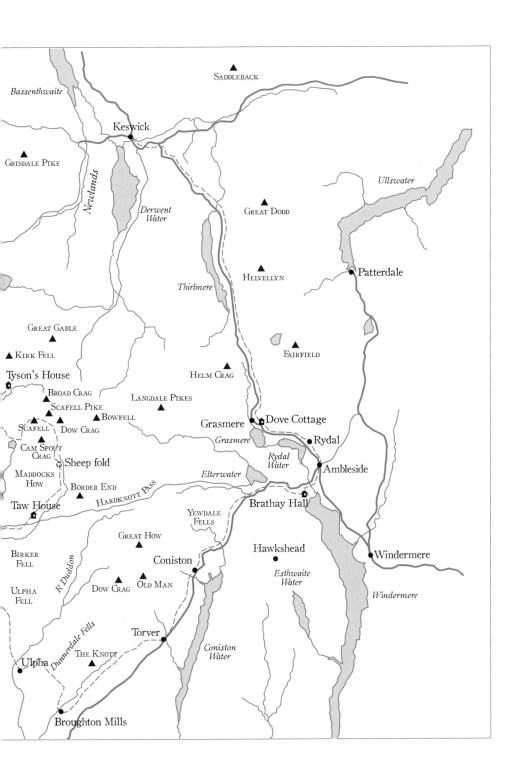

Bassenthwaite

SADDLEBACK

Keswick

GRISDALE PIKE

Newlands

Derwent
Water

Ullswater

GREAT DODD

HELVELLYN

Patterdale

Thirlmere

GREAT GABLE

KIRK FELL

FAIRFIELD

Tyson's House

BROAD CRAG

HELM CRAG

SCAFELL PIKE

LANGDALE PIKES

SCAFELL

BOWFELL

DOW CRAG

Grasmere

Dove Cottage

CAM SPOUT
CRAG

Sheep fold

Grasmere

Rydal

MADDOCKS
HOW

Rydal
Water

Ambleside

BORDER END

Elterwater

Taw House

HARDKNOTT PASS

Brathay Hall

YEWDALE
FELLS

GREAT HOW

BIRKER
FELL

R Duddon

Hawkshead

Coniston

Esthwaite
Water

Windermere

ULPHA
FELL

DOW CRAG

OLD MAN

Windermere

Dunnerdale Fells

Torver

Coniston
Water

Ulpha

THE KNOTT

Broughton Mills

Right: Coleridge's map
of his proposed route
for the nine-day walk,
1802, (N1206). Based on
Hutchinson's map.[11]

Below: Detail from 'Lakes
in Cumberland', from
Hutchinson's *History of
the County of Cumberland,*
1794.

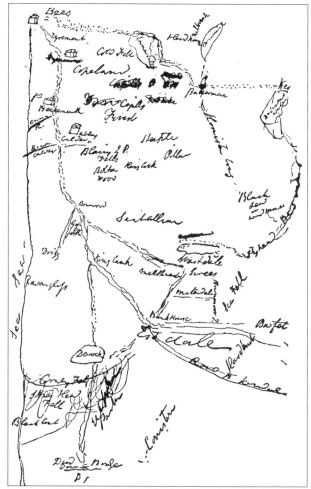

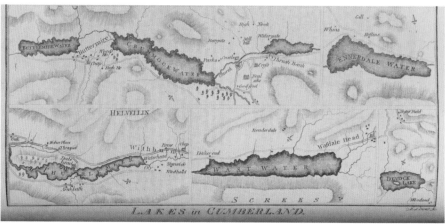

rapidly dissipated. In fact, his disappointment with the coast and cliffs of St Bees meant that he left immediately after a long walk along the shore. Leaving Egremont he determined to 'sleep at some place between Kings Camp & Wastdale Foot – going up the Irt', the northerly prong of his Trident. On this occasion he seems only to have intended to reach the foot of Wast Water, perhaps because he had already visited Wasdale Head with Wordsworth on the earlier walk, before returning 'into the Road on the South of Melthwaite Side by Burnt House' and arriving at Devock, skirting the southern edge of the Scafell ridge. At this point he tells himself 'When in Miterdale, try by all means to command a view of Ravenglass – Why not turn out of the road to the Sea and Muncaster Fell'. This was perhaps his best chance to see the great Trident formed by the three rivers that had so captured his imagination.

From here he planned to pass through into Eskdale and up onto Birker Fell, heading past Devoke Water and over Ulpha Fell to Duddon Bridge, before walking up the vale and sleeping 'if possible at the foot of Coniston'. His plan for the next day is nothing if not ambitious: 'Friday ascend Coniston, return thro' Eskdale, Burnmoor Tarn to Styhead, & sleep in Borrodale', returning to Keswick the next day. He does not mention it, but it would seem that it was on this leg of the journey that he planned to reach the summit of Scafell on his way to Styhead Pass.

In the event, of course, things turned out rather different, largely because once he reached the foot of Wast Water he was immediately swept up into the drama of the high fells towering above it, the 'naked Rock of enormous height', 'huge facing rock, more than half a mile of direct height', 'deep perpendicular ravines', 'huge fells … Yeabarrow … the Great Gavel', the whole sweep of peaks from Middle Fell, Stirrup Crag, Kirk Fell, Great Gable, and, towering above it all, 'Scafell Pyramid'; he was inexorably drawn to explore and discover these places and walked on to pass the night as he had with Wordsworth at Tyson's house in Wasdale Head. A great adventure lay ahead, and, from this point on, chance, as much as planning, dictated his route. Although he undertook this walk alone, on a couple of occasions he spent the best part of the following day learning the names of the features around him and taking a closer look at the area with his hosts for the night, with John Ponsonby in Ennerdale, an acquaintance of his landlord William Jackson, and then in Eskdale with Thomas Tyson's friend, John Towers.

DAY 1 (SUNDAY, 1 AUGUST): NEWLANDS – ENNERDALE

Coleridge left Greta Hall on Sunday morning, walking past Portinscale before turning up into Newlands, and the experience of the walk and his changing moods are caught in both the direct shorthand observations of the notebook entries and in the fuller, more reflective ones of his subsequent letters, two to Sara Hutchison and one to Robert Southey.[12] Full of energy and expectation he is looking around, noting names, places, reacting to the changing landscape, recording the things that catch his eye:

> Stoney Croft Bridge – Newlands, general character – house below the road, liveliness of the Vale – wildness of the Fells – yet even their stoniest parts softened down by the semi-circular Lines & bason-like concavities … cataract [Moss Force] is fine no doubt in a storm but extravagantly exaggerated by West & Gilpin …[13]
>
> I passed on thro' the green steep smooth bare Kescadale … came out on Buttermere & drank Tea at the little Inn, & read the greater part of *Revelations* … of the new Testament …

He repeats his description from the 1799 walk of the view up Buttermere, as an 'enormous Stone Bason, of which one half is gone', before turning up from Crummock Water to pass over to Ennerdale:[14]

> I passed by Scale Force, the white downfall of which glimmered thro' the Trees, that hang before it … and climbed until I gained the first Level – here it was "every man his own path-maker", & I went directly across it – upon soft mossy Ground, with many a hop, skip, & jump … observing the old Saying: where Rushes grow, a Man may go.

Following the old track, and no doubt having got his feet as wet as Palmer had done, he passed the becks flowing away down to Loweswater from either side of Hen Comb to his right, and Red Pike, the 'dolphin-shaped Peak of a deep red' to his left. He then 'reached an ascent, climbed up, & came to a ruined Sheep-fold – a wild green view all around me …I sate there near 20 minutes, the Sun setting on the Hill behind with a soft watery gleam'. A panoramic view to the north opens up, from 'the upper Halves of huge deep-furrowed Grasmire [Grasmoor, above Crummock Water] & the huge Newland & Buttermere Mountains, & peeping in from behind the Top of Saddleback'. On the Newlands side of Buttermere 'the Trees in [the] fields were the only

Trees to be seen,' before '[I] left the Sheep-fold with regret – for of all things a ruined Sheep-fold in a desolate place is dearest to me'.

Then, before descending into Ennerdale, he passed:

> a frightful craggy precipice with shivers [screes], & all wrinkled – & a chasm … [Herdhouse or Herdus] what a noble precipice it is the far-thest part black with green velvet moss cushions on the ledges / towards Buttermere, the half is a pale pink – and divided from the black by a stream of Screes – I never before beheld a more glorious view of its kind. I turn and look behind me – what a wonderful group of mountains – what a scene for Salvator Rosa …

He then walked on and passed the night at Long Moor 'two miles below the foot of the Lake' with Mr Jackson's friend John Ponsonby.[15]

Day 2: Ennerdale – St Bees

The next morning Mr Ponsonby 'went to the head of the Lake with me, the mountains at the head of this Lake & Wast-dale are the monsters of the Country, bare bleak Heads, evermore doing deeds of Darkness, weather-plots, & storm-conspiracies in the Clouds, their names Herd house, Bowness, Wha Head, Great Gavel, the Steeple, the Pillar, & Seat Allen.'

This 'Bowness', which Coleridge describes as 'Bowness higher and lower, high Bowness with Herdhouse forms a delightful angle of sheltered land', suggests he is referring to what is now known as Great Borne, while the con-tinuation 'Bowness the finest piece of savage rock-work, I ever saw – great bulging bullsheads of Crag with Stream of Shiver between the ravin[e]s in these Nesses, and between one fell & the adjoining one called raiks – Sheep clinging like flies to a grass' would seem to describe his 'lower Bowness', today called Bowness Knott, an outcropping lower down between Great Borne and the Ennerdale Water, which Wainwright describes as 'an untrodden chaos of steep crags and talus slopes'.[16] Sheep still cling like flies amongst the chaos.

After leaving Mr Ponsonby – a fund of particularly unpleasant tales of fox and wild cat hunts – late in the day, he walked 'thro' very pleasant Country' to Egremont and on to St Bees and got 'an apology for a [bed], at a miserable Pot-house; slept or rather dozed, in my clothes'.

He spent most of a rather disappointing day at St Bees; the morning was a 'wet woeful oppressive one – I was sore with my bad night', and while he enjoyed his walk down the beach 'a very nice hard Sand for more than a mile', St Bees Head 'scarcely bears a looking at', so he walked back to Egremont for the night.[17]

DAY 3: EGREMONT – WASDALE HEAD

On Wednesday, he left Egremont for Calder Abbey, 'an elegant but not very interesting Ruin', and 'turned eastward, up the Irt arriving in the afternoon at an Inn, a mile and a half from the Foot of Wast Water'. The view ahead was framed by 'the inverted arch formed by the rough fells before me' and beyond these 'the huge enormous mountains of Wast dale all bare and iron-red – and on them a *forest* of cloud-shadows, all motionless – a low Ridge intercepts the Lake from the eye'. Towering above them all were the massive forms of Seat Allen and Scafell which, 'facing each other, far above the other Fells, formed in their interspace a great Gap in the Heaven', a space full of promise which, together with the 'first downright summer Day', filled him with a new sense of urgency: 'Now I must go and see the lake.'

After a meal at the Inn he walked to the Lake, finding that as he approached the low ridge at its foot, 'The Lake is wholly hidden, till your very Feet touch it, and to a stranger the Burst would be almost overwhelming'.

In his notebook he exclaims on arriving 'O what a Lake', and then sits down to write one of the fullest descriptions of a landscape in any of his writings, accompanying it with a typically muddled up drawing: if the plan of the lake is right, then the captions and outline around them needs flipping over right for left. Nevertheless, as with so many of the rapidly sketched descriptions and drawings, what excites him about it is somehow clear:

> I am sitting at the foot almost – for three miles the Screes form its right bank, a facing of naked Rock of enormous height, & two thirds of its height downward absolutely perpendicular, & then slanting off in Screes, steep as the meal out of the Miller's grinding Trough … but in the middle of the Lake the Screes commence far higher up, & occupy two thirds of the height in the shape of the apron of a sheet of water … or rather an outspread fan – it is of a fine red streaking in broad streaks

Looking up Wast Water towards Wasdale Head [author].

'O what a Lake' was Coleridge's reaction on seeing this view of Wast Water, which he described as follows: 'At the top of the Lake two huge Fells face each other, Scafell on the right, Yewbarrow on the left – and between these Great Gavel intervenes, the head and Centre-point of the Vale', while 'for three miles the Screes form its right bank, a facing of naked Rock of enormous height, & two thirds of its height downward absolutely perpendicular, & then slanting off in Screes, steep as the meal out of the Miller's grinding Trough'.

thro' stone Colour, and when I first came, the Lake was like a mirror, & conceive what the reflections must have been, of this huge facing rock, more than half a mile of direct perpendicular height, with deep perpendicular Ravin[e]s, from the Top two thirds down, other Ravin[e]s slanting athwart down them, the whole wrinkled & torrent worn and barely patched with moss – and all this reflected, turned in Pillars, & a whole new world of Images, in the water.

At the top of the Lake two huge Fells face each other, Scafell on the right, Yewbarrow on the left – and between these Great Gavel intervenes, the head and Centre-point of the Vale …

Coleridge adds 'If the Lake itself were broader, and of more various outline, more Bays etc, I do not hesitate to think it would be the grandest object in the Country', and then goes on to list in detail the features and peaks of the ring of fells around the lake.

It is at this point that he had planned to turn back and make his way round to Mitre Dale, Muncaster Fell and Eskdale, but instead, elated by the views before him, drawn by the great gap in the Heavens and the spaces up on Scafell, and encouraged by the weather, instead of turning back he walked on up into Wasdale, and 'so on to Kirk Fell, at the foot of which is Thomas Tyson's House where Wordsworth and I slept November will be 3 years – & there I was welcomed kindly, had a good Bed, and left it after Breakfast.'

It would be wonderful to have witnessed Tyson's reaction to the sudden arrival of Coleridge, and in particular to the latter's suggestion that, rather than repeating his walk with Wordsworth of three years before, when they returned to Keswick over the challenging but well-trodden path to Styhead, he now intended to climb Scafell. Whatever he thought of the venture, Tyson seems to have attempted to fill in some of the gaps in the map Coleridge had cobbled together from Hutchinson's separate images, giving him both a detailed description of the topography of the summit and the best route up to it; certainly it will have been he who also suggested Coleridge should descend into Eskdale and lodge with his friend John Towers at Taw House. In any event, the plan for the following day represented the most ambitious ascent Coleridge had so far undertaken, and, as it turned out, proved to be a fitting climax to his adventures in the Lakes.[18]

Day 4: Wasdale Head – over Scafell – Eskdale

'Thursday morning, August 5th 1802 left T. Tyson's at Wastdale Head where I had been most hospitably entertained … move down the vale almost to the Lake Head, and ascended in the low reach between the Screes & Sca fell, and in about a mile came to Burnmoor Tairn.'[19] He then turned left and followed the Hardrigg Beck up towards the summit, 'now a Glead [Kite] Mews over-head', over relatively gentle slopes, before reaching the point where the bare, open fell side steepens sharply as it runs up to the summit. Here he turned to survey the wide panorama, following it round from Wasdale Head on his right, to Irton Fell, the fells forming Mitredale, Eskdale 'partly in sight', Birker and Ulpha Fells, Muncaster beside these, and the sea beyond, before taking on the steeper slope, 'Ascend, stooping, & looking at my shadow, stooping down to my shadow, a little shorter than myself.'

From here on up he:

climbed & rested, rested & climbed, till I gained the very summit of Sca' Fell – believed by the Shepherds here to be higher than either Helvellyn or Skiddaw … before me all the Mountains die away, running down west-ward to the Sea, apparently in eleven Ridges & three parallel Vales with their three Rivers, seen from their very Sources to their falling into the Sea, where they form … the Trident of the Irish Channel at Ravenglass …

In the original notebook entry recording this moment, the words are strangely moving: 'all before is the dying away of all the fells.'

All of these views were, perhaps, very much what he had hoped and expected to see, the Trident in particular, but it was when he then turned round and took in the view in the other directions that we really sense his excitement. Certainly he was the first person he knew who had ever seen this view, and he did his best to record what he saw and how he perceived his situation. His descriptions of what he saw are to say the least confusing, partly because in the notebook entries it seems he had misunderstood much of what Tyson had described to him and partly because he was clearly excited, desperately trying to capture an impression of what he saw. In addition to all of this, he also wrote what he says was 'surely the first Letter ever written from the Top of Sca' Fell!' to Sara Hutchinson, 'talking, talking, talking, even in that wilderness' as Holmes puts it, and in the letter he was able to correct some of the names that night under the guidance of John Tower at Taw House in Eskdale.

Confused as he may have been about the names, his first exclamation says it all about the impact of everything he saw: 'O my god! what enormous Mountains these are close to me.'

With his back to the sea, on his left he follows the line of 'Great Gavel, Kirk Fell, Green Crag [Red Pike?], & behind the Pillar, then the Steeple, then the Haycock', while on his right he sees 'Great End, Esk Carse [Hause], Bowfell', and straight ahead 'two huge Pyramids, nearly as high as Sca' Fell itself ... the hither one Broad Crag, and the next to it ... Doe Crag [Scafell Pike],' while on the hazy horizon he sees the fells receding away in the direction of Carrock and beyond.

Looking around to take in this panorama, apart from being 'hunger'd & provisionless', he also becomes aware that there are unmistakable signs of an imminent change in the weather: 'the wind is strong, & the Clouds hast'ning hither from the Sea – the whole air sea-ward has a lurid Look – we shall certainly have Thunder'. Even so, he is not ready to leave, and before thinking about a way down, he seeks out a more sheltered spot where he can really take in this experience, where he can write down his thoughts and reactions in his letter to Sara Hutchinson. Thus descending onto the saddle just below the first peak, he took temporary shelter from the wind behind 'another point, a great mountain of Stones'. Coburn identifies this as 'one of the rock towers above Deep Ghyll', and here Coleridge sits down at 'a nice Table of Stones', pen and paper ready.

There is some question as to exactly what happened next, but in his letter to Sara, Coleridge describes only looking down 'Directly thro' Borrodale, the Castle Crag, the whole of Derwent Water, & but for the haziness of Air I could see my own House – I see clear enough where it stands,' before starting his way down. In a letter written to William Sotheby about a month later, however, he claims that ' ... when I was on Sca'fell – I involuntarily poured forth a Hymn in the manner of the psalms,' and, whether he wrote this 'hymn' then or later is a matter of some debate. There is also some debate as to exactly how original his hymn was, since he went on to tell Sotheby that he wrote it 'accidentally lighting on a short Note in some Swiss poems, concerning the Vale of Chamouny'; either way, the context in which his poem, 'Hymn before Sunrise, in the Vale of Chamouni', is included in the letter, provides interesting insight into just what he experienced that day – more in fact than the poem itself. [20]

In his notebook entry about 'seeing' his house he had added 'I saw the spot where it was', making the link between where he was and his home even more specific. On Carrock Fell two years before, in a similar place of shelter amongst the rocks, he had 'sate for a long while sheltered as if I had been in my own Study', and now, for an instant, from his seat at the stone table on Scafell, that connection between his home and this 'home' in the landscape is re-established. This revelation, that this connection lies at the heart of life, is emphasized in the letter to William Sotheby in which he is discussing the fact that in contemporary blank verse poems about nature and the natural world:

> there reigns … a perpetual trick of *moralizing* every thing – which is very well occasionally – but never to see or describe any interesting appearance in nature, without connecting it by dim analogies with the moral world, proves faintness of Impression. Nature has her proper interest; & he will know what it is, who feels & believes, that every Thing has a Life of its own, & that we are all *one Life*. A Poet's Heart & Intellect should be *combined*, *intimately* combined and *unified*, with the great appearances of Nature …

To this he adds 'that this is deep in our Nature, I felt when I was on Sca'fell.' It was perhaps inevitable that this clarity about what he had experienced should have only come after some reflection, after he had had time to process it, but it is also perhaps not surprising that he should have registered it afterwards as all part of the same moment up there on Scafell. Equally, the fact that he then transferred the experience to the Alps, and almost certainly drew on the experiences, and perhaps the words, of another poet to express it in verse, does not alter the quality and importance of what he had understood, since it is this that sets his prose writing, notebooks and letters about the Lake Country apart from what had gone before. Just as his 'excursions' on the fells represented a new way of experiencing the landscape, the 'great appearances of Nature', around us, so his written accounts represented a new way of recording those experiences, recognizing them for what they actually are, that 'Nature has her proper interest'; that indeed, 'all before is the dying away of all the fells.'

On the day itself, however, he cannot linger. Coming out of his reverie, he faces immediate challenges of the changing weather, the fact that he has no food or real shelter, and the terrain before him – 'But O! what a look down just under my Feet! The frightfullest Cove that might ever be seen, huge perpendicular Precipices, and one Sheep upon it's only Ledge, that surely must be crag! Tyson told me of this place, & called it Hollow Stones.' He continues

'I must now drop down, how I may into Eskdale – that lies under to my right – the upper part of it the wildest & savagest surely of all the Vales that were ever seen from the Top of an English Mountain, and the lower part the loveliest.'

Opting not to attempt the vertical pitches in the lower half of Deep Ghyll, and perhaps uncertain as to where it would lead, Coleridge walked to the edge of the Cove till Eskdale was below him. Tempted by the relatively easy slope of the ground, 'the first place that was not direct Rock', he descended to the edge of Broad Stand and 'went on for a while with tolerable ease – but now … came (it was midway down) to a smooth perpendicular rock about 7 feet high – this was nothing.' After throwing his stick down ahead of him, 'I put my hands on the Ledge, & dropped down, in a few yards came just such another, I *dropped* that too, and yet another, seemed not higher … so dropped that too.'

At this point it began to dawn on him that perhaps this had not been such a good idea after all. He found himself to be sharing the ledge with 'a dead Sheep quite rotten' and '

> the stretching of muscles of my hands & arms, and the jolt of the Fall on my Feet, put my whole Limbs in a Tremble, and I paused, & looking down, saw that I had little else to encounter but a succession of these … So I began to suspect that I ought not to go on, but then unfortunately tho' I could with ease drop down …I could not *climb* [back], so go on I must … but every drop increased the palsy of my Limbs – I shook all over'.

By now he is increasingly aware that 'to return was impossible' and, further, that the next 'drop' was 'tremendous', both high and with too narrow a ledge at the bottom to land on safely, and if he proceeded he would have 'fallen backwards & of course killed myself'.

So, here for a moment he stopped, his body trembling uncontrollably, lay on his back, and:

> was beginning in my custom to laugh at myself for a Madman, when the sight of the Crags above me on each side, & the impetuous Clouds just over them … overawed me, I lay in a state of almost prophetic Trance & Delight – & blessed God aloud, for the powers of Reason & the Will, which remaining no Danger can overpower us! …I know not how to proceed, how to return, but I am calm & fearless & confident …

In this frame of mind he got up and began looking for ways down, studying the rock below until 'I glanced my eye to my left, & observed that the Rock was rent from top to bottom – I measured the breadth of the Rent, and found that there was no danger of my being *wedged* in, so I put my Knap-sack round to my side, and slipped down between two walls, without any danger or difficulty – the next Drop brought me down on the Ridge called the How.' Once out on the col, he retrieved his stick and takes stock. His body still trembling, even he realized that this had been a very close call. He had initially intended to carry on exploring and ascend 'Doe-Crag' [Scafell Pike], but given the reaction of his body, and since the weather was rapidly closing in, he opted instead to follow the stream down the mountain, round Cam Spout Crag, and descend into Eskdale.

Many years later Wainwright was to describe Broad Stand as 'The greatest single obstacle confronting ridge-walkers on the hills of Lakeland', an impossible place to ascend without climbing gear even after squeezing through the deep vertical cleft – Coleridge's 'Rent' in the rock. In retrospect, in his second letter to Sara Hutchinson relating his adventures on Scafell that day, he prefaced his account with his assessment of why he had undertaken such a dangerous descent, admitting, perhaps, how foolhardy it had been: 'There is one sort of Gambling, to which I am much addicted … It is this. When I find it convenient to descend from a mountain, I am too confident & too indolent to look round about … I wander on, & where it is first *possible* to descend, there I go – relying on fortune'. He refers again to this risk-taking in a third letter to Sara, written at the end of August, when on a 'glorious walk' he makes the dangerous scramble up the slippery rocks beside Moss Force, and comments 'I have always found this *stretched & anxious* state of mind favourable to depth of pleasurable Impression, in the resting Places and *lownding* Coves.'

That this impetuosity was something he had long recognized in himself is illustrated, I think, by a comment Coleridge made in a letter to William Godwin, some years before, when he writes that when 'An idea starts up in my head, away I follow it thro' thick & thin, Wood & Marsh, Brake and Briar.'

In fact, his matter of fact tone describing his descent from Scafell gives little suggestion of how risky the adventure had been, especially as the weather was closing in. Just how risky it was is confirmed, three years later, by a shaken Mr Luff, Coleridge and Wordsworth's friend in Patterdale, who was to report to the latter,

An event happened here last night which has greatly affected the whole village … The Body, or more properly speaking the Bones of a poor Fellow were yesterday found, by Willy Harrison, in the rocks at the head of Red Tarn. It appears that he was attempting to descend the pass from Helvellyn to the Tarn, when he lost his footing and was dashed to pieces. His name appears to have been Charles Gough [a Manchester artist], several things were found in his pockets; fishing Tackle, Memorandums, a Gold Watch, Silver Pencil, Claude Lorraine Glasses &c &c …[21]

In the light of this sort of tragedy, Coleridge had indeed seriously 'relied on fortune', but once down, he descended rapidly, passing the 'magnificent' waterfalls at Cam Spout before following the young Esk, past Sampson's Stones, and down beside the Esk falls, until he came to a 'village of Sheep-folds where he took shelter from the 'Thunder-shower – accompanied by such Echoes!' Huddled down in the sheep-fold, as the storm crashed around him, we sense that Coleridge had never felt more alive. Even after the adventures of the day, the distances he had travelled, no food, and probably soaking wet, his body aching and throbbing with a heat rash, he is exultant: 'Oh God! what thoughts were mine! O how I wished for Health & Strength that I might wander about for a Month together, in the stormiest month of the year, among these Places, so lonely & savage and full of sounds!'

He had walked for days, lacked sleep and food, but had just climbed the highest of the Lakeland mountains, faced down death, and had felt at home. His elation is clear. Just what the Towers at Taw House made of this sudden, wild-eyed arrival is not recorded, but he was welcomed in and stayed the night.[22]

DAY 5: TAW HOUSE, ESKDALE – ULPHA, DUNNERDALE

The next day Coleridge took a walk with his host, John Towers, back up the slopes above Taw House to locate an interesting stone that he had read about in William Hutchinson's *History of the County of Cumberland*. Coleridge describes this in his notebook as 'the four-foot Stone – on which there are the clear marks of 4 feet, the first a beast's foot … the next a Boy's shoe … the third a large dog's Foot …, the fourth a child's Shoe'. The crag names Coleridge gives amongst which the stone sat are now lost, as, it appears, is the location of the rock itself, but they are clearly the group of small out-crops on the open slopes 'which appeared in the mist' between Scale Gill, Cowcove Beck, High Scarth Crag, Green Crag, Heron Crag & Brock Crag,

Scafell Range from Birker Fell [author].

As he made his way over Birker Fell towards Dunnerdale, Coleridge described this view to the north 'huge Mountains … of a very wild, & various, & angular outline, running in ridges, rising in triangles, sinking in inverting arches, or darting down in Nesses – mountain seen behind mountain, either the backward overtopping the hither-ward, or the nearer mountain dipping down in an inverted arch or triangle'.

an area Coleridge calls 'Moddoch' or 'Maddock How' (another name now lost). Accompanied also by a young shepherd girl (out with her father, no doubt checking on the sheep after the thunderstorm) they found the stone and Coleridge duly measured the marks and carefully recorded all the details, before they returned to Taw House for a late lunch.

It is interesting that Coleridge should have been so intent on locating this stone, spending a good part of the day on it, especially given his experiences of the day before, but it is illustrative of an important element in how he saw these 'lonely & savage' landscapes. It is similar to his fascination with the pattern of the rivers and fells running out to Ravenglass, his 'Trident' – something that he mentions over and over again and drew twice in notebook entries and at least once in a letter. It is as though the appearance amongst the forms of the natural world of these patterns and shapes, the trident, the footprints, the animal prints, recognizable from our world, confirms for him that even though 'every Thing has a Life of its own', we are also 'all *one Life.*' That it is not only 'A Poet's Heart & Intellect' that should be seen as '*combined, intimately* combined and *unified*, with the great appearances of Nature', but also every aspect of our physical existence.

In addition, throughout the notebooks and his letters, he tells us of finding, sitting in and taking inspiration from that recurring reminder of human presence on the fells, the sheepfold. Sometimes with the company of Wordsworth, often alone, he sought these places out and, as already mentioned, wrote on this walk 'of all things a ruined Sheep-fold in a desolate place is dearest to me'. There is a sense in these words that here he felt safe, that he had found a 'home', like his rock shelter on Carrock Fell and his sheltered spot on the summit of Scafell with its stone table – 'a sort of natural porch' as he was later to describe it to Sotheby – a place where, even though 'every Thing has a Life of its own', and he felt his life '*unified*' with 'the power & "eternal Link" of Energy' he felt swirling through the landscapes around him. His use of the word 'porch' here also helps illustrate just what he meant by 'unified', since a porch is a liminal structure, a link between 'indoors' and 'outdoors', and he sees the sheepfold as playing a similar unifying role between our world and the world of nature.

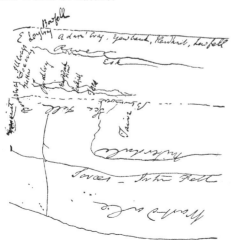

At some point during this day, either with the help of the shepherd or John Towers, Coleridge made a sketch map which identifies both the prominent features of the skylines seen from the valley through which they walked to find the stone, and locates the valley in relation to Scafell and the dales around.

While the shepherd and Towers may have supplied the names of what they were looking at, the overall layout of the map indicates just how strongly the image of the Trident influenced Coleridge's perception of the locality, the three dales of the Irt, Mitre & Esk rivers running in an organized parallel sequence. The skyline prominences are then named, looping round upper Eskdale, starting with the 'Tairns' (Tarns) which lie between Mitredale and Eskdale, up to Burnmoor Tarn (with Mitredale running up to meet it), the Scafell ridge with the prominent features of the summits, Broad Crag, Dow Crag (Scafell Pike), Ill Crag and Long Pike, curving on round the head of the valley to Bowfell and on down the skyline past Hardknott to Low Fell [possibly Border End]. Tucked up under the precipices of the summit of Scafell, Coleridge marks in 'The How', the col into which he finally escaped from Broad Stand, and below, this running down beside the Esk, the valley of Maddock How, location of the 'Four Foot Stone'.

It is quite possible that he created the map because he wanted to remind himself of the setting since, on seeing the footprints on it, the stone 'really does work on my imagination very powerfully & I will try to construct a Tale upon it, the place too is very, very wild.' It is equally possible that, as with the map he sketched of Wast Water two days before, on his first sight of the immense spaces and forms of Scafell and the landscape around it, he wanted to capture the topography and memory of the extraordinary adventure he had had when he got there and on the subsequent descent and aftermath. Certainly, he never made any sketch maps like these of any of the other places he visited.

Later that afternoon, he finally said goodbye to John Towers and set off for Ulpha, but, as the rest of the journey unfolds, it is not long before we get a sense that his mood has changed. As we have seen, the day before, sheltering from the violence of the thunder storm in the sheepfolds below Scafell, totally energized and excited, he had 'wished for Health & Strength that I might wander about for a Month together, in the stormiest month of the year, among these Places, so lonely & savage and full of sounds!' It is a remarkable sentence, and expressing the kind of experience that set his accounts apart from anything that had come before, but, as he leaves the high, wild places for the tamer fells below, and the end of his walk comes into sight, his mood of the day before evaporates as he senses the impossibility of ever having the health, strength, or indeed, freedom to live amongst 'savage' landscapes full of 'sounds'.

Although he wrote only a brief summary in a letter, this time to Robert

Southey, having 'proceeded that evening to Devoke Lake, & slept at Ulpha Fell', the subsequent journey that day is recorded in detail in the notebook.[23] Leaving the main road just before Eskdale Green, he crossed the Esk Bridge and walked up over Birker Fell until he 'crossed a moss, and ascended another & and came out upon Devoke Water, a good large Tairn with naked Banks, & a tiny Island covered with Sea Fowl ... & a bold view of the huge Mountains at the head of Wastdale directly across the Lake and in front of me' Caught up once again in the drama of these mountains, in spite of the fact that it was now late in the day, he paused to write his notes:

> huge Mountains ... of a very wild, & various, & angular outline, running in ridges, rising in triangles, sinking in inverting arches, or darting down in Nesses − mountain seen behind mountain, either the backward overtopping the hitherward, or the nearer mountain dipping down in an inverted arch or triangle.

From Devoke Water, he 'Passed over a common, wild, & dreary, and descending a hill came down upon Ulpha Kirk, with a sweet view up the River'. [River Duddon]. Here, his spirits seem to revive somewhat as he surveyed the vale, so different from the wild & remote fells he had just walked over. 'Ulpha Kirk is a most romantic vale ... the Kirk standing on the low rough Hill up which the Road climbs, the fields level and high, beyond that; & then the different flights of mountains in the back ground, with wild ridges to right and the left, like Arms & confining the middle view to these level fields on high ground is eminently picturesque.'

Day 6: 'Donnerdale Mountains' − Coniston

As he walked down into the vale of the Duddon the next day, Coleridge reached the bridge over the river and looked around him: 'A little step beyond the bridge, you gain a completely different picture − the houses and Kirk forming more important parts, & the view bounded at once by a high wooded rock ... I pass along for a furlong or so upon the road, the river winding thro' the narrow vale'. His attention was then caught by the drama of the rock crags up on Dunnerdale Fell, 'a very rocky Fell, yew-trees on the Rocks ... [the] outline most wildly saw-toothed, and sheep-tracks everywhere − O lovely, lovely Vale!'

The special nature of Dunnerdale had also worked its magic on Wordsworth, who knew it well from childhood, and Coleridge's joyful discovery of the

Dunnerdale from the Dunnerdale Fells [author].

As Coleridge made his way up and over the Dunnerdale Fells he was struck by the particular beauty of the landscape around him 'a very rocky Fell, yew-trees on the Rocks …[the] outline most wildly saw-toothed, and sheep-tracks everywhere – O lovely, lovely Vale!'

'lovely, lovely vale' in 1802 anticipated the sonnets that Wordsworth was to start writing about it in 1806. It was to be another fourteen years, however, before Wordsworth completed the cycle of thirty-four poems for publication in 1820, poems which have been seen as the 'last glow of his genius'. On his way, Coleridge notes 'behind me, right over the Dubbs, a fine water view'; 'Dubs' is northern dialect for 'deep dark pool in a stream and river', and one senses here that Coleridge, peering down into the smooth, deep stream will have recognized the inspiration behind some of the best known lines in the Wordsworth sonnets:

> For, backward, Duddon, as I cast my eyes,
> I see what was, and is, and will abide:
> Still glides the Stream, and will forever glide,
> The Form remains, the Function never dies.[24]

Coleridge then cut over Stickle Knot [Stickle Pike] on Dunnerdale Fell to Broughton Mills, and while his exact route is unclear, it brought him after a while into another 'lovely vale, & a Bridge covered with Ivy' and Coleridge then begins an extended description of this new view, a description which, like an unpunctuated stream of consciousness, is hard to follow with any topographic precision, but which both draws us in to share his sense of enclosure within the landscape, and also acts to illustrate the lack of precedent and indeed language for such descriptions:

> the vale completely land-locked by segments of circles folding in behind each other, before me a (strait) ridge slants across, the Hill on my right folds in a long *Ellipse* behind, while the Hill on my left in more of a segment of a circle folds in before it, so is it, with my back to the sea, & my face looking up the Stream that runs between alders and birch elms – the name of the Beck Little Beck, that springs out of Coe Moss ... Turning round ... the Hill that is now to my left & makes an elliptical line to my back, curves in a circle-segment, while the Hill on my right folds round about it ...

While it is not clear exactly where he was looking, we are nevertheless swept up in the swirls of circles, segments, slants, folds, elliptical lines, the beck, the enclosing alders and what he calls the 'birch elms'. Coleridge is writing as fast as he could, recording one impression after another, creating as he went a new style of writing, one which sought to convey the direct experience; not aesthetic 'sensitivity' to the 'sublimity' of his surroundings, but a sense of being there.

Perhaps because he is now approaching the last couple of days of the walk, or perhaps inspired by the details of Dunnerdale after so many days on the bleaker high fells, Coleridge seems more aware than ever of the physical presence of the landscape itself, of the sheer complexity of the interlacing elements that make up what we see. Further re-energized by a lunch of 'Oatcake & cheese, with a pint of Ale, & 2 glasses of rum & water sweetened with preserved gooseberries' at the ale house in Broughton Mills (where the publican seems to have recommended his heading for 'Mr Thomas Robinson's Black Bull, Conistone'), Coleridge sets off towards Torver, recording in bewildering detail the changing views, sights and sounds, to right and left of the road. Approaching and then passing the 'great bulging rocky Hill covered with wood, with two or three deep wooded Ravines in it' [perhaps 'The Knott' of Broughton Moor], he seems determined to capture exactly what the view is actually composed of, with:

> [the] unseen ever-heard Brook winding at its feet – between the road and the brook inclosed fields of steep descent … a Beck runs almost straight up to its Fountain Head – and a beautiful Road serpentizes over the Hill just above its head … it rises or seems to rise between 2 round stony Hills, each of which the Mountain-ridges now rise over, now sink under, in a jagged saw-tooth outline … thro' an inverted arch in the Fells, a very singular pike looks in …

Amongst the torrent of words here, sentences stand out, 'a gentle ascent, ferny Common – Steep on my right, the wider view on my left a descending Fell with green stony bulging Hills on either side, which unite at its head in a shelving ridge, over behind which a higher ridge shelves in the same Direction'; '3 Hills, the largest of which looks like a Paradise in the wild'; 'to my left a bleak Common, & stony Fells over which the Clouds are sweeping'; and he sums it all up 'it is a day of sun & Clouds, with a thousand Shadows on the Hills.'

He continued up this vale, through Torver, sights Coniston Water, 'doubtless a worthy Compeer of the Stateliest – an equal Coheir for Nature with Keswick, Wyndermere, & Ullswater', and takes in the great fells rising up to the Old Man accompanied by the waterfall of Levers Water, the great 'crescent of hills' from Dow Crag on the Seathwaite Fells, Brim Fell, the ridge to Great How and round to the Coniston and Yewdale Fells; all described amidst the 'broken Sunlights, Clouds and Storm', the high mountains of 'sternness and simplicity, one-coloured'.[25]

Days 7 – 9: Brathay – Grasmere – Keswick

In a breathless conclusion to the walk, and seven days after leaving Greta Hall, he arrives at Brathay, before returning home via Grasmere. After a final rambling entry that ends with comments concerning gardens and clipped yew trees, the notebook account of the walk ends. In his next letter to Sara Hutchinson about the trip, he announces that 'I am well, & have had a very delightful & feeding Excursion, or rather Circumcursion', before going on to elaborate on some of the details of these last few days of the trip. When he passes through Grasmere, the Wordsworths were, of course, away in France, and Dove Cottage appears cold and empty. After the euphoria of his ascent of Scafell, once he had left the mountain and was now back and thinking of his friends, Coleridge's mood is bleak:

> I wish, I wish, they were back … I slept at Bratha on Sunday night and did not go on to Grasmere, tho' I had time enough, and was not over-fatigued; … I did not like to sleep in *their* lonely House. I called the next day – went into the garden … but I did not go upstairs, nor indeed anywhere but the Kitchen. Partly I was very wet & my boots very dirty … I had small desire to go up![26]

Two letters, written later in August and early September to William Sotheby, are, however, more reflective and they indicate the central place the experience on the top of Scafell has come to occupy in his memories of the walk. It is clear that he has been thinking about what happened and is beginning to embellish it to create a more complete moment of spiritual and poetic revelation. In the first letter, Scafell is the only part of the walk he covers in any detail at all, the account of what came before and after being simply a list of places visited. Even more telling, however, is the second letter, that of 10th September,[27] by which time he has convinced himself that, such was the power of the moment of revelation of the depths of our 'Nature', that 'I involuntarily poured forth a Hymn …':

> O dread and silent Mount! I gazed upon thee,
> Till thou, still present to the bodily sense,
> Didst vanish from my thought: entranced in prayer
> I worshipped the Invisible alone.
>
> Yet, like some sweet beguiling melody,
> So sweet, we know not we are listening to it,
> Thou, the meanwhile wast blending with my thought,
> Yea, with my life and life's own secret joy:
> Till the dilating Soul, enrapt, transfused,
> Into the mighty vision passing – there
> As in her natural form, swelled vast to Heaven!

As we have already seen, there is some doubt as to whether this actually happened, and some doubt about the originality of his Hymn.[28] Nevertheless, the importance of that day is underlined by the fact that it seems it was his experience on the summit of Scafell that stayed with him after the trip and made a lasting impression on him.

Although full of plans for a further walk in the Alps on his return from the nine-day walk, hoping perhaps for even more dramatic experiences amongst the high peaks, it was in fact to be another year before he set out walking again, this time, in August 1803, on a trip to Scotland suggested by Dorothy and William Wordsworth.

7

'That poor, mad poet, Coleridge':
The final Walks, 1803

The Scottish trip had been suggested by the Wordsworths, who felt that a new adventure amongst the dramatic landscapes of Scotland in the collaborative spirit of their earlier walks would be good for both Coleridge's frame of mind and his health. Unfortunately it was not to be. On the one hand, the Wordsworths decided the three of them would travel by cart, and on the other, the tensions that were visible during their earlier walk to Nab Scar seem only to have grown. For Coleridge, travelling by cart meant sitting all day as they slowly plodded along the roads, giving him no opportunity to suddenly turn aside and explore something that caught his eye, to find the stimulating and unexpected, to get lost, challenge himself and take a gamble. In addition, as Dorothy had written of the Nab Scar walk 'we could not be all of one mind', and these tensions came to a head a few days into the trip, when Coleridge decided to leave the Wordsworths and continue on his own on foot; it would seem that too much had changed in their relationship for these three to recapture the experiences of their earlier walks together.

Yet the story of Coleridge walking in the Lake District is not entirely finished, since in September and October of 1803, following his return from Scotland, he did take two final walks and the differences between them illustrate, perhaps, the extreme polarities of his experiences in the Lakes. On the one hand, his grand scheme for a walk with Southey ended prematurely in the kind of sad muddle that typifies much of his life. On the other was a short, energetic outing with both Southey and William Hazlitt, during which he gives not just a remarkably clear-eyed assessment of the Lakes but also of himself. His account reads as a kind of fond farewell to the world that had been the focal point of his existence during those eventful years 1800 and 1802.

The 'Walking Tour' with Southey, September

Following the birth of his daughter Sara at Greta Hall in December 1802, Coleridge had again left the Lakes, and, after spending time in both the West Country and London, he returned for his fourth and last summer in Keswick in April 1803. It had long been Coleridge's dream that his friend Robert Southey should also move with his family to the Lakes, inviting him as early as the spring of 1801 to share the house at Greta Hall, and while Southey had visited with his family that summer, he soon returned south and the move never happened. In September 1803, however, Southey and his wife Edith, grieving the loss of a child, decided to visit the Coleridges at Greta Hall. Although at the time they appear not to have planned on staying long, the Southeys soon took over one wing, sharing the house with the Coleridges, and they continued to live there with Sara Coleridge and the children until Southey's death in 1843.

Following his own return from the trip to Scotland, Coleridge seems to have again determined to introduce Southey to the wonders of the high fells, and to this end he planned 'a Lakeland walking tour with Southey; Saddleback, Bowscale, White Water Dash, Caldbeck Fells, Uldale, Cockermouth, Mockerkin, Mosser, Loweswater, Mosedale, scale force, Bleaberry Tarn, High Stile, Scarf Gap, Hay Stacks, with a possible pillar, Steeple, Haycock coda.'[1] Far more ambitious than even his nine-day solo walk of the year before, he seems to have relished the chance to once again set out with a close friend to share the experience of exploring and discussing, composing lines, exclaiming in joy, and, all the time, wondering at the marvels around them. Typically, perhaps, he seems not to have paused to reflect on the wisdom of such an ambitious walk, of his imagination being, yet again, cramped and restrained by the moods and opinions of another, or indeed the physical effort that would be required.

Planning the route, poring once again over the maps in Hutchinson and West, Coleridge was as fascinated as ever by the shapes and forms he sees created by the webs of becks as they flow down and around the peaks and ridges. Lacking the contour outlines to give definition to the landforms that we are now so familiar with, he focuses instead on the intricate networks of streams, tarns and rivers which flow across the map. He notes, for example, that the 'Glenderamacken' combines with the numerous becks that flow into it 'making Souther Fell almost an island'. On the one hand these bring the physical landscape into relief, conjuring up images in his mind of what he will see (just as the Virgivian Trident had done earlier) and give form to the landscape setting through which they will pass; while on the other, in conjunction with the lines of roads and tracks, they provide the basis for interesting routes to follow.

The first day was to be Keswick to Caldbeck: the route would take them over Saddleback, along the ridge to Bowscale Fell, past Bowscale Tarn and down to Mosedale. From here they would walk back up beside the Caldew Beck under the scree slopes of Carrock Fell, and up past Swinside, before cutting up to the right and passing Coomb Height, Knott and Burn Todd. They would then 'descend close on White Water Dash', before turning back and heading for Caldbeck past High Pike, West Fell and Calebreck.

The second day was also clear to him, Caldbeck to Loweswater: the route would take them south-west to Uldale, round under Binsey to Bewaldeth, and past Isel Grange and Hewthwaite Hall to Cockermouth. From here they would head south towards Pardshaw, but turn off left to Aikbank and up over Mosser Fell to Asgill Knot and 'force a way ¼ of a mile to Water end'. They would then spend the night at either Water End or Loweswater.

After this, the third day remained somewhat unresolved. Coleridge's head full of alternative routes, he suggested ascending Mosedale by following Mosedale Beck up between Mellbreak and Loweswater Fell, before dropping down to visit Scale Force and climbing back up the ridge to Red Pike. From here they would follow the ridge to High Steel [High Stile] and High Crag and then either drop down to Buttermere 'to dine', or continue to Hay Stacks. From here the plan became even more vague, with a suggestion of dropping down into the head of Ennerdale, climbing Black Sail Pass, turning up to Pillar, and on to Steeple and Haycock before heading off to Seat Allen. From this point on, however, the rest of the trip, the route back to Keswick, and even the number of days was all left undecided.

Such was the grand plan, but we have to wonder whether Southey's heart was ever really in it, or whether Coleridge was really committed either. Coleridge's notes tell us that they set off at 10am, climbed Saddleback to 'Saddlback Tarn' [Scale Tarn], where he rediscovered the excitement he had previously felt on seeing it: 'I had quite forgotten the fearfully sublime Precipice & striding Edge on its ... Northern Side [Sharp Edge], and the colours of the little Tarn, blood-crimson, and then Sea Green etc, etc, etc '. It seems to have been windier than on his previous visit because, this time, he becomes captivated by the wind on the surface of the Tarn 'now Calm, now Ruffled Spaces, & nowhere more beautiful can you see the breeze-race, blowing a rich blue like the Peacocks neck over the Tairn, till where it comes near the blood-crimson, & then it turns into the most beautiful purple.'

The little drawing he includes in this entry clearly shows the outline of the 'sublime Precipice' with the jagged 'striding edge' running up it. But after this detailed observation of the Tarn, the notebook goes quiet. The walk north, down from Saddleback, over Bowscale Fell and on to Caldbeck, passes unrecorded. A line tacked on to the next day's entry – 'the Deluge of Stones from Carrock, on the road from Mossdale to Hesket, no stones immediately under the mountain, & a few on the left of the road' – suggests that they had skirted Carrock rather than including it in their walk, and they arrived in Caldbeck early enough in the day to spend a good part of the afternoon exploring the waterfalls of Caldbeck Howk. They, or at least Coleridge, since there is no mention of Southey being with him, find it interesting enough to return the next day. A detailed description of the waterfalls follows, but photographic rather than interpretive, lacking the imaginative reach of his earlier descriptions.[2]

Describing the 'Pool & the natural bridge with two Arches of unequal size', he writes 'the Stream thro' the larger Arch falls down after a twist or two in a noble waterfall under a pendant mass of Ivy, itself under a ceiling of Lime Trees,' and continues 'the second pool still more beautiful & wide & green and deep, and as sweetly o'er-canopied by Limes & Ashes, the Limes absolutely *showering* their yellow leaves'. Looking again at this second pool the next morning he describes as 'the best view of the whole underpart of this scenery … the water gushing out from under [a mass of rock], like a furious Gush of blood from a plethoric Artery fighting with the mossy buttress of this Sub-bridge', and continues with 'a beautiful opening, with the round faery Cauldron below it, whose wall forms a connection between this Turret, & the second Turret, equal in height, & much larger in diameter', while the water passes him in 'furious gushes' and 'another stream rushing'.

The fact that, by the afternoon of the first day, they had abandoned the original plan to walk back up the Caldew Beck from Mosedale to Whitewater Dash, and then on to Caldbeck, suggests that Southey at least was already tiring. Whether this was due to physical exhaustion or whether Coleridge's commentaries were overwhelming him, the walk was, by the second morning, already over. After investigating the falls at

Caldbeck Howk again, and returning to Caldbeck, Coleridge notes 'it seemed to threaten rain, Southey was weary & already homesick, so we turned off'. Instead of continuing to Cockermouth they walked down Bassenthwaite and 'returned about 5 o'clock in the afternoon.' Coleridge makes no further comment, and perhaps, in the end, he too was not really up to it, having enjoyed the anticipation, the excitement of looking at the map, his imagination running wild, rather more than the actual experience. It had been at least four years since he last enjoyed a long walk in company, when he and Wordsworth first explored the area in 1799; his great Lakeland experiences since then had all been alone, himself one to one with the landscape.

This would truly have been a sad and muddled end to Coleridge's walks in the Lakes, but fortunately for us, just four days later, Southey having evidently recovered, the two of them set off again, accompanied on this occasion by the essayist and journalist William Hazlitt, on what turned out to be Coleridge's last recorded walk amongst the fells. His commentary is particularly interesting because not only was the route a new one, with new sights to discover and describe, but it has a sense of being his farewell to the 'vale of Elysium', which, as much as any other in his life and writings, he had identified as a place where he felt at home; his place in the landscape.

WALK WITH SOUTHEY AND HAZLITT THROUGH BORROWDALE INTO WATENDLATH, OCTOBER

The notebook entry for 4 October 1803 reads: 'I walked with Southey and Hazlitt thro' Borrodale into Watendlath, & so home to a late dinner. Of course it was for me a mere walk; for I must be alone, if either my Imagination or heart are to be excited or enriched'.[3]

He seems to accept here that for him, walking had become a solitary joy, and that he was never again going to enjoy the kind of companionable walks that he had shared with the Wordsworths some five years before in the Quantocks. Since that time, his great, transcendental moments had all come when he was alone. Only then is his heart going to be enriched by what he experiences. Although in this instance he sets off with friends, there is no mention of them along the way. We get a sense, in fact, of Coleridge striding away from the others, and taking it all in on his own terms, with no record of interaction between the three. Instead, as the walk unfolds, we get a flurry of description, capturing both what he actually saw and a sense of the life that

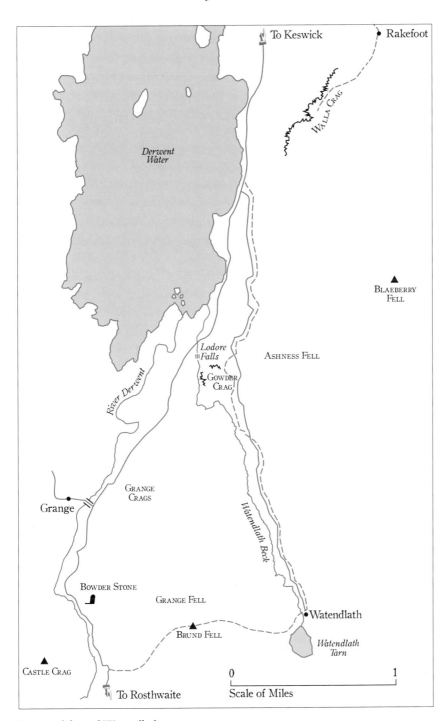

Borrowdale and Watendlath.

he now recognizes pulsing through the valley. Assessing the scenery as he goes along, he writes:

> I thought still more that if the Lake had pushed up into Borrodale, as far as the Bowder Stone, & if Borrodale were still better wooded, it would be distinguished from the Trossachs chiefly by its continuity of massiveness – tho' there is one vast Crag to the left, as you go up Borrodale, complete Trossachs, all the dislocation and multitude of outjuttings & precipices …

Preoccupied by these thoughts, he lost his way but, as ever, this in turn seren-dipitously brings him to yet another new, startling view: 'I ascended in the wrong place, but it led me to some glorious fantastic rocks – the mitre, the huge pyramid, & Peak Fantastic, with the lower Rock to the Right of it, between which two in a narrow defile I went, having in this Toilsome Climb two most singular & noble views of the Lake & Vale of Keswick …'

From his description, it would seem possible that he had missed the path over to Watendlath from Rosthwaite and climbed straight up to Brund Fell. Wainwright describes the summit of Brund Fell as follows: 'The Summit of Brund Fell is one of exceptional interest. A number of steep-sided rock towers rise oddly from the heathery top …'[4] and his accompanying drawing of it seems to illustrate Coleridge's 'glorious fantas-tic rocks – the mitre, the huge pyramid & Peak Fantastic.' In addition, Wainwright's won-derful drawing from the top of Brund Fell looking north over the top of the rocks gives us a priceless glimpse of the view over Derwent Water that Coleridge saw.

Looking north from the top of Brund Fell [A. Wainwright, *The Central Fells*].

And then, suddenly, from amongst the rocks he paused to look back down into Borrowdale, and his attention is suddenly caught by 'A whole Flight of small Birds [which] flung themselves down in a gale of wind into Borrodale like a *shoot* of stones – each Bird seemed to dart onwards by projection, & to descend by its own lifelessness & weight!'

Whatever his problems at this time, he had not lost the ability for his 'imagination and heart … to be excited or enriched', to suddenly catch sight of the wider sense of 'Life' moving through the valley, animating the great theatre setting of landscape, or his ability to capture that sudden moment in a rapid word sketch.

From Brund Fell, he walked down to Watendlath Tarn, and followed the stream down towards Lodore and Ashness, before turning off at the bridge and walking, it would seem, through the woods towards the precipice below Gowder Crag:

> This open Coppice brings [the Traveller] suddenly to the Edge of a finely wooded Precipice, with Lodore beneath him at a small distance on his Left, & on his right the Promontory of Birches on the Lake, the house at the Foot of Lodore, the Bridge, the Road seen in 3 different distances, so very beautiful – the Lake of Keswick – & Bassenthwaite – the height from the extreme steepness & direct plumb-down Look in the Lake seems vast – the breezes rush in pencil brushes over it – you *look down* on everything, & everything spreads in consequence, broad & long & vast! This is, I have no hesitation in saying it – the best, every way the best & most impressive View in all the Lake Country – why not in all the Island?

Just what his experiences of 'looking down' on everything, and everything 'spread in consequence, broad, long and vast', had meant to Coleridge is perhaps summed up in what Holmes describes as 'a magnificent evocation of his fell-walking … which turned it into a personal Romantic credo. It deserves its place, far more, one might think, than his 'Hymn before Sunrise', in any anthology for Lake District lovers' and which he quotes as follows:

> I never find myself at one within the embracement of rocks & hills, a traveller up an Alpine road, but my spirit courses, drives, and eddies, like a Leaf in Autumn: a wild activity, of thoughts, imaginations, feelings, and impulses of motion, rises up from within me – a sort of *bottom-wind*, that blows to no point of the compass, & comes from I know not whence, but agitates the whole of me; my whole Being is filled with waves, as it were, that roll & stumble, one this way, & one that way, like things that have no common master. I think, that my soul must have pre-existed in the body of a Chamois-chaser … The farther I ascend from animated Nature, from men, and cattle, & the common birds of the woods, & fields, the greater becomes the Intensity of the feeling of Life … In these moments it has

been my creed, that Death exists only because Ideas exist: that Life is limitless Sensation, that Death is a child of the organic senses, chiefly of the Sight; that Feelings die by flowing into the mould of the Intellect ... I do not think it possible, that any bodily pains could eat out the love and joy, that is so substantially a part of me, towards hills, & rocks, & steep waters. And I have had some Trial.

Holmes concludes, 'This is more than mere fell-walking, it is an evocation of the state of creativity. The process of inspiration, the outpouring of inner being, the artist's confidence in immortality, were all enacted for Coleridge in these wild, solitary journeyings.'⁵

On this last walk, however, surveying the view, it seems he accepts that he will not experience such landscapes again in the way he had, and passes on his final judgement on all the places he has seen. This certainty is then reflected in the final sentence in which he suddenly feels that he has another great poem in him: 'O surely I might make a noble Poem of all my youth nay *of all my Life.*'

This was, of course, not to be, but as he looks down on the vale of Keswick, he records that 'I worshipped with deep feeling the grand outline & perpetual Forms, that are the guardians of Borrodale, & the presiding Majesty, yea, the very Soul of Keswick'; such had been the impact of his time on the fells.

COLERIDGE'S LATER REPUTATION AND THE EMERGENCE OF FELL-WALKING AS A POPULAR PASTIME

That winter, in early January 1804, after a visit to Dove Cottage, Coleridge left the Lakes and he was not to return until 1806. By then, however, his health had declined as his addiction to opium grew. Although he had come to understand 'the grand outline & perpetual forms' of the mountains, and discovered in them the 'very Soul of Keswick', it was to be left to others to build on the experiences he had pioneered.

Although he visited the Lakes again on several occasions, in particular staying with the Wordsworths at their new home of Allan Bank in 1810, once he had left in early 1804, Coleridge's active engagement with the landscapes of the area was at an end. While Wordsworth, and then Southey, went on to be ever more closely associated with both the area and the romantic movement that had grown out of their time there, Coleridge, it seems, was rapidly forgotten, his participation and contribution fading from memory. Perhaps the single biggest factor in this was the fact that, while the others continued publishing books and poetry, Coleridge's writings on the Lakes, and, crucially, the contents of his notebooks, went unpublished and therefore unseen. As his personal problems, particularly the ever-present strain of his unhappy marriage, his doomed love for Sara Hutchison, his financial insecurity and his continuing addiction to opium came to steadily dominate his reputation, his insights and achievements in those ground-breaking walks of 1800 and 1802 slipped from the record, as did his very presence in the area.

The speed and extent of this process is, I think, vividly illustrated by the account in her *Journal* by Elizabeth Vassall, Lady Holland, who visited the Lakes in 1807. The *Journal* records the Hollands' visit to the Lake District in August of that year, and is of great interest both in terms of what caught Lady Holland's eye and who she is hoping to meet there. On 23 August, she tells us, they arrived 'late in the evening at Lowood Inn, by the side Windermere'.[6]

The next day Lady Holland 'sent an invitation to Wordsworth, one of the Lake Poets, to come and dine, or visit us in the evening. He came. He is much superior in his writings, and his conversation is even beyond his abilities … He is preparing a manual to guide travellers in their tour amongst the Lakes.' She then goes on to note that 'he holds opinions on picturesque subjects with which I completely differ, especially as to the effects produced by *white houses* on the sides of the hills; to my taste they produce a cheerful effect … His objection was chiefly grounded upon the distances being confounded by the glare of white.'

Having thoroughly enjoyed Wordsworth's company and arguing for her version of the 'picturesque' vision, the Hollands travel on towards Keswick. On the way, they are seriously underwhelmed by the midsummer falls at Rydal – 'a very feeble cascade at Sir Daniel Le Fleming's' – and reach 'Derwent Water' for dinner. Soon afterwards they have 'found Southey, who accepted our invitation. He is full of genius and poetical enthusiasm.' During their meeting, Southey invites the Hollands to Greta Hall and 'In the evening we visit his family; I was curious to see his interior. His house is excellent and beautifully situated. He seems much beloved by a numerous domestic circle of connections and friends; he is surrounded by heaps of old and valuable Spanish books.' After an evening spent with Southey and family, the Hollands leave Keswick on 26 August, to continue their journey into Scotland.

It would seem then, if this entry of 1807 and Palmer's anecdote of 1808 (that 'I am one of two people spoken of in this neighbourhood for their long perambulations (the other being a Mr Townley)'), are anything to go by, that only some three or four years after he left the Lake District, Coleridge had already been forgotten locally, and that his presence in the Lakes had passed into history. Elsewhere, however, and particularly in London, where his return to England after living in Malta and his current journalism were attracting attention, Coleridge remained a figure of interest. Having expressed no curiosity about him on her trip to the Lakes in 1807, by early 1808, and back in Holland House in London, Lady Holland writes in her *Journal*:

> I hear nothing but of Coleridge, which makes me regret not being acquainted with him … [after] his Commissaryship at Malta, he is returned to England, where he is supposed to employ himself in writing articles in the *Courier*.[7]

In the end, they seem never to have met, but we do catch a vivid glimpse of this still-talked-about Coleridge, who was then living in Highgate, in the following entry from 1823 in Elizabeth Grant's *Memoir of a Highland Lady*. At the time she is staying in Hampstead with an uncle and aunt, and writes:

> I must try and recollect the names of the few remarkable people I met with … Mr William Rose occasionally came to dinner, and that poor, mad poet, Coleridge, who never held his tongue – stood pouring out a deluge of words meaning nothing, with eyes on fire, and his silver hair streaming down to his waist. His family had placed him with a young doctor at Highgate, where he was well taken care of … .[8]

Thus it was that by 1823, Coleridge had become 'that poor, mad poet', his reputation and exploits eclipsed by tales of his eccentricities, his chaotic family life, his illnesses and his addictions. By the twentieth century this image of Coleridge had, if anything, hardened, and any of the compassion for his situation hinted at in Grant's description had been replaced by something altogether more dismissive.

In 1819 William Green published the first volume of *The Tourist's New Guide* to the Lakes, effectively an updated version of West's *A Guide to the Lakes* of 1778, and although written only nine years after Coleridge left the Lakes for the last time, he is only mentioned once, and that in the context of the debate 'as to the effects produced by *white houses* on the sides of the hills' which continued to preoccupy Wordsworth; no mention at all is made of his fell walks or indeed of his having lived in Keswick.[9] From this time on, as Wordsworth's reputation and indeed Southey's, as residents and poets of the Lakes, grew inexorably, Coleridge's faded rapidly, until by 1855, when Harriet Martineau wrote *A Complete Guide to the English Lakes*, Coleridge is not mentioned at all.

As she describes the various 'moderate' tours, suitable for ladies and gentlemen, Martineau, a resident of Ambleside, makes numerous references to Wordsworth – telling us for example that Loughrigg Fell, 'very easy and charming', will be 'well known to all readers of Wordsworth', or that Wordsworth's account of his ascent of 'Scawfell' is 'the best we have of the greatest mountain excursion in England'; and she refers also to Gray, Southey, Walter Scott and Hartley Coleridge. Martineau mentions Gray when describing the view from Castlerigg 'which made the poet long to go back again to Keswick', while Greta Hall is mentioned as 'Southey's abode', Dove Cottage is 'where the poet [Wordsworth] and his sister lived many years ago when Scott was their guest', and Nab Cottage, beside the road from Grasmere to Rydal, was where 'Hartley Coleridge lived and died.' As to Hartley's father, not a word.

Yet while Martineau makes no mention of Coleridge, there is one section in her book, 'A Day in the Mountains', which throws his exploits into a vivid light. Her description of the potential dangers of taking on the high peaks, and the precautions that need taking, indicate to us just how far ahead of his time Coleridge actually was. While she says that the 'ascent of Skiddaw is easy, even for ladies, who have only to sit on their ponies to find themselves at the top', she also relates a series of tales of people who have become lost, disorientated or injured, and who have only survived by good luck. Her final words of advice are that if you are going to ascend to the ridges and peaks, 'a map is essential … and in the case of an ascent of a formidable mountain, like Scawfell or Helvellyn, it is rash to go without a guide.'[10]

Following on in this tradition, in the 1880 Lake District guide book written by M.J.B. Baddeley (one popular enough to remain in print until 1978),[11] Coleridge makes only brief appearances as one of the poets who lived in the Lakes alongside Wordsworth. When he does finally appear in the guidebooks in his own right it is not as a pioneering walker, but as the 'poor, mad poet'. In the *Lake District* volume of Arthur Mee's *King's England Series* (1937),[12] for example, Wordsworth's presence looms large over the book. By page 3 we have quotations from his poetry and the county of Westmoreland has been introduced as 'the haunt of the poet who, above all the rest, looks Nature in the face and feels himself her child.' The author goes on to say 'Here he lies at rest, and his spirit is the magnet that draws men to this place.' On the other hand, Coleridge is not mentioned at all except when the guide reaches Keswick, and then the tone of his brief appearances is harshly unforgiving, making no mention of Coleridge's life in the Lakes until 1803 when he convinced Southey to join him in Keswick:

> In 1800 [to Greta Hall] came Coleridge to live, his best poems already writ-ten. To it in 1803 he invited Southey, a far finer man, and perhaps more of a man than a poet. For a little while their two families were together, Coleridge erratic and struggling to master himself, Southey methodical, thinking deeply, writing hard, and revelling in his books; and when the unstable Coleridge cut himself adrift it was Southey who for more than a generation kept this home going, bearing the burden of both families, winning fame as Poet Laureate, and earning the high respect and admiration of all.

The book continues: 'Presently Coleridge, unmanned by opium, set forth on his vague wanderings, and Southey was left in Greta Hall with three families to support', and with that note, any mention of Coleridge ceases. Indeed, as with Martineau, the book contains far more about 'the tragedy' of Coleridge's son Hartley than the 'unstable' father, and only Wordsworth, Southey and then Ruskin are credited with having explored and understood the unique qualities of the landscapes of the Lakes and written anything of lasting quality about them.

Although a partial collection of Coleridge's letters was published in 1895, it was not until the 1950s, with the publication of a full collection of the letters, edited with commentaries by E.L.Griggs (1956), followed by the notebooks by Coburn (begun 1957), that a much more balanced and detailed appraisal of Coleridge's time in the Lakes has been possible, and the importance of what he achieved more fully appreciated.

Yet, if by the early twentieth century Coleridge himself had largely been forgotten, his chosen activity of fell-walking finally started to come into its own, although it is clear that it took a while for 'walking' to be recognized as a legitimate 'activity'. As early as the mid-nineteenth century, mountaineering, particularly in the Alps, became an important or popular-enough pastime to require the formation of an official club. 'The Alpine Club' was founded in 1852, but it took until 1889 for the 'Scottish Mountaineering Club' to follow, and then another ten years or so before 'The Climber's Club' of England and Wales was founded.

Meanwhile, in the Lakes, two brothers, George and Ashley Abraham, professional photographers and keen climbers from Keswick, formed a partnership with the Welsh climber Owen Glynne Jones. They accompanied him as he pioneered a number of new routes in the Lakes, and published a photographic record of these, *Rock Climbing in the English Lake District*, in 1897. As the reputation of such climbers as Jones, who became widely known for his fearless style of climbing, steadily grew, the 1890s saw the Lake District become one of the focal points for the new sport.

Clearly, a large number of these mountaineers and climbers were also doing a great deal of walking up on the fells, to get themselves to their climbs, but, as yet, walking there for its own sake had not emerged as such a popular pastime. The first indication we have that this was changing came in 1902, when 'The Rucksack Club' was proposed, its aim being 'to facilitate walking tours and mountaineering expeditions'. Straightaway, enough people were interested for the idea to go ahead, and, once founded, the club's published rules stated its major aim was 'to encourage the pursuits of mountaineering, climbing and hill-walking'. From here things moved on rapidly for walking as a valid pursuit in itself, with the arrival of 'The Wayfarer's Club' in 1904, 'to encourage the pursuits of mountaineering, walking, ski-running, and cave exploration', and finally, two years later, came the 'The Fell & Rock Climbing Club of the English Lake District' (1906), founded by, amongst others, the Abraham brothers, which aimed to 'encourage ... the exhilarating exercise and sport of Fell Rambling and Rock Climbing in the Lake District'.

It may have taken almost 100 years from Coleridge's last walk, to its emergence as a popular way to explore the Lake District, and then almost another 100 for it to become the phenomenon it is today, but once it did, of course, countless people have come to understand the exhilaration and rewards of fell-walking that he had first glimpsed; and no one more so than the self-styled 'Fellwanderer' Alfred Wainwright, identified by Holmes as Coleridge's 'greatest inheritor'.

THE FELLWANDERER: ALFRED WAINWRIGHT[13]

A recurring presence throughout this book, Wainwright was born in Lancashire and initially visited the Lakes in 1930, aged 23. He never forgot his first view of Windermere and the fells beyond from Orrest Head, a spot which remained central to his experience and which he introduces on a final visit as follows:

> Orrest Head, for many of us, is 'where we came in' – our first ascent in Lakeland, our first sight of mountains in tumultuous array across glittering waters, our awakening to beauty. It is a popular walk, deservedly, for here the promised land is seen in all its glory. It is a fitting finale, too, to a life made happy by fellwandering. Dare we hope there will be another Orrest Head over the threshold of the next heaven?

Although he tells us he was not a religious man in any formal sense, the almost biblical language in this description gives us some indication of just what the lakes and fells of Lakeland meant to him. Without doubt, beyond the determination to see, understand and record in empirical and minute detail the incredible intricacies that went to make up these landscapes, there was another, more intuitive, even spiritual, dimension at work. In the Introduction to the first of the *Pictorial Guides*, Wainwright wrote that Lakeland's 'enchantment grows' and that 'this book is one man's way of expressing his devotion to Lakeland's friendly hills. It was conceived and is born, after many years of inarticulate worshipping at their shrines. It is, in truth, a love-letter.' Coleridge, who had written 'I worshipped with deep feeling the grand outline & perpetual Forms', would, one feels, have understood both the sense of 'inarticulate worshipping' and the vision that identified this place as the 'promised land', as he too had sought to express something intangible that he found here, sensing the ongoing conversations 'as if heaven & Earth were for ever talking to each other', and discovering the 'Godlikeness of this place'.

One senses too, that both Coleridge and Wainwright, in their different ways, would have understood the writings of one of the early pioneers of Chinese landscape painting, Tsung Ping (375-443). With approaching old age, and unable any longer to actually wander in the mountains, Tsung sought to bring them into his home by painting images of them, from memory, on his walls. 'Now', he wrote, 'I can only do my pictures and spread my colours over the cloud covered mountains. The reason for doing it has always been to transmit for future ages the hidden meaning which lies beyond all descriptions in words. The mind can grasp the contents of books, but that is not like strolling about and enjoying nature with the eyes.'[14]

If Coleridge had been an artist as well as a writer, as Wainwright was, would he too have sought 'to transmit the hidden meanings which lie beyond all descriptions by words'? His little sketches of shapes, lines and shadows scattered amongst the words of the notebook certainly indicate that now and then, as language failed him, he felt it necessary to transmit exactly what it was that caught his eye, rather than attempt a written description. But, beyond this, he would most certainly have identified with the joys and rewards of both 'strolling about' and 'fellwandering'.

In 1797, in reply to Paul Postlethwaite's question, as they sat together on Loft Crag, 'wot a broughtin yoa here?' Joseph Palmer had replied 'Curiosity, Paul.' It is clear that, as Coleridge sat looking out at the mountains from his study window in 1800, curiosity was certainly one of the motives that led him to undertake his series of walks, as indeed it was for many visitors at the time, and remains so today. It is equally clear, however, that what Wainwright called the 'enchantment' of Lakeland also steadily cast its spell over him, and that his growing awareness under this spell that these places had 'hidden meanings' about the nature of existence itself, was accompanied by both a sense of pure 'Joy' powered by his deepening respect and sense of awe for the natural world. In a world increasingly happy to accept the vapid phrase 'because it is there', as a valid reason for climbing a mountain, or adventuring into the landscapes of the natural world, Coleridge's descriptions of his walks seem to offer something that has been lost, and which could be of value as we try, today, to create a more considerate and mutually self-sustaining relationship with the 'wild places of Nature'.

Notes

CHAPTER 1

Introductory quotation from Chinese Zen
master Yun-men Wen-yen (864–949), taken
from *Zen Baggage*, Bill Porter, Counterpoint
(Berkeley, 2009), p.289.

1   Powell and Hebron, 2010, Catalogue 1: After
    George Smith (1700–73), *The Caudbec Fells*,
    1747.
        This catalogue for the Wordsworth Trust's
    exhibition is invaluable for presenting the
    chronology of the artists and discussing the
    development of the content of their images.
    The present discussion of the development of
    the Picturesque tour draws on, among other
    things, both the essays by Cecilia Powell and
    Stephen Hebron and the catalogue entries by
    Powell contained in it.

2   Anon XXI: *A New Description of Matlock,
    Pool's Hole, Winander-mere*, published in
    Gentleman's Magazine, Vol. 18, Dec. 1748,
    pp.562–3. Passages quoted from p.563.

3   *A Descriptive Poem addressed to Two Ladies, at their
    return from viewing the mines near Whitehaven*,
    London, 1755. Dr John Dalton (1709–63) came
    from the village of Dean, Cumberland, situated
    between the western fells and Workington.
    Hunt and Willis, 1988, p.191.

4   Quoted in Roberts, 1996, p.241. The brief
    survey of the life of John Brown (1715–66)
    that follows is based on William Roberts's
    detailed account, Roberts, 1996, Part 1,
    pp.4–71.

5   *A Description of the Lake at Keswick (And the
    adjacent Country) in Cumberland Communicated
    in A Letter to a Friend* was given this
    elaborate title when 'first published in the
    London Chronicle of 24–26 April, 1766 …
    and re-published as a separate pamphlet in
    Newcastle some time in 1767 … Further
    editions followed: in Kendal in 1770; in
    Kendal again in 1771; in Whitehaven in 1772;

in London in 1772.' Roberts, 1996, p.237 and
n.1.

6   'a plausible conjecture', 'the first major piece
    of prose writing': Roberts, 1996, pp.33 and
    60–61, and Roberts, 2001, p.136.

7   'Active Fancy travels beyond Sense'. These
    lines provide something of a mystery as to
    whether they are quoted from a poem or
    some other piece of writing, whether he
    is referring to something someone said, or
    whether Brown simply coined them himself
    to emphasize the nature of what he calls
    'agreeable perplexity'. Roberts notes: 'It has
    proved impossible to locate this "quotation",
    which might have been helpful in dating the
    Description … the English Poetry database has
    been consulted, without success. It is possible
    that Brown invented the "quotation" – which
    would be an interesting device.' Roberts,
    1996, p.238, n.3.
        It is also interesting to note that Brown
    specifically refers in these lines to 'Active
    Fancy', a phrase which we find repeated in
    Thomas Whately's account of the land-
    scape developments at Hagley Hall in his
    Observations on Modern Gardening of 1770. In
    this he writes that 'the excellencies both of a
    park and of a garden are … happily blended
    at Hagley,' creating 'a scene of real magnifi-
    cence and grandeur'. He then concludes that
    'through all the rest of the place, the two
    characters are intimately blended; the whole
    is one subject; and it was a bold idea to
    conceive that one to be capable of so much
    variety; it required the most vigorous efforts
    of a fertile fancy to carry the idea into exe-
    cution.' Whately, ed. Symes, 2016, pp.157–64
        Although Whately's book was not
    published until 1770, as the editor Michael
    Symes points out, 'the material may have been
    gathered over a number of years,' and visiting
    Hagley at an earlier date means Whately may

well have heard accounts of the work that was carried out there from 1748 until Lyttelton's death in 1773; if so, the central role played there of Fancy, whether 'active' or 'fertile', may well have been mentioned.

8 'particular acquaintances' and 'Gray's efforts': Mack, 2000, pp.576 and 495. 'read and admired': Murray, 2012, p.21.

9 Mack, 2000, p.613.

10 This account of Gray's *Journal* is based on the text and commentaries added to each entry in *Thomas Gray's Journal of his visit to the Lakes in October 1769*: Roberts, 2001.

The passages quoted here follow Gray's progress from Day 2 until Day 9, and can be found between pp.33–89. Note: Roberts follows the original text and does not capitalize all the initial letters of new sentences.

11 *Journal*, p.46: Interesting to note here that this is the second time Gray uses the word 'nodding' to describe the setting of a rock. Previously, on Day 3 [p.39], he had passed a house called Hill-top in the valley of St John's in the Vale, and noticed beside it 'a great rock like some antient tower nodding to its fall'.

Roberts, in his interesting Commentary, writes: 'Gray's phrase about the huge rock next to [the house] "nodding to its fall", sounds like a quotation and indeed it is; it comes from Pope's *Essay on Man* and is meant to hint at a downfall due to fate.' Later in his account of this day [p.47], Gray also quotes Dante and refers to the shrouded landscapes further up Borrowdale, out of sight beyond Castle Crag, as an 'ancient kingdom, the reign of Chaos & old Night', calling on powerful images from Milton's *Paradise Lost*.

This drawing on literary and artistic references was, like the use of a Claude glass, a key part of the process by which tourists were able to transform the otherwise meaningless chaos of the world of nature into something of cultural value – to create the potential whereby 'Fancy travels beyond Sense / And pictures things unseen' as Brown had recommended.

12 'Catchidecam' is written as 'Catstye Cam' by the Ordnance Survey and 'Catstycam' by Wainwright.

13 See Roberts, 2001, pp.138–43, for a useful brief account of these other tourists, including Arthur Young, William Hutchinson, and Thomas Pennant.

Thomas West, *A Guide to the Lakes Dedicated to the Lovers of Landscape Studies and to All who have visited, or intend to visit, The Lakes in Cumberland, Westmoreland and Lancashire*, by the Author of the *Antiquities of Furness*, London & Kendal, 1778.

Thomas West (1720?–79) was 'a Jesuit priest … serving as a chaplain at Titeup Hall near Dalton in Furness, [who] wrote and published the *Antiquities of Furness* in 1774.' [Powell and Hebron, 2010, p.55] As the subject matter of his first book suggests, one of West's original contributions to the actual content of the tour was to add sites of antiquarian interest to the itinerary. Conveniently, West also added an Addenda which included the full texts of the writings that had first introduced the world to the Lake District: Article 1: Brown's *A Description of the Lake at Keswick (And the adjacent Country) in Cumberland Communicated in A Letter to a Friend*, Letter; Article 2: Dalton's *A Descriptive Poem addressed to Two Ladies;* and Article 3: Gray's *Journal*.

14 'discussed at some length': Mitchell, 2010, p.8.

William Gilpin (1724–1804) was born in Carlisle and after attending Oxford University was ordained in 1748. In the 1750s he was headmaster at Cheam School, London, and continued to pursue a lifelong interest in art and drawing. Following an annual series of summer tours, begun in the late 1760s, Gilpin began publishing his series of 'Guides', which included the *Observations on the River Wye* and *Observations, relative chiefly to Picturesque Beauty*.

The quotations used here are taken from Gilpin's *Observations on the River Wye 1770*, Pallas Athene, London, 2005, pp.17, 23, 25, 26.

15 'Tourists & Travellers: women's non-fictional writing about Scotland 1770–1830', Elizabeth Hagglund, March 2000, Degree Thesis, University of Birmingham [etheses.bham.ac.uk/12941/1/Hagglund00PhD.pdf accessed 21/4/16] p.143.

16 Joseph Palmer, Preface, *A Fortnight's Ramble to the Lakes by A Rambler in 1792*.

17 S.T. Coleridge, N760. June/July 1800.

It would appear that when he wrote this, Coleridge was visiting the Wordsworths and that Dorothy, sitting with him, also saw the ladies passing, Gilpins in hand: 'A coroneted Landau went by, when we were sitting upon the sodded wall. The ladies (evidently Tourists) turned an eye of interest upon our little garden and cottage.' Monday 9 June 1800, *Journals of Dorothy Wordsworth*, Selincourt, ed., Vol. 1, p.46.

CHAPTER 2

1 *A Fortnight's Ramble to the Lakes, by a Rambler in 1792*, Hookham & Carpenter, London, 1792, 2nd edn of 1795, and a 3rd edn in 1810, to which were added his accounts of his ascent of the Langdale Pikes (1797) and his winter visit to Scale Force waterfall (1798).

The 1792 first edition has been republished by Rosalind and Hugh Preston of Preston Publishing, complete with a short biography, glossary and notes, and it is this edition that is used for the present book. *A Fortnight's Ramble to the Lakes by a Rambler*, ed. R. & H. Preston, Preston Publishing, 1990 (paperback). The 2nd and 3rd edns are available online.

'so completely hath the Regiment ... ' quoted from 3rd edn, p.382.

'Inherited the Palmer estates ... ' quoted from Preston, 1990, p.105.

'the confusion of ideas ... ' quoted from Preston, 1990, p.104.

2 See Lefebure, 1970, p.131. It is worth noting, however, that, although notes on Palmer's life indicate that he was 'severely wounded' during the Siege of Gibraltar, no specifics are given, and Palmer himself does not mention any injury in the 1792 *Ramble*. He notes only that the descent from Helvellyn was 'difficult, being incommoded by loose stones, small rocks, or dry hard ground' and that 'I was obliged to press so hard against my stick, the ball of my hand was much blistered.' [Preston, 1990, p.83] It is only in the Preface to the 2nd edn that he mentions he had to undertake these rambles 'with but one arm to trust to', and adds later that Helvellyn was particularly difficult 'as I only had one arm to depend to '. Given Palmer's reticence in describing his injuries and the severity of what had clearly happened to one arm, it is quite possible that the injuries actually went beyond this, and that some of his physical dependency on his guides at the more exposed moments during some of the ascents and descents from the heights was due to this rather than an exaggerated sensitivity to the sublime.

3 'The grand crescent': a view now often overlooked, which Wainwright, who initially agrees with Palmer, calls *The Fairfield Horseshoe* and describes as 'a great horseshoe of grassy slopes below a consistently high skyline, simple in design and impressive in altitude', but then, in a telling example of how sensibilities have changed, concludes that it 'lacks those dramatic qualities that appeal most to the lover of hills.' See AW 1, Fairfield 2 and 3.

'Fairfield swells in Alpine pride': Thomas West, *Guide to the Lakes*, 1784, p.59.

4 *Tourists & Travellers: women's non-fictional writing about Scotland 1770–1830*, Elizabeth Hagglund, March 2000, Degree Thesis, University of Birmingham [etheses.bham.ac.uk/12941/1/Hagglund00PhD.pdf accessed 21/4/16] p.141.

5 It is interesting to note that Wainwright, writing 163 years later, implies that not much has changed here, and describes this route as 'the shortest way ... [but] very steep and rough for 2,200 feet ... [it] is not attractive and ... walkers with weak ankles should avoid it.' AW 1, Helvellyn 7 and 9.

We also find mention in Wainwright of 'Whelpside Gill Spring' ['Brownrigg Spring'], which Palmer was so grateful to find. His description tells us not only that it does still 'offer unfailing supplies of icy water', but also that 'few visitors to Helvellyn know this spring (the source of Whelpside Gill)', which indicates that Palmer too may well have missed it had Partridge not known about it. AW 1, Helvellyn 22.

6 Palmer, 3rd edn, 1810, Ch. IX, pp.82 and 179.

7 Palmer, ibid, pp.197–274.

8 In fact while Loft Crag is 2270m, and Pike o' Stickle 2190m, Harrison Stickle is actually higher at 2403m.

9 Palmer, 3rd edn, 1810, Appendix No. 1, Revisit to Buttermere, January 1798, pp.385–407.

10 Palmer's *Windermere, A Poem* was published in 1798 (under his original name Joseph Budworth), and his re-visit to Scale Force was originally published in the *Gentleman's Magazine*, January 1800, Vol. LXX, p.18.

11 The Coleridge children: Hartley (1796–1849), born Clevedon; Berkeley (1798–99), born Nether Stowey; Derwent (1800–83), born Greta Hall; Sara (1802–52), born Greta Hall.

12 *The Notebooks of Samuel Taylor Coleridge*, Vol. 1, 1794–1804, 2 volumes: *Text* and *Notes*, ed.

Kathleen Coburn, London, 1957.

13 Holmes, 1989, p.281 and n.

14 *Collected Letters of Samuel Taylor Coleridge*, ed. Griggs 1956–71, Vol.2, Letter 451 to Sara Hutchinson, 6 August 1802.

15 *Coleridge: Early Visions*, Holmes 1989, p.328. This is the first volume of Holmes' 2-volume biography of Coleridge, of which the second volume is *Coleridge: Darker Reflections*, Harper Collins, 1998.

16 L450, to Sara Hutchinson, 1–5 August 1802.

CHAPTER 3

1 *The Poetical Works of S.T. Coleridge*, The Lansdowne Poets Series, Frederick Warne, p.vii. This is an undated edn of c.1890s. The title page tells us that this is 'reprinted from the earlier editions with memoir, notes etc.', but does not specify which earlier editions or who wrote the introductory memoir 'The Life and Poetry of S.T. Coleridge' from which this quote is taken.

2 CL49 to Samuel Butler, c.14 June 1794, Cambridge.

The route of the Welsh Tour took them as follows: Oxford – Gloucester – Ross – Hereford – Llanfyllin – Llangynog ['Llanvunnog'] – Bala – Llangollen ['Llanvillin'] – Wrexham – Ruthin –Denbigh – St Winifred's Well, Holywell – Rhuddlan Castle – Abergele – Conway – Penmaenmawr – Beaumaris – Caernarvon – Snowdon – Harlech – Cader Idris – Aberystwyth – Llandovery (where Hucks, exhausted, perhaps, by Coleridge's restless energy and non-stop conversation, left to return home) – Brecon – Abergavenny – Monmouth – the Wye Valley – Tintern – Chepstow – Bristol.

3 Holmes, 1989, p.61.

4 All these excerpts from CL51 to Robert Southey, 13 July 1794, Wrexham.

5 CL52 to Henry Martin, 22 July 1794, Caernarvon.

6 L349 to William Godwin, 8 September 1800, Greta Hall.

7 Holmes, 1989, p.62.

8 Holmes, ibid, p.106.

9 Holmes, ibid, p.137, *Letters*, I, p.308.

10 The following quotes all from *Biographia Literaria*, ed. J. Shawcross, 2 vols, Oxford, 1907, 1979. Quoted in Holmes, 1989, p.161.

11 For Coleridge's accounts of the Tour of Harz Mountains see *CL* 280–82, and N 410–18.

Map 4: The Route of the Harz Mountains walk 11–18 May 1799:

11th: Göttingen – Hessen Driesch – Wage [Waake] – Rudolphshausen – Womarshausen – Gieboldshausen – Poele [Pöhlde] – Schlatchfeld [Scharzfeld]

12th: Einhornhöhle – Neuhof – Lauterburg – Andreasburg

13th: Rauschenbach – Oder Teich – Little Brocken – The Blocksburg / Great Brocken – Elbinrobe

14th: Rubelland – River Bode – Hüttenrode – Blankenburg

15th: Got lost leaving Blankenburg, eventually found Werninger [Wernigerode] – Drubeck – Hartsburg – Goslar

16th: Goslar, a day in Goslar.

17th: Claustal

18th : Lehrbech – Osterode – Catlenburg – Göttingen

The 'Brocken Spectre': Coleridge describes this as 'a curious phaenomenon which occurs occasionally when the air is filled with fine particles of frozen Snow, constituting an almost invisibly subtle Snow-mist, and a Person is walking with the sun behind his Back. His shadow is projected and he sees a figure moving before him with a glory around its Head. I have myself seen it twice.' MS Journal of Coleridge's German trip, quoted in Coburn, *The Inquiring Spirit*, 1951, p.243.

12 'MS Journal': Coburn describes this as a 'foolscap manuscript of Coleridge's visit to Germany' in the Berg Collection, NYPL. N410 f.21, CL280 to his wife Sara Coleridge, 17 May; N411 f.24, CL280 again; N412 f.25 and *Note*.

13 CL281, Mrs Sara Coleridge, 17 May 1799.

14 The waterfalls: N415, f.25 and CL280.

15 CL281 and Clement Carlyon , MD, *Early Years and Late Reflections*, 2 vols., 1836, Vol. I, p.51, quoted in Holmes, 1989, p.230.

16 N415 f.26 (Rubelland), N416, 417 *Notes* and CL282.

17 CL282.

18 N418 f.28 Descriptions of the landscape from Clausthal to Catlenburg [Katlenburg] and Holmes, 1989, p.234.

19 'He and Chester': Holmes, 1989, p.236 and N412, f.26.

CHAPTER 4

1 'pikteresk Toor': see N508, and CL405. It was on this walk that Coleridge finally lost his 5-foot-long carved walking stick.

For descriptions of this walk see N494–563; CL299 (a letter to Dorothy written jointly by Coleridge and Wordsworth) and 300; and EL124 (William Wordsworth to Dorothy).

2 See N494 for Croft-on-Tees.

3 See N495 for Egglestone Abbey.

4 Coleridge writes of John Wordsworth in his section of CL299, and his description of him is quoted in Holmes, 1989, p.247.

5 It is worth pointing out in the context of their descriptions of the landscape, that Thomas Gray's *Tour through England and Wales* (1799) had just been published and the two may well have already have read it. While they did not carry a Claude Glass to filter the raw landscape and provide the perfect 'view' as Gray and Gilpin had done, they nevertheless interpreted the views in terms of artistic composition.

Coleridge's descriptions of Haweswater are from N510 and Wordsworth's part of their joint letter to Dorothy, CL299.

6 N511.

7 Helm Crag: N515; Helvellyn, CL299 (Wordsworth) and N515 (Coleridge). John Wordsworth was leaving for sea and would then have continued on down to Patterdale and round Ullswater to Penrith.

8 Churnmilk Force: N516. It is not clear which fall this actually refers to but it may have been the upper waterfall at Rydal, which Wordsworth says they visited 'the same evening (after climbing Helvellyn)': EL124 (Wordsworth). It is then in CL299 that he tells Dorothy about Dove Cottage.

9 For extract from *Windermere* by Palmer, see N527.

10 'Exquisite network of Film': N518. The word 'instinct' is used here in the sense of 'animated' (*see* OED).

11 'Mist as from a Volcano': N529. This vision of water 'rolling' like a wheel was to become central to Coleridge's written descriptions of waterfalls. Richard Holmes comments on this image 'Water as usual made him metaphysically aware of the underlying energies of nature, and transcendental implications, as if a waterfall was a kind of perpetual Brahman

prayer-wheel', Holmes, 1989, p.332.

12 Ouse Bridge: N536.

13 For description of the subsequent walk to Buttermere: N537.

14 For details at Crummock Water and Buttermere: N538 and 539.

15 Description of Scale Force Waterfall and the following walk to Wasdale Head: N540. It is worth noting that in this entry Coleridge starts using the word 'Ness', 'the grand Ness' and 'the Ness', a word which the OED defines as 'a promontory, headland or cape', i.e. it is usually used to reference coastal landforms. There is, therefore, in this reference to the coast, an interesting sense of Coleridge's emerging consciousness that each of these great ridgelines and the buttresses that run down their sides, represent the end of something, of looking from one world into another, threshold points in an unfolding experience, which is something new in his writing about landscapes; quite possibly this was partly the result of the discussions they were having as they walked along.

16 Ennerdale and Wasdale Head: N540. The walk up Ennerdale: N541 f.34 and f.33.

17 The descent from Styhead Pass: N541.

18 Matterdale Common and the hat in the field: N549.

19 Account of the walk round the Great Promontory to Scalehow Force: N551–553.

20 N556.

21 For the Notebook entries listing the peaks in view, see N778–780.

Drawing of the Greta River and the House: CL344 to Samuel Purkis, 29 July 1800, Greta Hall.

22 CL341 to Josiah Wedgwood, 24 July.

23 CL343 to James Webb Tobin, 25 July 1800, Greta Hall.

24 CL344 to Samuel Purkis, 29 July 1800, Greta Hall.

25 CL348 to Thomas Poole, 14 August 1800, Greta Hall.

26 CL349 to William Godwin, 8 September 1800, Greta Hall.

27 CL362 to Josiah Wedgwood, 1 November 1800, Greta Hall.

28 L444 to William Sotheby, 13 July 1802, Greta Hall.

29 CL210 to Thomas Poole, 16 October 1797. See Appendix 2 for fuller extracts from the River Otter poem, 'Reflections on having left

a place of Retirement' and 'This Lime-Tree Bower My Prison'.

30 See CL197 to Robert Southey, July 1797, Nether Stowey.

31 CL238 to George Coleridge c.10 March 1798, Stowey, after a visit to Ottery.

CHAPTER 5

1 N720; Coburn suggests 'simile' for an unreadable word.

2 Description of Dungeon Ghyll Force: N753.

3 Ascent of Skiddaw: The date of this ascent is not certain. It is not mentioned in the Notebook, but will have been on or just before 14 August 1800, the date of his subsequent letter to Thomas Poole, in which he mentions it. Holmes, 1989, p.280, and CL pp.618–19.

4 The walk up Saddleback [Blencathra]: N784, *Notes*: 'The tour up Saddleback appears to have been made alone, and if so, it was either 7–8 August when Wordsworth went back to Grasmere, or after 17 August. The Wordsworths arrived at Keswick on the 8th and left on the 17th.'

Wainwright notes that Blencathra 'is one of the grandest objects in Lakeland', and although he adds disapprovingly that it is 'better known unfortunately as Saddleback,' that is how Coleridge knew it and so how it is referred to here.

5 'An eminently beautiful object is Fern': N785.

6 'As I sate in the side of Skiddaw': N790.

7 2 walks round the Bannerdale Crags N793, N797 and N797 *Notes*.

8 'collected local stories': N797.

9 AW 5, Bannerdale Crags 8.

10 Helvellyn Ridge to Grasmere, N798.

11 'Styx Top': Stick's Pass, which carries the path from Glenridding on Ullswater over to Stanah and Legburthwaite, where it joins the road from Grasmere to Keswick.

12 Or, as Wainwright described it, 'Rough scrambling in the gill', AW I, Helvellyn 9.

13 DWJ, I, 31 August 1800.

14 DWJ, I, 1 September 1800.

15 'skimming the lake like Swallows': N799.

16 AW 3, Harrison Stickle 10.

17 Wordsworth's comments on 'Christabel': 'I had no notion', EL, 141; 'it is my wish', EL, 144; 'I found that the Style of the Poem', EL, 150.

18 The 'Coledale Fells': This group of summits and ridges, that run from Rowling End to Grisdale Pike, on either side of Coledale Beck above Braithwaite and Stoneycroft Gill above Newlands, do not seen to have a collective name. Wainwright in his introduction to 'The North Western Fells' [AW 6] calls them simply 'the central sector' of this area, and since Coleridge does not give them a collective name either, 'Coledale Fells' has been selected for clarity. For Coleridge's descriptions, see N804 for the walk on 9 September and N805 for that of 12 September.

19 From: *Samuel Taylor Coleridge: A Narrative of the Events of his Life*, by James Dykes Campbell, 1894; Basil Savage, Highgate, London, 1970. Quoted in Holmes, 1989, p.283.

20 Coburn suggests that he was actually looking at the series of falls on Sourmilk Gill as it twists and tumbles down from Bleaberry Tarn on the far side of the valley, rather than Scale Force, but it could well be either.

21 N834 *Notes*.

22 Back o'Skidda: Notebook entries: 1st Day: N825; 2nd Day: N828, and CL360 to Humphry Davy, in which he gave a full account of this extraordinary day.

23 AW 5, Bakestall 2. Wainwright does not use this kind of language lightly, and his description catches much of the atmosphere of this dramatic place.

24 AW 5, Bakestall 9.

25 N825.

26 CL360 to Humphry Davy, 18 October 1800, from Greta Hall.

27 N834.

28 Holmes, 1989, pp.280 and 283.

29 L390 to William Godwin, 25 March 1801, from Greta Hall.

30 Coleridge's Preface to the 1816 edition of 'Christabel', included in PW, p.111.

31 Holmes, 1989, p.290.

32 N *Notes*, Introduction, p.xix, 21 June, 1823.

CHAPTER 6

1 N875.

2 N948 and N949.

3 Walla Crag walk: N1160.

4 The weather: DWJ, 16 April 1802.

5 DWJ, 22 April 1802.

6 N1164.

7 DWJ, 23 April, 1802. Dorothy's almost mystical observation here, 'not man's hills, but all of themselves', gives a clear indication of the groundbreaking nature of her *Journals*.

8 For mention of the creation of the 'Moss hut at the top of the orchard' see DWJ, entries for May 1802, and Preface to DWJ, Vol. 1, p. ix.

9 For Wainwright's walk on Nab Scar, see AW 1, Nab Scar 4.

10 The 'walk to St Bees': L449 to Robert Southey, 31 July 1802, Greta Hall. See William Hutchinson's *The History of the County of Cumberland*, 2 vols, Carlisle 1794.

11 Coleridge's hand drawn map: N1206. The 'Vergivian Trident': N1205, where Coburn spells this 'Virgivian', pertaining to Virgil.

12 Coleridge's trip is related in N1207–1219, written up in L450 (1–5 Aug) and N1220–1222 in L451 (6 August), both written to Sara Hutchinson; and N1222–1228 in L452 (9 August), written to Robert Southey.

13 Thomas West, *Guide to the Lakes*, 4th edn, 1789; William Gilpin, *Observations … Cumberland and Westmoreland*, 1792.

14 He leaves any description of both Moss Force [which he calls Buttermere Halse Fall] and Scale Force which he passes next day, to a separate letter to Sara Hutchinson: L456.

15 Day 1, quotes in sequential order: N1207, 1208.

16 AW 7, Great Borne 5.

17 Day 2: L450 and N1209.

18 Day 3, quotes in sequential order: N1212, L450, N1213, L450.

19 Wasdale Head to Burnmoor Tarn: N1214. This route follows the old 'corpse' road from Wasdale over to Eskdale. See AW 4, Scafell 4. This was in fact a very straightforward route, in considerable contrast to his descent; Tyson may well have advised the former, but almost certainly not the latter.

20 'I involuntarily poured forth a Hymn': L459. The full quotation from this letter reads: 'I involuntarily poured forth a Hymn in the manner of the *Psalms*, tho' afterwards I thought the Ideas &c disproportionate to our humble mountains – & accidentally lighting on a short Note in some Swiss poems, concerning the Vale of Chamouny, & its Mountains, I transferred myself thither, in the Spirit, & adapted my former feelings to these grander external objects.' The whole issue remains a little murky.

21 'There is one sort of Gambling': L451. 'I have always found this stretched and anxious state of mind': L456. 'An idea starts up in my head': CL, Introduction by E.L. Griggs, p. xxxv. 'An event happened': EY276, 23rd July, 1805.

22 Day 4, quotes in sequential order: N1216, L450, N1217, L450, N1218, L459, L459, L450, L451, L451 and L456.

23 Day 5, summary of day: L452 to Robert Southey, 9 August. Detail of journey: N1222–1225.

24 'deep dark pool in a stream or river': N1225 *Notes*. 'Still glides the stream', William Wordsworth, 34 Sonnets on the River Duddon.

25 Day 6, summary of day: N1225–1228.

26 End of the walk: L453 to Sara Hutchinson, 10 August.

27 Two letters to William Sotheby, L457 (August 26th) and L459 (early September).

28 *Hymn before Sunrise, in the Vale of Chamouni*, first published in *Morning Post*, 11 September 1802.

Lines 11–23: In *The Poetry of Samuel Taylor Coleridge*, [PW] p. 376, the editor notes 'This is an expansion, in part, of a translation of Frederika Brun's *Ode to Chamouny*, dedicated to Klopstock.'

CHAPTER 7

1 A Walk with Southey, 29–30 September 1803: N1518–1520.

2 The waterfalls of Caldbeck Howk: N1519 and 1520.

3 'Walk with Southey and Hazlitt thro' Borrodale into Watendlath': N1610.

4 AW 3, Grange Fell 6.

5 L916 to Tom Wedgwood, 14 January 1803, as quoted by Holmes, 1989, p. 343.

6 Elizabeth Vassall, Lady Holland: *Journal of Elizabeth Vassall, Lady Holland*. Vol. 2, 1799–1811, pp. 230–32 [available online: https://archive.org/stream/journalofelizabo2holl#page/n9/mode/2up (accessed 14-8-2016)].

7 'I hear nothing but of Coleridge', Vassall, *ibid*, p. 237.

8 Elizabeth Grant, *Memoirs of a Highland Lady*, Vol. II, p. 182.

9 William Green, *The Tourists New Guide; containing a Description of the Lakes, Mountains*

and *Scenery in Cumberland, Westmoreland, and Lancashire*, 2 vols, 1819 and 1822.

10 Harriet Martineau, *A Complete Guide to the English Lakes*, Garnett, Windermere, c.1860.

11 Mountford John Bryde Baddeley, *Thorough Guides. The English Lakes*, Dulau & Co., 1880.

12 Arthur Mee, *The Lake District, The Classic Guide*, pp. 107, 112. From *The King's England* Series, 1937, paperback reprint, Amberley Publishing, 2014.

13 *Fellwanderer*, the title of Wainwright's auto-biography of 1966 and the term he used to describe how he saw his trips to the Lake District.

Alfred Wainwright (1907–91) MBE, born in Blackburn, Lancashire, worked as a local government accountant. He moved perma-nently to the Lakes in 1941, when he took a job with Kendal Borough Council from which he retired in 1967. From his first visit to the Lakes in 1930, on a walking trip with a friend, until he retired, his visits to the Lakes took up many of his weekends. And each evening he worked on the painstakingly hand-written and illustrated pages of the books. The first volume of the *Pictorial Guides to the Lakeland Fells* was begun in 1952, and in the end the series ran to seven volumes, the last of which appeared in 1966.

These books were followed after his retirement by *Pennine Way Companion* (1968), *A Coast to Coast Walk* (1973), a walk that he largely pioneered, and one last volume on the Lakes, *The Outlying Fells of Lakeland* (1974). In this final volume Wainwright records his memorable first sight of the Lakes in 1930, when, together with his friend, he ascended Orrest Head. He evokes the experience in one of the most moving passages of the entire series. 44 years after the event, he had never forgotten it and what it meant to him.

14 Tsung Ping (375–443), quotation from Li Tai Ming Hua Chi, second part, chapter vi. Written by the T'ang era historian Chang Yen-yüan, it was completed in 845AD; this translation is taken from *The Chinese on the Art of Painting*, Osvald Sirén, Schocken Books, 1963.

Bibliography

ABREVIATIONS

AW Wainwright, A., *A Pictorial Guide to the Lakeland Fells,* 7 volumes (Kendal, 1956–65)

CL *Collected Letters of Samuel Taylor Coleridge,* ed. E.L. Griggs (Oxford, 1956) Vol. I: 1785–1800. *See also abbrev* L

EY *The Letters of William and Dorothy Wordsworth, The Early Years 1787–1805,* ed. E. de Selincourt, 2nd edition (Oxford, 1967)

L *Collected Letters of Samuel Taylor Coleridge,* ed. E.L. Griggs, Oxford, 1956. Vol. II: 1801–06

N *The Notebooks of Samuel Taylor Coleridge,* ed. Kathleen Coburn (London, 1957), Vol. I: 1794–1804

PW *The Poetical Works of S. T. Coleridge,* The Lansdowne Poets Series (London, c.1890s)

COBURN, KATHLEEN, ed., *Inquiring Spirit, a new presentation of Coleridge* (London, 1951)

COBURN, KATHLEEN, ed., *The Notebooks of Samuel Taylor Coleridge* (London, 1957), Vol. I: 1794–1804 [N]

DE QUINCEY, T., *Recollections of the Lakes and the Lake Poets,* ed. David Wright (Harmondsworth, 1970)

ELWIN, MALCOLM, *The First Romantics, Wordsworth, Coleridge, Southey* (London, 1947)

GITTINGS, R. and MANTON, J., *Dorothy Wordsworth* (Oxford, 1985)

GRANT, ELIZABETH, *Memoirs of a Highland Lady*, ed. Andrew Tod (Cannongate Classics, 2005)

GRIGGS, E.L, ed., *Collected Letters of Samuel Taylor Coleridge* (Oxford, 1956), Vol. I: 1785–1800 [CL]

GRIGGS, E.L, ed., *Collected Letters of Samuel Taylor Coleridge* (Oxford, 1956), Vol. II: 1801–06 [L]

HOLMES, RICHARD, *Coleridge: Early Visions* (HarperCollins *Publishers*, 1989)

HOLMES, RICHARD, *Coleridge: Darker Reflections* (HarperCollins *Publishers*, 1998)

HOWE, H.W., *Greta Hall. Home of Coleridge and Southey,* with revisions by Robert Woof (Daedalus Press, Norfolk, 1977)

HUDSON, ROGER, ed., *Coleridge among the Lakes & Mountains* (London, 1991)

HUNT, JOHN DIXON and WILLIS, PETER, eds., *The Genius of the Place: The English Landscape Garden 1620–1820* (paperback edition, London, 1988)

LEFEBURE, MOLLY, *Cumberland Heritage* (London, 1970)

MACK, ROBERT L., *Thomas Gray: A Life* (New Haven and London, 2000)

MEE, ARTHUR, *The Lake District: The Classic Guide, The King's England* series, first published 1937 (Amberley Publishing, 2014)

MITCHELL, JULIAN, *The Wye Tour and its Artists* (Logaston Press, 2010)

MURRAY, JOHN R., *A Tour of the English Lakes with Thomas Gray & Joseph Farington RA* (Frances Lincoln, 2012)

PALMER, JOSEPH, *A Fortnight's Ramble to the Lakes, by a Rambler in 1792*, ed. R. & H. Preston (1st edn 1792, republished by Preston Publishing, 1990). 2nd edition 1795, 3rd edition 1810.

PALMER, JOSEPH, *Windermere, A Poem* (1798) (ReInk Books, 2017, print on demand, SN Books World, India)

The Poetical Works of S. T. Coleridge. The Lansdowne Poets Series (London, c.1890s) [PW]

POWELL and HEBRON, *Savage Grandeur and Noblest Thoughts: Discovering the Lake District 1750–1820* (The Wordsworth Trust, 2010)

ROBERTS, W.G., *A Dawn of Imaginative Feeling, The Contribution of John Brown (1715–66) to Eighteenth-Century Thought and Literature* (Carlisle, 1996)

ROBERTS, W.G, ed., *Thomas Gray's Journal of his visit to the Lake District in October 1769* (Liverpool University Press, 2001)

SYMES, MICHAEL, *The Picturesque and the Later Georgian Garden* (Bristol, 2012)

THOMPSON, E.P., *The Romantics, England in a Revolutionary Age* (New York, 1997)

WAINWRIGHT, A., *A Pictorial Guide to the Lakeland Fells,* 7 volumes (Kendal, 1956–65) [AW]

WHATELY, THOMAS, *Observations on Modern Gardening,* Introduction and Commentary by Michael Symes (Woodbridge, Suffolk, 2016)

WORDSWORTH, DOROTHY, *Journals of Dorothy Wordsworth,* ed. E. de Selincourt, 2 volumes (London, 1970)

WORDSWORTH, WILLIAM and DOROTHY, *The Letters of William and Dorothy Wordsworth, The Early Years 1787–1805* ed. E. de Selincourt, 2nd edition (Oxford, 1967) [EY]

Index